Biblical Hermeneutics

A Guide for Studying the Bible

Dr. Harold A. Kime

ISBN-13: 978-1986310840
ISBN-10: 1986310841
BISAC: Religion / Biblical Criticism & Interpretation / General

DEDICATION

To my colleagues in the Bible and Theology Department of Lancaster Bible College who have faithfully taught the Word of God to generations of Christians. I especially want to acknowledge Dr. Gordon Johnston who now serves at Dallas Theological Seminary for his contributions to the materials dealing with biblical genres. I also want to thank Dr. Robert Spender for his efforts in editing the materials dealing with Old Testament genres.

PREFACE

In the early years of my ministry at Lancaster Bible College the curriculum included a two-credit course in Bible Study Methods. I was privileged to teach this course but soon realized that the course lacked sufficient depth for students to become skilled in biblical interpretation. In those early years the curriculum included a course in biblical hermeneutics but it was available only to students in our pastoral studies program. It also was a course that was mainly theoretical and apologetic, arguing for an historical-grammatical methodology. There was little emphasis given to actually training students in the methodology.

In the early 1980's the Bible and Theology department made a significant pedagogical change in its curriculum. Rather than a Bible curriculum that basically told students what the Bible meant, this new pedagogy was founded on the proposition that students should primarily be trained in developing the skills for proper interpretation of the Scriptures and only secondarily instructed on the meaning of Scripture. Thus, we moved from a deductive approach to an inductive approach, convinced that if a student was trained properly in biblical exegesis, they would arrive at the right interpretive conclusions.

So, biblical hermeneutics was revised to provide students with the knowledge and skills necessary for rightly dividing the Word of truth. I was given the responsibility to create this course. I chose to use two books that have become foundational to me. "Biblical Hermeneutics" by M. S. Terry provided the principles for interpretation and "Methodical Bible Study" by R. A. Traina provided the basic methodology for learning how to study Scripture.

The present work has added to these two volumes by attempting to provide more recent contributions to the field of biblical interpretation and by providing more specific guidelines and procedures to the methodology. Today, the historical-grammatical method has been expanded into the historical-grammatical-rhetorical-theological method. New fields such as discourse analysis have provided more systematic approaches to understanding the Bible as literary works. These new approaches cover a broad spectrum of hermeneutical issues from new ideas about the meanings of words to sweeping ideas about genre analysis and theological interpretation.

This work is designed for the classroom but it can also be used to train laypersons how to effectively read and study Scripture. My prayer is that a new generation of Christians will become workmen who are not ashamed, rightly dividing the Word of Truth.

Harold A. Kime
April, 2018

CONTENTS

Chapter 1   Introduction to Biblical Hermeneutics 1

Chapter 2   The Role of the Methodology 27

Chapter 3   Biblical Research Tools & Strategies 39

Chapter 4   The Historical Background 49

Chapter 5   The Occasion for Writing 57

Chapter 6   The Author's Purpose 63

Chapter 7   Discourse Analysis 71

Chapter 8   Paragraph Analysis 85

Chapter 9   Grammatical Analysis 97

Chapter 10   The Meaning of Words 109

Chapter 11   Figures of Speech 135

Chapter 12   Genre Analysis 145

Chapter 13   Theological Analysis 155

Chapter 14   The Application Process 161

Chapter 15   Gospel Genre 171

Chapter 16   Parables of Jesus 179

Chapter 17   New Testament Epistles 185

Chapter 18   Biblical Narrative 193

Chapter 19   Biblical Law 201

Chapter 20   Hebrew Poetry 209

Chapter 21   Psalms 221

Chapter 22   Proverbs 231

Chapter 23   Prophetic Discourse 239

Chapter 24   Apocalyptic Literature 249

Chapter 25   Typology 255

             Index of Terms 263

Chapter 1

Introduction to Biblical Hermeneutics

Outline

What is Biblical Hermeneutics?..2

The Need for Hermeneutics...3

Four Key Elements in Interpretation..4

The Nature of the Scriptures...5

English Translations..10

Role of the Interpreter..15

Role of the Holy Spirit..20

Summary...22

Review Questions...25

References...26

Learning Objectives

After completing this chapter, you should be able to

- ❑ Define hermeneutics and state its goal.
- ❑ Explain why hermeneutics is needed.
- ❑ List the four key elements in interpretation.
- ❑ List and define the key concepts related to the nature of Scripture.
- ❑ Identify the key scripture passages that reveal the nature of Scripture.
- ❑ Discuss the factors that influence a translation.
- ❑ Discuss the three basic approaches to translation.
- ❑ List the four criteria for choosing a translation.
- ❑ Discuss which translation of the Bible is best.
- ❑ Identify the spiritual and intellectual qualifications of the interpreter.
- ❑ Discuss the impact of subjectivity on interpretation.
- ❑ Discuss the various views concerning the work of the Spirit in illumination.

What is Biblical Hermeneutics?

Basic Definition

The term, hermeneutics, comes from the Greek verb, ἑρμενευω (*hermeneuo*), which means to interpret or to translate. In the New Testament it is most often used to introduce the translation of a Hebrew term into Greek. In the example below, the underlined English words translate the verb, *hermeneuo*.

> "The virgin will be with child and will give birth to a son, and they will call him Immanuel" – <u>which means</u>, "God with us."
>
> Matthew 1:23

> **Biblical Hermeneutics**
> The discipline that provides the principles and guidelines for interpreting the Bible

Biblical Hermeneutics is the discipline that provides the principles and guidelines for interpreting the Bible.

> **Hermeneutical Principle**
> A rule that must be followed if one is to properly interpret

A **hermeneutical principle** is a rule that one must apply for consistent interpretation. For example, one important principle of interpretation is that the meaning of a word in a statement is determined by its context. Take for instance the word, bill. It has several possible meanings (invoice, paper money, legal proposal). Only by examining the context in which the word is used can one determine which meaning the author intended. The context determines the meaning.

> **Hermeneutical Guideline**
> A procedure that must be followed if one is to properly interpret

A **hermeneutical guideline** is a procedure that one must follow for consistent interpretation. For example, one important guideline for understanding the meaning of words is to discover the word's range of potential meaning using a good dictionary. Assume for instance, that you do not know the possible meanings of the word, bill. Before you can attempt to interpret this word in a given statement, you must look up its possible meanings in a dictionary.

> **Hermeneutics**
> Both a science and an art

Hermeneutics: Both a Science and an Art

Terry suggested that hermeneutics is both a science and an art[1]. As a study of the nature of communication and how to understand communication, hermeneutics is a philosophical science. As a skill learned and refined through experience, hermeneutics is an art. The practitioner must learn to apply the principles and guidelines discovered through the study of communication.

As a science, hermeneutics:

- Is an orderly method or process to be learned.
- Sets forth sound principles for interpretation.
- Is objective in nature.

As an art, hermeneutics:

- Seeks to develop skills to be applied
- Utilizes the principles in actual Bible study
- Is subjective in nature

Goal of Interpretation: The Author's Intended Meaning

It might seem obvious that the primary goal of interpretation is to discover the author's intended meaning. However, many modern scholars either deny that the intended meaning can be understood or deny that it should be the primary goal of interpretation. Some suggest that our primary goal should not be to discover the author's original intent but to establish a current relevant understanding. For the purpose of this book, we will assume that our goal is to discover the intended meaning of the author. For a fuller discussion of this issue, you might want to read the article written by Elliott E. Johnson[2].

> **Goal of Interpretation**
> To discover the meaning intended by the author

The Need for Hermeneutics

At first one might think that the study of hermeneutics is not necessary. Can't you merely read the Bible and understand it? Doesn't God provide the believer with the correct interpretation? Bible scholars agree that the use of sound hermeneutical principles is necessary for correct interpretation. Moises Silva[3] provides an excellent discussion of the need. For our purposes, four examples should be sufficient to establish the need.

> **Hermeneutics Needed Because of**
> - Direction required
> - Diligent study required
> - Differences between original and modern readers
> - Differing interpretations

Direction Required

The story of Philip and the Ethiopian eunuch in Acts 8:26-40 illustrates that interpretation is not always the obvious result of reading. The eunuch was sitting in his chariot, reading the book of Isaiah when Philip approached. Philip asked him if he understood what he was reading. The eunuch replied, "How can I unless someone explains it to me?" (Acts 8:31) The eunuch was able to read the words but he did not understand what he was reading. There were gaps in his understanding he could not bridge. Philip's direction was required.

Diligent Study Required

The story of the Berean Christians in Acts 17:10-12 is another story that illustrates the need for applying hermeneutical principles. When Paul arrived in Berea, he began to preach in the synagogue. The Bereans received his message and "examined the Scriptures every day to see if what Paul said was true." (Acts 17:11) A simple reading of the Scriptures was not sufficient. They needed to make a thorough study. Likewise, we must be diligent to rightly divide the Word of Truth (2 Tim. 2:15).

Differences between Original and Modern Readers

Difficulty in interpretation is often due to different perspectives between the modern readers and the original readers. The story of the marriage of Ruth and Boaz (Ruth 4:1-15) illustrates this difficulty. To marry Ruth, Boaz needed to purchase the land owned by Naomi and to do this he needed to have another near kinsman relinquish his right to purchase the land. All of this is strange and confusing to the modern reader. The authors of scripture wrote between two and three thousand years ago. Since our world is different from their world, it is often difficult to understand what they wrote. Some scholars write of the distance between the original readers and us[4]; others write of the gaps between the original readers and us[5].

These gaps in history, culture, and language must be overcome if we are to understand the author's intended meaning. Hermeneutics provides us with the principles and procedures for filling in these gaps.

Differing Interpretations Demonstrate the Need

If correct interpretation was a natural result of reading and was provided to the Christian by God, then we would expect that in most instances Christians would agree on what the Bible says. However, this is not the case. It is true that honest Bible-believing Christians agree on the basic gospel message. Yet, these same Christians often disagree in many areas of biblical teaching. For instance, simple verses like John 3:16 can be debated. In what sense does God love the world? Does world refer only to the elect or to every person? Such differences often result from differences in hermeneutics.

Four Key Elements in Interpretation

Four Key Elements
- Scriptures
- Interpreter
- Holy Spirit
- Methodology

To interpret the Scriptures, four key elements should be considered, the Scriptures themselves, the human interpreter, the Holy Spirit, and the hermeneutical methodology that is used.

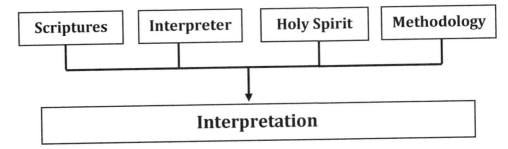

Figure 1.1
Four Key Elements in Interpretation

The Scriptures

Biblical hermeneutics has both similarities and differences from general literary hermeneutics. The similarities are due to the fact that the literary qualities of Scripture are consistent with the literary qualities of genre equivalent literary texts written during the same historical and cultural timeframe. The differences are due to the nature of the message presented in the Scriptures. The Bible claims to be the word of God. Later in this chapter we will examine the nature of the Scriptures and discuss differences in translations.

The Interpreter

The interpreter's knowledge, abilities, presuppositions and prejudices greatly affect interpretation. Later in this chapter we will consider the role of the interpreter, including qualifications as well as how subjectivity can affect interpretation.

The Holy Spirit

One reason that God has given His Spirit to believers is so that we might receive help in appropriating scriptural truth. The question remains, however, as to what kind of help the Holy Spirit provides, and as to how this help relates to the interpreter's own responsibility in applying the principles and procedures of hermeneutics. This question will be probed later in this chapter.

The Hermeneutical Methodology

Differences in interpretation of Scripture can often be traced to differences in hermeneutical method. Not all interpreters use the same principles and guidelines. It is essential that one become aware of one's own methodology; be committed to that methodology; and apply it to the text consistently. In Chapter 2 we will discuss the role of the methodology and suggest an appropriate methodology.

The Nature of the Scriptures

The Importance of the Nature of Scripture in Hermeneutics

Our presuppositions about the nature of the literature we are studying will dramatically affect our approach to understanding it. Take for example the difference in approach we would have in interpreting a document if we thought the document was the deceptive propaganda of an enemy instead of the truthful statement of a friend. Instead of employing a hermeneutic of trust, we would employ a hermeneutic of distrust. As a result, we would interpret very differently. Our hermeneutical methods are directly related to our beliefs about the nature of the literature we study.

> **Principle:**
> Our hermeneutical methods are directly related to our beliefs about the nature of the literature we study

This principle is just as true in the interpretation of the Scriptures. Take, for instance, the presupposition that the miracles ascribed to Jesus and his disciples never happened and that they were added by the early church during times of persecution to encourage the saints and bolster faith. Such a presupposition led liberal theologians in the 19th century to develop the hermeneutical principle of demythologizing Scripture. To them a correct understanding of the Bible required the removal of all the mythological legends that the early church had added to the story about Jesus. Their goal was to get back to the historical Jesus, the grand teacher. As a result, they created a Jesus that was not divine and a religion that was not supernatural.

Four Key Concepts

To correctly interpret the Bible, we must be convinced that it is the inerrant Word of God, that it is God's supernatural revelation of himself, and that we must acknowledge its authority in our lives. In the following discussion we will develop these thoughts under four key concepts, *revelation*, *inspiration*, *inerrancy*, and *authority*.

> **Key Concepts Related to the Nature of Scripture:**
> - Revelation
> - Inspiration
> - Inerrancy
> - Authority

Revelation

Definition

Revelation can be thought of as a process and a product. As a process, revelation was the process in which God sovereignly communicated His invisible, hidden thoughts to the human authors of Scripture, the prophets and apostles. This definition is limited to the supernatural revelation of God found in the Scriptures. It does not include the revelation of God in creation (Rom. 1:18-20), in the human spirit (Rom. 1:14-15), or in Spirit-related experiences (1 Cor. 12:2-4). The Bible makes it clear that God fundamentally revealed himself to mankind through the creation of Scriptures (Heb. 1:1-2; 1 Cor. 2:9-13) and that no other revelation of himself is necessary or sufficient for a relationship with him (Rom. 10:17).

As a product, revelation is the truth about God contained in the Scriptures. It is important to understand that not everything found in the Scriptures is revelation. For instance, Acts 23:26-30 is a note from a centurion, Claudius Lysias to the governor, Felix. Though these verses provide some interesting historical background, they do not contain any revelation about God. On the other hand, in Col. 1:15, a passage filled with revelation, Paul states that Jesus is "the image of the invisible God, the firstborn of all creation."

Key Passages

1 Corinthians 2:6-13

From 1 Corinthians 2:6-13 we can see three important facts. First, God's wisdom is unknown to the world (2:7). It is "a secret" and "hidden". Second, it is unknowable by the world apart from divine disclosure (2:9). This wisdom cannot be discovered empirically "no eye has seen and no ear has heard" or rationally "no mind has conceived." People can neither observe it nor reason their way to it. Third, God through His Spirit revealed it (2:10). Thus, the knowledge of God required a supernatural revelation.

Hebrews 1:1-2

According to Hebrews 1:1-2, God revealed himself progressively to a select group of individuals (1:1) and this process of revelation is now complete (1:2). The mention of the prophets indicates that this revelation was not given to every person but only to a select group. The prophets in turn were to share this revelation with others. The main way that they could share it with future generations was to write it down in the form of scripture. Also, God did not reveal everything about himself at one time. He spoke "in many times and in various ways." Revelation was progressive. He continued to give more and at times greater revelations throughout the Old Testament. Finally, God gave his last written revelation. Jesus Christ is both the one through whom the final revelation has come and about which the final revelation speaks. The final message has been given.

Conclusions

- Man could not know God unless God revealed himself.
- God did reveal himself through the prophets in the Old Testament Scriptures.
- The revelation of Jesus Christ in the New Testament in God's final revelation.

Inspiration

Definition

Inspiration was the process in which God sovereignly guided, controlled, and superintended the human authors of Scripture to ensure that what they wrote was exactly what He intended and revealed to them.

Inspiration is limited to the original writers and does not include any work of God in the mind or heart of the reader. The Scriptures are inspired, not the interpreter of them. Additionally, inspiration is limited to the original manuscripts. Translations of the Scriptures were not inspired, that is, God did not sovereignly guide the translators of Scripture. Translations reflect this inspiration when they accurately represent the original.

> **Inspiration**
> The process in which God sovereignly guided, controlled, and superintended the human authors of Scripture to ensure that what they wrote was exactly what he intended

Key Passages

2 Timothy 3:16

From 2 Timothy 3:16, several points can be made. First, inspiration encompasses all scriptures. We use the term, **plenary**, to describe this. Second, inspiration encompasses the words of Scripture, not merely the concepts. We use the term, **verbal**, to describe this (1 Cor. 2:13). Third, inspiration makes God the ultimate author of Scripture (Heb. 3:7; 4:7). It is God-breathed, θεοπνευστος, *theopneustos*.

> **Inspiration – Key Passages**
> ● 2 Timothy 3:16
> ● 2 Peter 1:21

2 Peter 1:21

2 Peter 1:21 helps us to understand the relationship between the human and divine aspects of the authorship of Scripture. The biblical message did not originate with the human author. It came solely from God. However, this does not mean that God dictated the messages to the human authors. Rather, the human authors were "carried along by the Holy Spirit." Much like when we pick up a pen and write, the Holy Spirit picked up the human instrument and wrote. Just as my writing exhibits some characteristics of the pen I used, such as color and thickness, so also the Scriptures exhibit some characteristics of the human authors such as rhetorical style and vocabulary. God controlled the process without hindering the unique human character traits of each author.

Conclusions

- Inspiration was plenary and verbal.
- God is the ultimate author of Scripture.
- The messages in Scripture are from God, not from men.
- Inspiration was not dictation but allows for the writer's individuality.
- Like revelation, inspiration is a finished process, the product of which is Scripture.

Inerrancy

Definition:

Inerrancy is the teaching that the Bible is without error.

Many scholars, faced with the seeming inconsistencies between science and statements in Scripture wrestle with the idea of inerrancy. Some deny the inerrancy of Scripture and instead substitute the concept of **infallibility**, stating that the Bible is trustworthy in all that it affirms about God and his will. It seems better to refine the idea of inerrancy as Dockery

> **Inerrancy**
> The teaching that the Bible is without error

8

does when he states that Scripture "is completely true in all that it affirms, to the degree of precision intended by the author's purpose, in all matters relating to God and His creations."[6] Take for example, the claim by the meteorologist that sunrise this morning will be at 6:45 AM. Any scientist knows that the sun does not rise. The earth turns. Yet, this is a true claim when we understand that the description is phenomenological, not scientific. In our experience then sunrises. So, proper interpretation of Scripture is necessary to discover the inerrant teachings of Scripture. When science and Scripture seem to contradict, either we have faulty scientific conclusions or incorrect interpretation of Scripture. See the article by Lemke for a fuller discussion of the topic of inerrancy.[7]

Inerrancy – Key Passage
- John 17:17
- Numbers 23:19
- 1 Samuel 15:29

Key Passages:

John 17:17

In John 17:17, the Lord does not say that the Scriptures contain truth, but rather that they are truth. In this we see the difference between inerrancy and infallibility. Infallibility only teaches that Scripture contains truth. It allows for some errors in areas that are not theological. Yet, Jesus affirms inerrancy when he affirms that Scripture is truth.

Numbers 23:19; 1 Samuel 15:29

God cannot lie (Num. 23:19; 1 Sam. 15:29). Thus, the Scriptures, since God authored them, must be true. This is a reasonable conclusion. Indeed, a high view of inspiration requires a high view of inerrancy. Conversely, if you have a lower view of inerrancy, you will ultimately have a lower view of inspiration also.

Conclusions

- The Scriptures are true in all that they affirm.
- Seeming contradictions between science and Scripture exist either because of faulty scientific conclusions or faulty interpretation of Scripture.

Biblical Hermeneutics: A Guide for Studying the Bible

Authority

Definition:

Authority is the teaching that the Scriptures have the absolute and supreme right over the lives of all people, revealing what we must believe (doctrine) and how we must live (practice).

This ultimate authority is not shared with any other. One of the key tenants of the Reformation against Catholicism was that Scripture alone must be the ultimate authority. All authority found in the church is delegated and secondary. That is to say, the church derives its authority from the Scriptures and therefore we must go back to the Scriptures to understand and know God. We cannot merely listen to the teaching and dictates of the church or of any theological system.

> **Authority**
> The teaching that the Scriptures have the absolute and supreme right over the lives of all people

Key Passages:

Isaiah 7:7; Isaiah 8:20

Isaiah 7:7 and Isaiah 8:20 are typical for the Old Testament and demonstrate that the prophets' authority came from a Sovereign Lord. They did not appeal to the authority of the government or to the authority of Jewish religion. They appealed to the authority of God.

> **Authority – Key Passage**
> • Isaiah 7:7
> • Matthew 7:29
> • 2 Peter 1:19-21

Matthew 7:29

In Matthew 7:29 we see a great contrast in authority. The Jewish teachers based their teachings on the authority of others rather than on the Scriptures. Jesus, however, taught with authority. The lesson here is that authority is inherent in God, not in the teachings of men. In contract to the Jewish teachers, Jesus appealed to Scripture as his authority (Luke 4:4, 8, 12).

2 Peter 1:19-21

In 2 Peter 1:19-21, Peter appeals to two great authorities, the authority of eyewitnesses and the authority of Scripture. For him, the eyewitness accounts made even surer the prophecies of old. He had seen them fulfilled with his own eyes. Today, we do not have the direct authority of the eyewitnesses, instead we have the authority of the sure Word of God.

Conclusions

- The prophets, Jesus, and the disciples saw Scripture as authoritative.
- No organization or theological system should replace the authority of Scripture in our lives.
- We must always base our beliefs on the Scriptures.

English Translations

The Issue

It is best to study the Bible using the original Hebrew and Greek texts. However, few people will actually do this. It takes years of training and study to become proficient in these ancient languages. Most people will study the Bible using a translation.

For those who will study the Bible using an English translation, a clear problem arises. Which English translation should you use? You are confronted with many options. Our purpose here is to help you sort through the issues involved in choosing a translation and to provide you with a set of useful criteria for selecting translations.

Before we begin our discussion, we should define a few terms. We will use the term, **text**, to refer to a copy or edition of the Scriptures in their original languages. We will use the terms, **translation** and **version**, interchangeably to refer to a copy or edition of the Scriptures in another language. Though some scholars reserve the word, version, for translations directly from the original Greek or Hebrew texts, we will not press this distinction.

Factors That Influence a Translation

As we begin to compare translations, we quickly realize that translations can be very different. Why? We can identify four factors that influence the translation.

> **Factors That Influence Translation**
> - Hebrew and Greek Text
> - Interpretive Difficulties
> - Age of the Translation
> - Approach to Translation

- The Underlying Hebrew and Greek Text
- Interpretive Difficulties
- The Approach to Translation
- The Age of the Translation

Four Translations Compared

Before we consider these factors, let's first look at four translations of 1 Corinthians 7:36 and note the difference in each.

King James Versions	But if any man think that he behaveth himself uncomely toward his virgin, if she pass the flower of her age, and need so require, let him do what he will, he sinneth not: let them marry.
New American Standard Version	But if any man thinks that he is acting unbecomingly toward his virgin daughter, if she should be of full age; and if it must be so, let him do what he wishes, he does not sin; let her marry.
New International Version	If anyone thinks he is acting improperly toward the virgin he is engaged to, and if she is getting along in years and he feels he ought to marry, he should do as he wants. He is not sinning. They should get married.
Contemporary English Version	But suppose you are engaged to someone old enough to be married, and you want her so much that all you can think about is getting married. Then go ahead and marry. There is nothing wrong with that.

The most significant difference in the versions relates to whether Paul is talking about a father and his daughter or an engaged couple. The NASB refers to a daughter, the NIV and CEV refer to an engaged couple, and the KJV does not indicate either. Second, there are subtle differences in the way the CEV expands the description of the man's motivation in the expression, "all you can think about is getting married." The other readings suggest that there is something compelling the man to marry, but they do not suggest what it is. Finally, some versions are easier to read than others. The CEV and NIV are quite readable. The NASB seems stiff and formal. The KJV is quite difficult to read especially because of its archaic language.

From these observations we can draw three conclusions about translations. First, translations often make interpretive decisions. The act of translation naturally involves some interpretation. The question is how much. Those translations that include more interpretation tend to be easier to read but also limit the reader's choices about the meaning. Second, some translations include extensive expansions designed to make the meaning more obvious and clear to the reader. These expansions are not distinguishable from the parts of the translation that are more literally bound to the original language. Finally, the translations that are more readable tend to be the ones with more interpretations and expansions.

> **Three Conclusions about Translations**
> - Translations often make interpretive decisions
> - Translations often include expansions for clarity
> - Translations that include interpretations and expansions are easier to read

The Underlying Hebrew and Greek Texts

One reason why translations differ is because different translations are based on different Hebrew and Greek Texts. These differences, called *variants*, are most noticeable when comparing the KJV or NKJB with other modern translations. The above example does not demonstrate this problem. However, when comparing the KJV rendering of Romans 8:1 to modern translations the problem can be seen. The clause, "who walk not after the flesh, but after the Spirit" found in the KJV is missing from modern translations because the underlying Greek clause is missing from the older Greek manuscripts.

Interpretive Difficulties

One of the major factors that resulted in different translations of 1 Corinthians 7:36 is a difficulty in interpretation. The language of the passage is ambiguous. The text only mentions a virgin but does not indicate if the virgin is the man's daughter or fiancée. In this instance, the translator must decide either to leave the passage ambiguous and thus more difficult to read, or to include an interpretation with the translation. When translators disagree about the meaning, translations will also differ.

The Age of the Translation

Another factor that resulted in different translations in 1 Corinthians 7:36 is the age of the translation. The King James Version was made in 1611. The English language has gone through many changes since that time. Clearly, the age of this translation directly contributes to the differences with the other translations. To get the most out of Bible study, we need to use an up-to-date, modern translation.

The Approach to Translation

The final factor that resulted in different translations of 1 Corinthians 7:36 is the approach or goal in translation. Some translators have the goal of making an easy-to-read, clear translation, while other translators have the goal of translating in such a way that the wording of the translation is as close as possible to the original Hebrew or Greek, even if that means sacrificing readability and clarity.

Three Basic Approaches to Translation

Three Basic Approaches to Translation
• Formal Equivalency
• Dynamic Equivalency
• Paraphrase

An understanding of the different approaches to translation is vitally important. Fee and Stuart discuss three basic approaches or theories to translation. They include formal equivalency, dynamic equivalency, and paraphrase.[8]

Formal Equivalency

Formal Equivalency
Attempts to represent each word in one language with an equivalent word in another language

Formal equivalency creates a word for word translation. It represents each word in the original language with an equivalent word in the receptor language. This type of translation is often called a **literal translation**. Because of the differences in languages, exact formal equivalency is not possible. For example, an exact formal equivalency of John 3:16 would be:

> So for loved the God the world, so that the son the only He gave, in
> order that all the believing into him not might perish but have life eternal.

Formal equivalency strives to represent the structure of the original text as accurately as possible in another language. This includes word meanings, the order of the words in a sentence, and the grammatical structure of the sentence. An interlinear Hebrew or Greek Bible will illustrate how a literal 'word for word' translation might read.

The advantage of formal equivalency is that it includes far less interpretations than do other types of translations. However, it is normally less readable.

Dynamic Equivalency

Dynamic Equivalency
Creates a thought for thought translation

Dynamic equivalency creates a thought for thought translation. The goal is to represent the meaning of the original statement in the clearest possible way, not to replicate the structure of the original language in the translation. Since the Greek and Hebrew languages differ significantly from English, the result is a translation that is often very different in structure from the original. To illustrate this, we can compare the number of sentences in the KJV, NASB, NIV and CEV translation of Ephesians 1:3-14.

Greek	KJV	NASB	NIV	CEV
1	3	5	7	13

Clearly, there was little attempt on the part of the translators of the CEV to retain the grammatical structure of the original. In a sense, the chart represents a spectrum moving from least dynamic (KJV) to most dynamic (CEV).

For another example, let's look at 1 Thessalonians 1:3 in these same translations.

King James Versions	Remembering without ceasing your work of faith, and labour of love, and patience of hope in our Lord Jesus Christ in the sight of God and our Father;
New American Standard Version	constantly bearing in mind your work of faith and labor of love and steadfastness of hope in our Lord Jesus Christ in the presence of our God and Father,
New International Version	We continually remember before our God and Father your work produced by faith, your labor prompted by love, and your endurance inspired by hope in our Lord Jesus Christ.
Contemporary English Version	We tell God our Father about your faith and loving work and about your firm hope in our Lord Jesus Christ.

The CEV exhibits the most structural differences, followed by the NIV. The KJV and NASB are very similar and follow the structure of the Greek more closely. Note also how the NIV expands the triplet with the words, produced, prompted, and inspired. Both the CEV and NIV move the expression, "in the presence of our God and Father" to the beginning of the verse and thereby relate it to the act of remembering. The CEV goes so far as to explain that this remembering in the presence of God must refer to prayer, that is, "telling God."

Clearly dynamic equivalency incorporates a significant amount of interpretation. This is a great advantage for those who would have difficulty understanding without the interpretation. However, at the same time, this is a potential danger since it eliminates other viable interpretations of the text.

Paraphrase

A **paraphrase** is a radical rewording of a passage rather than a direct translation. Often a paraphrase will attempt to discover the idea of a whole passage and then to set forth that idea using a contemporary setting. For instance, one might attempt to reproduce the story of the Good Samaritan in a modern city setting.

Paraphrase
Radical rewording of a passage rather than a direct translation

A paraphrase can be helpful in communicating the basic truths of Scriptures to an audience with little understanding of biblical culture. However, as Brisco warns[9], you should not use a paraphrase as a study Bible because it contains extensive expansions, alterations, and commentary.

Criteria for Choosing a Translation

We have discovered that translations differ for several reasons. The next obvious question to ask is, "Which translation is best?" There is no easy answer to this question. Certainly, there are some translations that we should reject, and it is best to choose one translation as your primary translation for personal study and memorization. However, the best advice is to use several translations for Bible study, selecting ones that are appropriate for the task. You should select a translation that:

Select a Translation that is
- Modern
- Scholarly
- Orthodox
- Appropriate for Study

- Is modern and up-to-date.
- Is based on good scholarship.
- Has no unorthodox theological bias.
- Is appropriate for your study.

The Age of the Translation

Language is constantly changing. It is essential that you choose a translation that is up-to-date. This is the major problem with holding onto the King James Version. In spite of attempts to update some of the wording, the basic text remains outdated. For those who grew up with this classic translation and who memorized so many of its verses, an alternative would be to use The New King James Bible. It retains much of the style of the King James and is based on the same original texts.

The Scholarship of the Translation

The task of translating the Bible is a difficult one that requires tremendous scholarship. A committee of scholars who are skilled in the original languages, biblical interpretation, and translation theory produces the best translation. You should inquire about the qualifications of the translators before you decide on a translation. Often information about the translators and the process they employed in creating the translation is available in the preface of the translation. You can also find information in scholarly journals and publications.

The Presuppositions of the Translators

We have seen that translations always include some interpretation and often include quite a bit of it. So, we must be cautious about translations that are the product of those who reject the clear teachings of Scripture. For example, *The New World Translation*, produced by the Jehovah's Witnesses, translates John 1:1 as follows:

> In the beginning the Word was, and the Word was with God, and **the Word was a god.**

The bold is added for emphasis. Jehovah's Witnesses, who deny the deity of Christ, clearly bias the translation.

The question of gender-neutral translations is also related to the presuppositions of translators. Should translations avoid using the masculine gender? Is it better to talk about God as our parent rather than our father? Most likely this issue will become a major area of debate in future years.

The Purpose of Your Study

After you eliminate translations that lack scholarship or that include inappropriate biases, you are still left with many possibilities. You should not limit yourself to just one selection. It is best to select a translation that is appropriate for a specific task. You learned above that translations based on formal equivalency more closely retain the grammatical structure of the original language and introduce less interpretations and expansions. Because of this they are preferred when we are performing detailed structural analysis. *The New American Standard Bible* or the *English Standard Version* is a good choice. However, a dynamic equivalency is easier to understand and read. It should be preferred for surveying large sections of Scripture to get the over-all purpose and plan of that section. For this, *The New International Version* is a good choice.

Conclusion: Not One Translation but Many

In conclusion, as your primary translation, you should select a scholarly translation that is fairly literal. However, a good Bible student will have a number of translations and will use them often, selecting the more literal translations when performing in-depth analysis, and selecting the more dynamic translations when performing a quick survey.

You should also consider your audience. For instance, those working with children may need to use a very readable translation, even a paraphrase, while those working with older adults may need to use the King James Version. We should be deferent to our audience when we communicate the truth of Scripture, yet during our study, we should use the most scholarly translations possible.

> **Which Translation for Study?**
> A scholarly, fairly literal translation for general use, supplemented by more dynamic translations

The Role of the Interpreter

Above we introduced four key elements in interpretation: the Scriptures, the interpreter, the Holy Spirit, and the methodology. Now we will develop the role of the interpreter more fully. At the very outset we must be aware that the interpreter is intimately involved in the process of interpretation. Recall that hermeneutics is not only a science but also an art. The interpreter actively applies the principles of hermeneutics in an attempt to understand the text. As Mickelsen states,

> "An interpreter brings to bear upon the text all that he is, all that he knows, and even all that he wants to become...Knowing this, we must try to be so molded by God that the distortion brought about by our subjectivity will be at a minimum."[10]

We will begin with a review of the qualifications of the interpreter necessary to be a skilled Bible scholar. Then, we will examine the effects of our subjectivity on interpretation so that we can minimize any distortions in interpretation that subjectivity might create.

Qualifications of the Interpreter

To be a capable interpreter, you must exhibit both spiritual and intellectual qualifications. In 2 Corinthians 3:5-6, Paul states that it is God who makes us adequate for the task of serving him. In contrast, Peter speaks of those whose spiritual lives are so far from God that they fail completely at interpretation (2 Peter 3:16). We must make every effort to present ourselves approved in the work of interpretation (2 Tim. 3:16).

Spiritual Qualifications

To properly interpret God's Word, you must know Jesus Christ as your Savior and have an intense desire to know His Word and a humble heart to respond in obedience to it.

> **Spiritual Qualifications**
> • Salvation
> • Spiritual Longing
> • Obedience

Salvation

The Scriptures make it clear that only Christians, who are indwelt by the Spirit of God, can fully grasp and properly evaluate the Scriptures (1 Cor. 2:14-16). The unbeliever can understand the basic meaning of the Scriptures but can never properly evaluate them. Full appreciation that comes from a deep awareness of the truth contained in the Scriptures requires the Holy Spirit, who indwells the believer.

Spiritual Longing

The interpreter must have a passion for God's Word. David writes, "My soul is consumed with longing for your laws at all times" (Psalm 119:20) and again, "How I long for your precepts" (Psalm 119:40). The work of interpretation requires diligence (2 Tim. 2:15) that is driven by a desire to know the meaning of Scripture.

Obedience

James instructs us to be doers of the Word and not hearers only who deceive themselves (James 1:22). The ultimate goal of Bible study is response. Failure to respond to God's word will lead to self-deception and misunderstanding about the ultimate meaning of Scripture.

Intellectual Qualifications
- Logical Thinking
- Well Educated
- Acquainted with original languages

Intellectual Qualifications

In Ezra 7:6, Ezra is described as a skilled scribe. The description seems to be more related to his general ability and diligence than to his spiritual qualifications. Along with spiritual qualifications, it is clear that an interpreter must also exhibit certain intellectual qualifications. You must be logical, well-educated, and acquainted with the original languages.

Logical Thinking

Paul often appeals to his readers to use their minds in following his arguments (1 Cor. 11:13). So too, the Lord asked Israel to reason with Him as he argues his case (Isa. 1:18). If we are to understand the Scriptures, we must be mature in our thinking (1 Cor. 14:19). A logical mind needs to be developed. It does not necessarily come naturally. You need to be trained in logic and rational thought.

Well-Educated

The Bible is an historic book in which the reader encounters people from different cultures. It is a book of literature, filled with unique genres and literary features. It is a book of profound thoughts that have occupied the minds of people for generations. To fully understand it, you need to be well-educated in the arts. The interpreter should be an historian, a philosopher, a linguist, a sociologist, and a literary scholar. Acquaintance with these disciplines will greatly contribute to your ability to interpret.

Acquainted with the Original Languages

The Bible was written in Hebrew, Aramaic, and Greek. It is best studied in these languages. At times, the subtle meaning of the text is difficult to completely represent in a translation. At other times, a translation includes interpretations that might not be the intent of the original. Clearly, it is more likely that the interpreter will discover the correct interpretation when an understanding of the original languages is employed.

The Effect of Subjectivity on Interpretation

Definition of Subjectivity

Subjectivity
Those things internal to the interpreter that affect interpretation

---

By **subjectivity** we mean those things internal to the interpreter that affect interpretation. They include the things we know, our pre-understandings; the things we believe, our presuppositions; and the things we feel, our prejudices.

To illustrate the concept of subjectivity and its effect on interpretation, consider how a stone-age tribal people living deep in the Amazon rainforest would understand a picture of an astronaut walking on the moon. They would most likely misinterpret the picture, creating in their minds the most bazaar ideas. The problem is that their minds are not prepared to process accurately what they saw. First, they would lack knowledge of the modern world; and secondly, they would attempt to understand based on what they know and believe about their own world.

For a fuller explanation of subjectivity, read the material presented by Klein, Blomberg, and Hubbard.[11] They discuss the presuppositions and the pre-understandings of the interpreter necessary for correct interpretation.

Three Aspects of Subjectivity

Pre-understandings – Informational Aspect – What We Know

Our **pre-understanding** is the knowledge that we have previously acquired in life through prior education, training, and experience. Our pre-understanding influences interpretation in several important ways.

Pre-understanding Shapes the Way We Understand New Information

Our pre-understanding is the basis for all future new understanding. We learn the unknown, new knowledge, in the light of the known, previously understood knowledge. Whether we are aware of it or not, we filter all new information through the grid of our pre-understanding. Thus, our prior knowledge and previous experiences shape the way we see the world and understand new information.

Pre-understanding Is Sometimes Reliable at Other Times Unreliable

We interpret all subjective experiences and evaluate all objective data on the basis of our own pre-understanding. Some portions of our pre-understanding may be accurate. Unfortunately, other portions of our pre-understanding may be inaccurate or incomplete. When our pre-understanding is complete and accurate, it can be a reliable tool in evaluating and correctly interpreting new information. When our pre-understanding is incomplete and inaccurate, it is an unreliable tool in evaluating and interpreting new information.

Pre-understanding Affects Our Ability to Interpret Scripture

Inevitably, our pre-understanding will affect our ability to understand and interpret the Scriptures. Pre-understandings influence the questions we ask and the kind of answers we form. As a result, our pre-understandings can either be an aide or a hindrance. When our pre-understanding of Scripture is somewhat complete and accurate, it will enable us to be accurate interpreters. When our pre-understanding of Scripture is incomplete or inaccurate, it will distort our interpretations.

Presuppositions – Ideological Aspect – What We Believe

Presuppositions are the ideas or beliefs that we assume are true or which we take for granted. Our presuppositions form our worldview, that is, our conception of what we think the world is and how we believe it operates.

Most Important Presuppositions – Our Beliefs about God & Scriptures

The most important presuppositions relating to biblical interpretation are those that we hold concerning God and the Scriptures and concerning the correct method of interpreting the Scriptures. Earlier in this chapter you learned about the need for the interpreter to believe in God and have a saving relationship with Him. In the prior chapter you learned about divine revelation, inspiration, inerrancy, and authority. Later, you will learn about the

> **Three Aspects of Subjectivity**
> - Pre-understandings
> - Presuppositions
> - Prejudices

> **Pre-understanding**
> The knowledge that we have previously acquired in life through prior education, training, and experience

> **Presuppositions**
> The ideas or beliefs that we assume are true or which we take for granted

proper method of interpretation. These form the key presuppositions essential for correct interpretation.

Other Presuppositions Also Important

Other presuppositions can also have an effect on our ability to interpret. This most often occurs when our current beliefs lead us to reject an interpretation before we perform a thorough study. Take for instance, Paul's statement in 1 Corinthians 2:6:

> We do, however, speak a message of wisdom among the mature, but not
> a wisdom of this age or of the rulers of this age, who are coming to
> nothing.

Some reject the idea that the mature in this passage refers generally to Christians as opposed to unbelievers, based on their presupposition that only some Christians can validly be called mature. When such a presupposition closes our minds to other possibilities, it can be destructive. One needs to be open to other possibilities and then to perform research to see if these possibilities are valid.

Prejudices – Attitudinal Aspect – How We Feel

Our **prejudices** are our attitudes and inclinations that have already been formed in our past. To a large extent, our prejudices determine in advance how we will feel about something. They dictate our opinions.

When our prejudices are positive, they precondition us to view something or someone in a positive light. When they are negative, they precondition us to view the same in a negative light. For instance, people whose fathers abused them or failed to love and care for them may have a difficult time understanding the concept that God is our Father. The issue is one of feeling. They never experienced love and tenderness in their father's presence, only fear. So, for them it becomes difficult to understand the relationship expressed when God calls us His children.

Impact of Subjectivity on Interpretation

The Prevalence of Subjectivity in Interpretation

Cornelius van Til notes that everyone has so many presuppositions that it is impossible for anyone to be completely neutral. We must recognize that we cannot escape a certain amount of subjectivity in our efforts to interpret the Bible. No one ever interprets anything without an underlying set of assumptions. Those who claim that they have discarded all their presuppositions and that they always study the biblical text in a purely and totally objective manner are either self-deceived or grossly naive.

The Subtle Nature of Our Subjectivity

Unfortunately, most people are not aware of their subjectivity nor are they aware that they tend to use it in a totally unconscious manner. Accordingly, a professor at another college once said, "The problem with many freshmen is that they don't know that they don't know!"

The Impact of Our Subjectivity upon Interpretation

An insightful and honest interpreter once remarked, "Wonderful things in the Bible I see, most of them put there by you and me." Subjectivity is so powerful that interpreters tend to find in a text precisely the meaning, and only that meaning, they expect to find. Our subjectivity serves as a blinder to observation. Our pre-understandings and presuppositions are especially powerful in coloring our interpretations of controversial passages and subjects. We must be aware of our presuppositions and pursue objectivity with the evidence.

Prejudices
Our attitudes and inclinations that have already been formed in our past

Subjectivity Inescapable
We cannot escape a certain amount of subjectivity.

Subjectivity Subtle
We are often unaware of our subjectivity

Subjectivity Very Powerful
Especially powerful in coloring our interpretations of controversial passages and subjects

The Benefits and Liabilities of Our Pre-understandings

The Benefits of Pre-understandings: Prerequisite Knowledge

When our pre-understandings are correct, they can help us correctly interpret and understand new things since we cannot learn new truths without prerequisite knowledge of elementary truths. The Scriptures themselves presuppose that its readers are bringing some prior pre-understanding to the biblical text. For example, in order to correctly understand the New Testament, we must have some degree of prior pre-understanding of the Old Testament. If and when our pre-understandings are correct, they serve as a launching pad for greater depths of new understanding in the Scriptures (e.g., 2 Tim. 3:14-17; 2 Peter 1:3-6).

Benefits of Pre-understanding
When correct they help us interpret and understand.

The Liabilities of Pre-understandings: Unintentional Subjectivity

Pre-understandings that are incorrect and invalid distort both observation and interpretation. When Bible study is controlled by incorrect pre-understandings the result will most likely be incorrect interpretation. As a result, failure to control our presuppositions, even if unintentional, is harmful to correct interpretation.

Liabilities of Pre-understanding
Pre-understandings that are incorrect distort both observation and interpretation

Strategy for Controlling Subjectivity

Because we are all conditioned by our own subjective presuppositions, we might erroneously conclude that we are doomed to subjectivity and that we can never interpret Scripture in an objective manner. The key is to take steps to control our subjectivity. A strategy to do so will include the following:

- Become aware of your presuppositions.
- Seek God's Help in Reshaping Your Thinking.
- Use an Objective Hermeneutical Method.

Strategy for Controlling Subjectivity
• Become aware of your presuppositions • Seek God's Help in Reshaping Your Thinking • Use an Objective Hermeneutical Method

Become Aware of Your Presuppositions

Before we begin to study a passage, we need to discover and acknowledge what our presuppositions are about that passage and what we would like our conclusions to be. We must consider all the social, racial, political, economic, and religious factors that color our thinking.

We must test, critique, and evaluate our presuppositions in the light of an objective study of the passage. We must be willing to reject or modify any presuppositions that are found to be unacceptable in light of the objective evidence.

Seek God's Help in Reshaping Your Thinking

We must seek God's help to reshape our hearts and minds so that our thinking is in harmony with the perspective of Scripture so that the distortion brought about by our own subjectivity will be minimized (e.g., Rom. 12:2-3). Before we even begin to study a passage, we must pray, asking the Spirit to free us from our presuppositions in order to observe the biblical text honestly and without bias. We must ask God to give us humble hearts and open minds.

Use an Objective Hermeneutical Method

To safeguard ourselves against our prejudices and biases in interpretation, we must use a hermeneutical method that will minimize our tendency to read into the text what we want to see. We must use an interpretive approach that is objective in nature and that will force us to reckon with the data in the text. We need to start with an inductive approach.

Once we have studied a passage inductively, we should check our conclusions against the conclusions of other biblical scholars. We need to find out how past scholars throughout church history have interpreted the passage. We must allow their studied insights to critique our views and interpretive conclusions. We should also compare our interpretations with those of contemporary Christian scholars, allowing them to critique our interpretations to look for any mistakes and blind spots.

The Role of the Holy Spirit

Earlier we introduced four key elements in interpretation: the Scriptures, the interpreter, the Holy Spirit, and the methodology. Now we will discuss in a fuller way the critical question, "What role does the Holy Spirit have in our understanding of Scripture". At one extreme are those who teach that the Holy Spirit so opens the mind of the believer that no academic study of Scripture is necessary. Indeed, it can be destructive. At the other extreme are those who see no place for the subjective working of the Spirit in the mind or heart of the interpreter. Rather, they teach that interpretation requires a completely objective, rational process. The Scriptures do not suggest either extreme.

Definition of Illumination

> **Spiritual Illumination**
> The work of the Spirit in making the heart receptive and helping the believer to properly evaluate the message

The term, illumination, means enlightenment, clarification, or explanation of what is not understood or known. The phrase, **spiritual illumination**, refers to the work of the Spirit in helping believers either understand, evaluate or judge the truthfulness of Scripture and how it applies to their lives. When we are dealing with the work of the Spirit in illumination, we are seeking to clarify the role of the Spirit in the process of interpretation and application. The key question is, "Does the Spirit help the believer understand the meaning?" We reject this idea, preferring rather to see the role of the Holy Spirit as making the heart receptive and helping the believer to properly evaluate the message. For a full discussion of this view, see Roy Zuck's article.[12]

Scripture teaches that the Spirit illumines every believer (e.g., 1 Cor 2:14; 1 John 2:27). However, this does not mean that Christians do not need to learn how to study and interpret the Bible. Nor does it mean that the work of the Spirit in illumination replaces the need for hermeneutics and interpretation. The work of the Spirit in illumination is more closely related to application and reception of the Scriptures than to understanding and interpretation. When the Christian studies the Bible, the Spirit takes the interpreted passage and enlightens the Christian about its relevance and authority in his or her life and makes the believer open and receptive to its message.

Biblical Teaching about Illumination

Spiritual Illumination is Necessary to Accept the Message of Salvation: 1 Corinthians 2:14

> **1 Cor. 2:14**
> • Spirit helps person accept spiritual truth
> • Spirit helps person evaluate spiritual truth

> The man without the Spirit does not accept the things that come from the Spirit of God, for they are foolishness to him, and he cannot understand them, because they are spiritually discerned.

1 Corinthians 2:14 makes it clear that a full grasp of Scripture requires some work by the Spirit, since, apart from the illumination of the Spirit, man does not accept the basic gospel message. However, this passage does not suggest that the illumination of the Spirit is necessary for intellectually understanding of the Bible. Rather, it is needed to render the

heart humble, open and receptive to the gospel message. Thus, the Spirit's work in illumination does not deal with the objective, cognitive interpretation of Scripture, but with the subjective transformation of the human heart when confronted with the truthfulness and authority of Scripture. The Spirit does not interpret Scripture for the unbeliever. Rather, the Spirit helps a person welcome the Word of God, and spiritually appraise its truthfulness and authority over one's life.

Commonly Misunderstood Passages

The following passages have often been used to support the idea that illumination includes the work of the Holy Spirit in providing the basis interpretation of a passage. When properly understood, they do not support this idea.

> **Commonly Misunderstood**
> - 1 John 2:27
> - Psalm 119:18
> - John 14:26

1 John 2:27

> As for you, the anointing you received from him remains in you, and you do not need anyone to teach you. But as his anointing teaches you about all things and as that anointing is real, not counterfeit- just as it has taught you, remain in him.

The Spirit's illumination, His anointing, makes all believers spiritually capable of understanding and perceiving the basic truths of Scripture. Therefore, believers have no need for new revelations, as the false teachers were claiming (1 John 2:18-27). However, this passage does not claim that the Spirit's illumination guarantees that every believer will correctly interpret every passage in the Bible all the time. That is contrary to experience, church history, and the teaching of Scripture itself. This passage does not suggest that every passage in the Bible will be crystal clear to all believers, only that all can generally understand its basic message. Thus, 1 John 2:27 does not imply that believers merely need to pray for the Spirit to lead them into the correct interpretation of Scripture. This kind of illumination relates only to the basic truths of Scripture.

Psalm 119:18

> Open my eyes that I may see wonderful things in your law.

Psalm 119, as a whole, focuses on obedience to the commands of God. The psalmist never asks for help in interpreting the Law. However, in this passage he asks for spiritual help in obeying and applying Scripture to his life. The psalmist is not so much asking God for objective interpretation of the Word of God, as much as for subjective enlightenment about its relevance and application to his life. He wants to see how the general principles of the commands of God could be applied to the specifics of his everyday life. The psalmist is asking God to help him discern those areas in his life that need to come into obedience to the commands of God. Thus, spiritual illumination helps the believer see the relevance of what he intellectually understands about the Scriptures.

John 14:26

> But the Counselor, the Holy Spirit, whom the Father will send in my name, will teach you all things and will remind you of everything I have said to you.

John 14:26 and other similar passages (John 15:26; 16:13) are often misunderstood by some people to be describing the work of the Spirit in teaching the Word of God to believers. However, it is best to understand these passages as relating only to the work of the Spirit in inspiring the apostles to write the New Testament. These passages do not relate to the illumination of believers. Therefore, they do not teach – as some people erroneously claim – that all believers can perfectly interpret any passage if only they are Spirit led. These passages have nothing to do with spiritual illumination of believers in general, only with the inspiration of the apostles.

What the Spirit Does and Does Not Do in Interpretation

What the Spirit Does Not Do

- The Spirit does not do the work of interpreting the meaning of a biblical passage for the interpreter.

- The Spirit does not mystically supply the information needed by the interpreter to interpret. Rather, the interpreter must discover this information through diligent study and research.

- The Spirit does not reveal the correct interpretation of a passage simply on the basis of us praying for the interpretation apart from the work of interpretation. Prayer is important in the interpretive process, not to give us the interpretation, but to make us humble and open enough to accept the correct interpretation.

- The Spirit does not give to some interpreters a hidden or novel meaning that is divergent from the normal, literal meaning of a passage.

- The Spirit's work in illumination does not guarantee that anyone's interpretation will be 100% accurate if they are simply Spirit-led.

What the Spirit Does Do

- The Spirit gives the believer the desire, hunger and motivation to study the Scriptures, including the drive and diligence required in this study (1 Peter 2:1-3).

- The Spirit works on the hearts of believers to make them welcome the meaning of correctly interpreted Scripture, and to make them receptive to its authority in their lives (1 Cor. 2:14).

- The Spirit helps believers discern how the correctly interpreted Word of God should be applied to specific situations in the everyday life of the believer (Psalm 119:18).

Summary

Hermeneutics is the discipline that provides the principles and guidelines for correctly interpreting the Bible. As such, it is both a science and an art. Its goal is to discover the intended meaning of the author. Hermeneutics is necessary because modern readers of the Bible are separated in time from the original readers. This may result, in different interpretations of a passage. The Bible suggests that proper understanding of the Scriptures requires the direction and diligence that hermeneutical methods provide.

Four key elements must be considered in interpretation, the Scriptures, the interpreter, the Holy Spirit, and the hermeneutical methodology. Our beliefs about the Scriptures directly affect our approach to interpreting them and to responding to them. To correctly interpret them we must be convinced that they are the inerrant, inspired Word of God. Four key concepts embody this conviction, revelation, inspiration, inerrancy, and authority.

Revelation is both a process and a product. As a process, revelation was the process in which God communicated to man his hidden and invisible thoughts. As a product, revelation is the truth about God contained in the Scriptures. Key passages on revelation are 1 Corinthians 2:6-13 and Hebrews 1:1-2.

Inspiration was the process in which God guided and controlled the writing of Scripture. Like the process of revelation, inspiration is historic. Jesus is God's final revelation; the Scriptures are complete. Key passages on inspiration are 2 Timothy 3:16 and 2 Peter 1:21.

Inerrancy teaches that the Bible is without error. Those who see conflicts between science and statements in the Bible deny inerrancy, replacing it with the idea of infallibility. A better approach is to understand that when the Bible is correctly interpreted in light of the author's intent and degree of precision, it will not conflict with the truth of God in nature. Key passages on inerrancy are John 17:17, Numbers 23:19, and 1 Samuel 15:29.

Authority is the teaching that the Scriptures have the absolute right over our lives. No other authority whether church or theological system should be given the same weight of authority. We must always return to Scripture as the source of ultimate truth. Key passages on authority are Isaiah 7:7, Matthew 7:29, and 2 Peter 1:19-21.

The student must select between a wealth of translations that differ significantly. They differ due to four factors that influence translation: differences in the underlying Hebrew and Greek texts, interpretive difficulties that often lead translators to choose between different interpretations, different approaches to translating, and the age of the translation.

A translation reflects one of three approaches to translating. Formal Equivalency attempts to represent each word in one language with an equivalent word in another language, retaining as much of the grammatical structure of the original language as is possible. Dynamic Equivalency produces thought for thought translations that are more concerned about clarifying the ideas represented in the original text than retaining the structure of the original text and thus include many interpretations and expansions. Paraphrases are a radical rewording of a passage rather than a direct translation and should not be used for in depth Bible study.

A good translation is modern, scholarly, unbiased, and appropriate for the type of study desired. A student should use several translations. One's primary translation should be a fairly literal translation. We must also keep in mind our audience.

Both spiritual and intellectual qualifications are needed to be a capable interpreter. Spiritually, the interpreter must have true salvation, have a spiritual longing for God's Word, and have a humble heart to obey God. Intellectually, the interpreter must have a logical mind, a balanced education, and an acquaintance with the original languages.

Our subjectivity, those things internal to ourselves that affect interpretations, includes our pre-understandings, our presuppositions, and our prejudices. Pre-understanding refers to the knowledge we possess, presuppositions are the beliefs that we affirm, and prejudices are the feelings we express. Though subtle in nature, our subjectivity is a prevalent and powerful factor in interpretation. It is beneficial when correct but destructive when incorrect. To control our subjectivity, we should become aware of our presuppositions, seek God's help in reshaping our thinking, and employ an objective hermeneutical methodology.

Spiritual illumination is the work of the Holy Spirit in making the heart ready to receive the truth of Scripture and helping the believer to properly apply the message of Scripture. Key passages related to illumination are 1 Cor. 2:14; 1 John 2:27; and Psalm 119:18. Interpretation is the work of the believer. Only after the believer arrives at a proper understanding of the Scripture does the Holy Spirit illuminate.

Key Terms

Authority
Dynamic Equivalency
Formal Equivalency
Hermeneutics
Hermeneutical Guideline

Hermeneutical Principle
Illumination
Inerrancy
Infallibility
Inspiration

Paraphrase
Pre-understanding
Prejudices
Presuppositions
Revelation
Subjectivity

Review Questions

1. What is hermeneutics?
2. What is the difference between a hermeneutical principle and a hermeneutical guideline?
3. In what sense is hermeneutics a science?
4. In what sense is hermeneutics an art?
5. What is the primary goal of interpretation?
6. What gaps exist between the modern and original readers of Scripture?
7. What are the four key elements in interpretation?
8. Why are our presuppositions about the Scriptures relevant to Hermeneutics?
9. What are the four key concepts relating to the nature of Scripture?
10. In what sense can we consider revelation both a process and a product?
11. What three important facts about revelation can we draw from 1 Corinthians 2:6-13?
12. What passage of Scripture clearly indicates that God is no longer giving new revelations about himself to men?
13. How is the concept of the inspiration of the writers of Scripture different from the idea of an artist being inspired in his work?
14. In what two important ways can divine inspiration be described?
15. What key passages of Scripture teach divine inspiration?
16. How is the idea of inerrancy different from the idea of infallibility?
17. What passage of Scripture clearly teaches inerrancy?
18. What it meant by the authority of the Scriptures?
19. What three examples do we have to demonstrate that authority should be placed in the Scriptures and not man-made systems?
20. What four factors explain the differences in translations?
21. Why are some translations more readable than others?
22. What three approaches are used in creating a translation?
23. What are the advantages and disadvantages of a literal translation?
24. What are the advantages and disadvantages of a dynamic translation?
25. What four criteria should be used when choosing a translation?
26. Explain why a student should use more than one translation?
27. What are the three spiritual qualifications of the interpreter?
28. What are the three intellectual qualifications of the interpreter?
29. What do we mean by subjectivity in interpretation?
30. What are the three aspects of our subjectivity?
31. What are the key presuppositions that are essential for correct interpretation?
32. How does our subjectivity impact our ability to interpret?
33. How can subjectivity be either beneficial or harmful?
34. What steps can be taken to control our subjectivity?
35. What is meant by spiritual illumination?
36. What is the relationship between illumination and interpretation?
37. What were the views of Luther and Calvin on illumination?
38. How does 1 Corinthians 2:14 explain illumination?
39. Explain why 1 John 2:27 does not teach that illumination eliminates the need for personal study into the meaning of Scripture?
40. For what does David ask in Psalm 119:18?
41. What does the Spirit do, and not do in interpretation?

References

[1] Terry, Milton S. *Biblical Hermeneutics*. Grand Rapids: Zondervan Publishing House, 1974. pp. 19-22.

[2] Johnson, Elliott S. "Author's Intention and Biblical Interpretation", Hermeneutics, *Inerrancy, & the Bible*. Grand Rapids: Zondervan, 1984. pp. 407-428.

[3] Silva, Moises and Walter C. Kaiser, Jr. *An Introduction to Biblical Hermeneutics*. Grand Rapids: Zondervan, 1994. pp. 15-25.

[4] Klein, William W., Craig L. Blomberg, and Robert L. Hubbard, Jr. *Introduction to Biblical Interpretation*. Dallas: Word Publishing, 1993. pp. 12-16.

[5] Ramm, Bernard. *Protestant Biblical Interpretation*. Grand Rapids: Baker Book House, 1970. pp. 4-7.

[6] Dockery, Russel. *The Doctrines of the Bible*. Nashville: Convention Press, 1991. pp. 80

[7] Lemske, Steve W. "The Inspiration and Truthfulness of Scripture." *Biblical Hermeneutics*. Ed. Corley, Bruce, Steve Lemke, and Grant Lovejoy. Nashville: Broadman & Holman Publishers, 1996. pp. 147-164

[8] Fee, Gordon D. and Douglas Stuart. *How To Read The Bible For All Its Worth*. Grand Rapids: Zondervan Publishing House, 1993. pp. 34-40.

[9] Brisco, Thomas V. "Translations and Hermeneutics", *Biblical Hermeneutics, A Comprehensive Introduction To Interpreting Scripture*. Corley, Bruce, Steve Lemke, and Grant Lovejoy, eds. Nashville: Broadman & Holman Publishers, 1996. pp. 199-200.

[10] Mickelsen, A. Berkeley. *Interpreting The Bible*. Grand Rapids: Wm. B. Eerdmans Publishing Company, 1963. pp. 65-66.

[11] Klein, William W., Craig L. Blomberg, and Robert L. Hubbard, Jr. *Introduction To Biblical Interpretation*. Dallas: Word Publishing, 1993. pp. 87-116.

[12] Zuck, Roy B. "The Role of the Holy Spirit in Hermeneutics", *Bibliotheca Sacra, Vol. 141*. Dallas: Dallas Seminary Publications, 1984. pp. 120-130.

Chapter 2

The Role of the Methodology

Outline

Introduction 28

Key Concepts 28

Inductive and Deductive Methodologies 30

The Four Basic Steps of the Inductive Method 32

The HGRT Method 34

Summary 37

Review Questions 38

References 38

Learning Objectives

After completing this chapter, you should be able to

- ❑ Define the key concepts: exegesis, eisegesis, interpretation, theology, application, and exposition.
- ❑ Distinguish between an inductive and a deductive method of interpretation.
- ❑ Explain when to use inductive and deductive methodologies.
- ❑ List the four steps in inductive Bible study.
- ❑ Explain why the HGRT method is valid.
- ❑ Identify the four principles of the HGRT method.
- ❑ Describe the four principles of the HGRT method.
- ❑ Identify the four theological characteristics of the Bible and the principles that relate to them.

Introduction

In Chapter 1 we introduced four key elements in interpretation: the Scriptures, the interpreter, the Holy Spirit, and the methodology. In this chapter we will begin to learn more about a proper methodology for interpreting the Scriptures. First, we will discuss key concepts related to that methodology and then we will discuss the differences between an inductive and a deductive methodology. Next, we will introduce the basic steps in inductive Bible study. Finally, we will formally introduce the HGRT methodology that we will use throughout the rest of our study.

Key Concepts

To discuss a methodology for interpretation, we need to begin by defining some key terms. Important to our understanding are the following:

Key Concepts
- Hermeneutics
- Exegesis
- Interpretation
- Theology
- Application
- Exposition

- Hermeneutics: The Principles of Interpreting the Bible
- Exegesis: The Practice of Interpreting the Bible
- Interpretation: The Product of Exegesis
- Theology: The Product of Correlating the Teachings of the Bible
- Application: The Process of Discerning the Relevance of the Bible
- Exposition: The Process of Communicating the Biblical Message

Hermeneutics: The Principles of Interpreting the Bible

Hermeneutics
The discipline that provides the principles and guidelines for correctly interpreting the Bible

In Chapter 1 we learned that hermeneutics is the discipline that provides the principles and guidelines for correctly interpreting the Bible. The goal of studying hermeneutics is to learn sound principles of interpretation and to acquire the interpretive skills necessary to study the Bible correctly.

Exegesis: The Practice of Interpreting the Bible

Exegesis is the actual practice of interpreting the Bible, based on sound hermeneutical principles. The term, exegesis, comes from a Greek word that means to draw the meaning out of the text. The practice of exegesis assumes that meaning resides in the text and that the goal of interpretation is to draw out that meaning.

The opposite of exegesis is **eisegesis**, which means, to read into a text. When we interpret the Bible, our method should be exegetical, allowing the Bible to speak for itself. Eisegesis occurs when we base our interpretation on our predetermined theology or presuppositions.

To do effective exegesis, we must understand and use the principles of sound hermeneutics. The goal of exegesis is to apply hermeneutical principles properly in an attempt to determine the original historical meaning of the author in the light of the historical and literary contexts.

> **Exegesis**
> The actual practice of interpreting the Bible, based on sound hermeneutical principles

Interpretation: The Product of Exegesis

Interpretation is the interpreter's understanding of the author's originally intended meaning. It is the product of exegesis and hermeneutics. If hermeneutics is like a recipe for a cake; exegesis is the act of baking the cake; and interpretation is what comes out of the oven.

For an interpretation to be correct, it must be based upon careful exegesis that is governed by sound hermeneutical principles. The goal of interpretation is to discern the original historical meaning intended by the biblical author for his original audience.

> **Interpretation**
> The interpreter's understanding of the author's originally intended meaning

Theology: The Product of Correlating the Teachings

The term, **theology**, is from the Greek words, θεος (*theos*) meaning God and λογος (logos) meaning word or message and means the study of God. Theology is the systematic summary and presentation of all that the Scriptures teach about its various subjects. As such theology can be considered a product.

However, theology also involves the process of determining how the theological themes that are revealed in individual passages in the Bible fit together to form overall biblical doctrines. The teachings of each passage must be integrated and correlated with similar teachings elsewhere in the Bible.

For our theology to be biblical and accurate, it must be based upon sound hermeneutical principles and the exegesis of every passage pertaining to a particular subject. The goal of theology is to produce a theological synthesis or summary of all the major theological themes in the Bible.

> **Theology**
> The systematic summary and presentation of all that the Scriptures teach about its various subjects

Application: Discerning the Relevance of the Bible

Application seeks to determine the relevance of a passage to our lives, and the ways to put that passage into practice. Exegesis deals with what it meant, the original historical meaning, while application deals with what it means, the contemporary significance.

The goal of application is to identify the universal principles contained in the text and then to act upon those principles in a manner that will bring our lives into obedience to the Word of God.

> **Application**
> Seeks to determine the relevance of a passage to our lives, and the ways to put that passage into practice

Exposition: The Act of Communicating the Biblical Message

Exposition is the act of communicating the meaning of the text along with its relevance to a present-day audience.

If hermeneutics is like a cookbook, and exegesis is the action of baking the cake, theology is like putting the icing on the top of all the parts of the cake, and exposition is like serving the cake.

Effective exposition and teaching of the Word of God requires more than a dynamic speaker or communicator. You must first:

- Master the principles of hermeneutics
- Practice accurate exegesis of the biblical text
- Produce sound and balanced interpretations
- Correlate your conclusions into a consistent theology
- Determine the relevant applications

Exposition must be based upon sound hermeneutical principles, careful exegesis, reasoned and biblically balanced interpretations, consistent theological conclusions, and contemporary principles of application.

Inductive and Deductive Methodologies

Distinction between Inductive and Deductive Methods

The Nature of Reasoning

Reasoning is the process of thinking in which we draw conclusions from other statements or observations. For instance, if on Sunday morning, I wake up and see that it is raining, I might conclude that attendance at church will be down. I have reasoned this.

Reasoning takes place in one of two ways, inductively or deductively. In **inductive reasoning**, we draw a general conclusion from the observation of many specifics. For instance, when we were children, we saw in real life or in pictures many cows, and they all had four legs. Our minds concluded that all cows have four legs, even the ones we never saw. In **deductive reasoning**, we apply a general principle to a specific situation and draw a conclusion about that situation. For instance, if asked how many legs Mr. Smith's cow had, our response would be four, even though we never saw Mr. Smith's cow. We reason that since all cows have four legs, it must be so that Mr. Smith's cow also has four legs.

These two methods of reasoning are also used in studying the Scriptures. We need to understand how and when to use each method.

The Inductive Approach to Interpretation

In the inductive approach to interpretation we begin by first observing the specifics of a biblical text and then we draw conclusions about its interpretation from these specifics. We allow the evidence of the biblical text to speak for itself. We delay any judgments and conclusions until we have carefully and impartially examined all the data.

The goal of the inductive approach is to discover the meaning of the biblical text. The inductive method is objective and impartial because it employs exegesis, not eisegesis. It forces us to listen to the Scriptures rather than to dictate to the Scriptures.

The Deductive Approach to Interpretation

In the deductive approach to interpretation we employ our presuppositions and conclusions and tend to interpret based on these conclusions. Ours presuppositions may affect our ability to observe accurately or to be open to interpretations that do not fit into our prior conclusions.

For example, in 1 Corinthians 15: 29 Paul asks, "Now if there is no resurrection, what will those do who are baptized for the dead?" Mormons interpret this to teach that it is possible to be baptized for others who have died to insure their place in heaven. Though this interpretation seems feasible based on the language of the passage, we reject it because it contradicts the clear teaching of Scripture that no one, except Jesus Christ, can provide eternal life for another (Acts 4:12). Our rejection is based on deductive reasoning.

> **Deductive Approach**
> We employ our presuppositions and conclusions and tend to interpret based on these conclusions

Normally Use the Inductive Approach

Several reasons lead us to conclude that we should logically use an inductive method of Bible study before using a deductive approach. First, inductive reasoning logically precedes deductive reasoning. Before we can deduce that Mr. Smith's cow has four legs, we must have concluded inductively that all cows have four legs. Second, inductive Bible study is based on first-hand observation of the text, while deductive Bible study is based on second-hand conclusions. Finally, inductive Bible study helps to control subjectivity, while deductive Bible study allows for uncontrolled subjectivity.

> **Normal Approach**
> Use an inductive method of Bible study before using a deductive approach

However, the deductive approach to interpretation does have a valid place in interpretation. For instance, we can conclude that, since God inspired all Scripture and since God does not lie or contradict himself, no proper interpretation of a passage will contradict the rest of Scripture. This general conclusion can be used to validate an interpretation of a specific passage. In this case we use a deductive method to eliminate certain improper interpretations.

Four Basic Steps of the Inductive Method

In the classic work, *Methodical Bible Study*, Robert Traina proposed four basic steps in inductive Bible study[1]. We present them below with one slight modification. We have reversed the order of the last two steps. They are as follows:

Four Steps in Inductive Bible Study
- Observation
- Interpretation
- Correlation
- Application

- Observation
- Interpretation
- Correlation
- Application

Observation: What Does It Say?

Observation is noting what is and is not present in the biblical text and being aware of what needs to be explained. Observation is more than seeing or reading. Observation is the process of recognizing and becoming mentally aware of what you see. The purpose of observation is to saturate yourself with the content of a passage.

Observation
Observation is noting what is and is not present in the biblical text and being aware of what needs to be explained

We can observe with different focuses and at different speeds. We can focus on words, structure, literary form, and even general atmosphere. We can spend hours observing a single verse or quickly scan a whole book. Changes in our pace and focus will affect our ability to observe.

Since observation is the basis for interpretation because it supplies the raw data for interpretation, observation must precede interpretation. Additionally, the more we observe, the fewer mistakes in interpretation we will make. The more time we invest in observation, the less time we may need in interpretation.

Questions can be used to help us focus our observations. The general question to ask is, "What does it say?" It is important also to ask, "What doesn't it say?" These kinds of questions are called observational questions. The more observational questions we learn to ask, the better job we will do at observation.

Interpretation: What Does It Mean?

As mentioned above **interpretation** is the interpreter's understanding of the author's originally intended meaning. As such, **interpretation** is an explanation of the meaning, intent, significance and implications of what has been observed. Traina suggests that interpretation takes place in three phases or at three levels. Basic interpretation seeks to discover the basic meaning intended by the author. However, we can also go beyond basic meaning, attempting to discover why an author says something or what the author implies by what he says.

Interpretation
An explanation of the meaning, intent, significance and implications of what has been observed

Interpretive questions help us move from observation to interpretation. The basic question to ask is, "What does it mean?" Interpretive questions can be distinguished from observational questions by noting that interpretive questions can only be made after an observation is made. They follow observation. On the other hand, observational questions lead us to make observations rather than to probe into their meaning. Other import interpretive questions include ones like these: "Why did the author say that?" and "What are the implications of what the author said?"

Correlation: How Does It Fit Together?

Correlation is the process of determining how the interpretation of an individual passage fits into the greater literary and theological context. At a literary level, correlation attempts to discover how the interpretation fits into the context of the book in which it is written. At a theological level, correlation attempts to discover how the interpretation fits into the context of the whole Bible. As such, correlation is based on the assumption that statements in the Bible are not isolated statements but part of a greater whole.

The general question to ask in correlation is, "How does it fit together?" We can also ask more specific question like, "How does this passage fit into the larger context?" and "How does the interpretation of this passage relate to the broader teachings of the Bible?"

> **Correlation**
> The process of determining how the interpretation of an individual passage fits into the greater literary and theological context

Application: How Should I Respond?

As mentioned above, **application** seeks to determine the relevance of a passage to our lives, and the ways to put that passage into practice. The goal of Bible study is not simply to determine what the Bible says, but ultimately how it applies to our lives. In application we seek to discover the universal principles found in the text and then to find relevant ways to put those principles into practice.

The general question to ask in application is, "How should I respond?" To do this we should ask, "What are the universal, timeless principles contained in this passage?" and "What are ways that these principles can be acted upon in my life?"

Application must be based upon proper interpretation and correlation. If we do not interpret the Bible properly, we cannot apply it properly.

> **Application**
> Seeks to determine the relevance of a passage to our lives and the ways to put that passage into practice

The Importance of the Steps and the Sequence

Do Not Skip Any of the Steps.

The reason many Christians have difficulty in studying the Bible is because they leave out one or more of the steps. Skipping one or more of the steps is like leaving out one or more of the ingredients from a recipe when you are cooking.

Follow the Steps in the Correct Order.

The order of the steps is crucial and generally should not be reversed or changed. The process however is like a spiral where each step may lead the interpreter to return to prior steps. Following an incorrect order is like using the right ingredients to bake a cake but putting them in at the wrong time and in the wrong order.

The HGRT Method

Earlier we learned that an inductive method of interpretation should be our primary method of interpretation. Now we will associate this literal, inductive method with the HGR Method, argue for its validity, and explain its three principles. Finally, we will expand the HGR Method to include a more deductive, theological principle. We end up with the HGRT method.

Dual Authorship of Scripture
A Rationale for the HGRT Method

Dual Authorship Explained

Our presuppositions about the nature of the Scriptures directly affect our approach to understanding them. In Chapter 1 we learned that the Bible contains God's primary revelation of himself to man and that God inspired the human authors, controlling them in such a way that their writings are said to be God-breathed. Yet, God did not dictate Scripture to them, but rather allowed the human authors to express their thoughts in their own words and within the context of their own culture. As such the Bible has two authors, God and man. We can describe the Bible in the following way.

> **The Bible is God's communication to man, through man's methods of communications.**

Starting with this assumption, a set of principles for the interpretation of Scripture logically follows.

Principles Derived from Human Authorship

The human authorship of Scripture suggests that the Bible should be interpreted using the same method of interpretation that we use to understand basic human communication. Three principles of this normal method are critical.

The Historical Principle

Historical Principle
Interpret using the historical context

We interpret a statement using the historical context in which the statement was first made. For example, look at the following words from the *Star-Spangled Banner.*

> And the rocket's red glare,
> The bombs bursting in air,
> Gave proof through the night,
> That our flag was still there.

We might ask the question, "What is the rocket's red glare?" We would be quick to correct a child, who in response described the bright glare of a modern rocket being launched into space. Indeed, it is normal, when teaching children this song, to explain to them the historical circumstances surrounding its creation.

The Grammatical Principle

We interpret a statement using the conventions of language such as word meaning, grammar, and literary context. Let's again consider the words of the *Star-Spangled Banner* given above. We would conclude, based on the grammar of the statement, that it was the glare that was red, not the rocket and that the glare illuminated the night sky to reveal a flag still located where it was earlier. These conclusions are based on using the principles of language.

Grammatical Principle
Interpret using the conventions of language

The Rhetorical Principle

We also interpret a statement in light of the kind of literature in which it is contained. Each unique kind of literature is called a literary genre. For instance, the *Star-Spangled Banner* is a poem. It is for the sake of the poetry that the author includes rhyme and rhythm. We consider the purposes and structures of the genre to better understand the message. For example, the poetic parallelism between the first two lines suggests that the bombs are mentioned mainly because they illuminated the sky.

Rhetorical Principle
Interpret in light of the literary genre

Conclusion

We conclude that proper interpretation requires that we interpret within the historical context, that we use the rules of language, and that we consider the unique form of literature. Thus, we should use the historical-grammatical-rhetorical method. This method has several important characteristics.

Characteristics of HGR Principles
- Universal
- Objective and Rational
- Inductive

- This method is universal and governs all forms of normal communication. The principles are not special rules that apply only to the Bible.

- This method is objective and assumes that the author's meaning can be uncovered using the objective, rational methods of language.

- This method is inductive. It begins with no assumptions about the meaning of the text and then draws out general conclusions about the meaning from observing the history, grammatical context, and literary form.

Theological Principle Derived from Divine Authorship

Since the Bible is the Word of God, its message is unique in character. It cannot be treated like other messages. The Bible is uniquely theological in nature, and therefore, we must interpret the Bible using a theological principle. Let's examine four aspects of the theological nature of the Bible and note the related theological principle.

Theological Principle
Interpret in light of its unique theological nature

Clarity of Scripture

When God inspired the Scriptures, His goal was not to conceal truth, but to reveal it (1 Cor. 2:10-13). Thus, it only makes sense to conclude that the basic message of the Bible is understandable. This suggests that if there are two equally possible interpretations of a passage, we should accept the clear and sensible meaning. In addition, clear and easy-to-understand passages can help us understand the less clear and difficult-to-understand passages.

Clarity of Scripture Theological Principle
Accept the clear and sensible meaning

Inerrancy of Scripture

God cannot lie and does not make mistakes. Thus, the Bible is inerrant and when properly interpreted will not conflict with truth of any kind. We must however, understand biblical statements at the degree of precision intended by the author. The Bible is not a scientific textbook but a record of human experience. As such, we must not use the precision of science as the standard for evaluating the accuracy of Scripture.

Inerrancy of Scripture Theological Principle
Proper interpretation will not conflict with truth of any kind

Unity of Scripture

**Unity of Scripture
Theological Principle**
No proper interpretation of a
passage will conflict with the
general teaching of the Bible

Since God controlled the process of inspiration from start to finish, we can conclude that the Bible has a perfect unity. Because the Bible is unified in all that it says, no proper interpretation of a passage will conflict with the general teaching of the Bible, called the **Analogy of Faith**. This also suggests that we should interpret the unknown in the light of the known.

Progressiveness of Scripture

**Progressiveness of Scripture
Theological Principle**
Later statements have
superseded some earlier
statements

Since God chose to reveal himself progressively over a long period of time, some statements in Scripture may be limited in scope to the time in which they were written. Later revelation may supersede earlier revelation. For instance, the OT commands to sacrifice animals (Lev. 1-7) have been superseded in the NT by the sacrifice of Christ (Heb. 9:1-28).

Conclusion

**Characteristics of
Theological Principle**
• Specific to the Bible
• Deductive

We conclude that proper interpretation of the Bible requires that we interpret it in light of its divine origin. We must interpret using theological principles. This method has two important characteristics.

- This method is special and applies only to the Bible.

- This method is deductive. We begin with conclusions about what the character of our interpretations must be. As such, this method must be used with caution.

The HGRT Method Summarized

HGRT Method
• Historical
• Grammatical
• Rhetorical
• Theological

We conclude that four general principles should govern our interpretation of Scripture. The first three principles are based on the fact that men wrote the Bible. They are the historical, grammatical, and rhetorical principles. The final principle, the theological principle, is based on the fact that God wrote the Bible. From these four principles we get the acronym, HGRT. Thus, the HGRT Method is the Historical-Grammatical-Rhetorical-Theological Method.

Figure 2.1
The HGRT Method

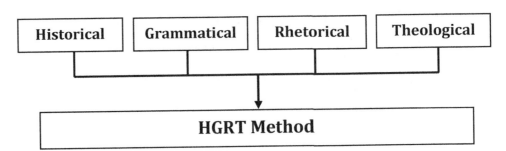

Summary

To discuss a methodology for interpretation, several key concepts must be understood. Hermeneutics is the discipline that provides the principles and guidelines for correctly interpreting the Bible. Exegesis is the actual practice of interpreting the Bible, based on sound hermeneutical principles. Interpretation is the interpreter's understanding of the author's originally intended meaning. Theology is the systematic summary and presentation of all that the Scriptures teach about its various subjects. Application deals with the principles and processes for determining how the Scriptures relate to our lives. Exposition is the act of communicating the meaning of the text along with its relevance to the present-day audience.

We reason both inductively and deductively. The inductive approach to interpretation begins by first observing the specifics of the biblical text and then drawing conclusions about its interpretation. The deductive approach to interpretation employs a person's presupposition and conclusions and tends to interpret based on those conclusions. Normally we should use an inductive approach.

The inductive methodology includes four basic steps: observation, interpretation, correlation, and application. No step should be skipped. The steps should be followed in order, though it is common to return to steps in a recursive fashion.

The HGRT Method of interpretation follows naturally from our assumption that the Bible is both the work of man and the work of God. As human communication, we must interpret it historically, grammatically, and rhetorically. As a divine message, we must interpret it theologically.

Key Terms

Analogy of Faith	Eisegesis	Inductive Reasoning
Application	Exegesis	Interpretation
Correlation	Exposition	Literary genre
Deductive Reasoning	Hermeneutics	Observation
Doctrine	HGRT Method	Theology

Review Questions

1. What is the difference between exegesis and eisegesis?
2. What is the goal of interpretation?
3. How is theology related to correlation?
4. How is application related to exposition?
5. What is the difference between inductive and deductive reasoning?
6. Why should an inductive approach to interpretation precede a deductive one?
7. What are the four basic steps of the inductive method of Bible study?
8. How do we use questions to help us when using the inductive method of study?
9. Why is it important to follow the steps of the inductive method in their proper order?
10. What is meant by the dual authorship of Scripture?
11. What three principles of interpretation are derived from the fact that the Bible was written by men?
12. What principle of interpretation is derived from the fact that the Bible was written by God?
13. What is meant by the historical principle?
14. What is meant by the grammatical principle?
15. What is meant by the rhetorical principle?
16. What is meant by literary genre?
17. What are the three characteristics of the HGR principles?
18. What are the four theological characteristics of the Bible and the principles that relate to them?
19. What does the Analogy of Faith mean?
20. What are the two characteristics of the theological principle?

References

[1] Traina, Robert A. *Methodical Bible Study*. Wilmore, KY: Asbury Theological Seminary,   1952.

Chapter 3

Biblical Research Tools & Strategies

Outline

Introduction 40

Research Strategy 40

    Move from the General to the Specific 40

    Use Scholarly Sources 41

    Use the Right Tool for the Task 41

Types of Research Tools 41

    General Topical Tools 41

    Bible Survey Tools 42

    Bible Commentaries 42

    Word Study Tools 42

    Historical Background Tools 43

    Periodicals and Abstracts 43

Selected Bibliography 44

Summary 48

Review Questions 48

Learning Objectives

After completing this chapter, you should be able to

- ❑ Suggest ways to perform meaningful research.
- ❑ Identify the tools useful for biblical research.
- ❑ Identify the right tool for the right research task.

Introduction

The HGRT methodology requires knowledge of the historical settings of the Scriptures, familiarity with the languages in which the authors wrote, and an understanding of ancient literary genres. To gain this knowledge, we must perform biblical research. This unit provides guidelines on how to perform this research and explanations of the various tools that we can use. We begin by explaining research strategy.

Research Strategy

> **Research Suggestions**
> - Move from General to Specific
> - Use Scholarly Sources
> - Use the Right Tool for The Task

To perform meaningful research that will enhance your understanding and make using the HGRT Method beneficial, we must use proper methods and tools. Here are some suggestions that will help you to perform meaningful research.

Move from the General to the Specific

The rule of thumb for basic research is to begin with general works and proceed to more specialized works. For example, if we want to study angels in the Bible, we would begin reading an article on angels in a Bible dictionary or encyclopedia. This will give us a general overview on the subject. We would then note the major areas of emphasis such as *Angels in the Old Testament, Angels in the New Testament, The Angel of the Lord,* etc. We would also check for a bibliography of more specific works.

Next, we would refine our topic and perform an in-depth study using more specialized tools. We might use a concordance to discover all the instances where angels are mentioned in the Bible and we might read books specifically about angels. In any case, the direction is from a more general tool to more specific tools. In this way specific ideas are built upon a broad foundation.

Use Scholarly Sources

Many Bible study tools are available to us. Unfortunately, much of what is available is not scholarly. Sometimes the materials lack depth. At other times, they contain unfounded opinions not based on solid research. It is imperative that we use well-respected scholarly sources. One important mark of a scholar is an awareness of scholarly tools.

Here are some sources to avoid. Do not use the notes in a reference Bible. Do not use devotional commentaries. Do not use the concordances in the backs of Bibles. Do not use sermon notes, church literature, etc. Do not use English dictionaries.

Here are some sources to use. Use scholarly Bible dictionaries and encyclopedias. Use scholarly, exegetical commentaries. Use exhaustive concordances. Use lexicons and theological wordbooks. Use theology texts.

Use the Right Tool for the Task

Not all Bible study tools are designed for the same purpose. As mentioned above, general-purpose tools are designed for general introductions to topics. They should not be used for in-depth research. A common mistake in performing a word study is to use the dictionary in the back of a concordance. This is not the right tool. A lexicon should be used for this purpose. As we continue our study, we will learn more about what tools to use for various research tasks. Below is a general introduction to tools and their tasks.

Types of Research Tools

A biblical scholar is well acquainted with scholarly tools. It will take many years to become acquainted with all the tools. However, it is beneficial to begin by understanding some of the basic categories of tools.

General Topical Tools

General topical tools provide articles on basic scriptural topics; historical, geographical, and cultural backgrounds; persons and places; and theological concepts. The two most commonly used tools in this category are Bible dictionaries and Bible encyclopedias.

Bible dictionaries are one-volume encyclopedias of biblical topics. Since they are one volume, they cover the topics in a limited way. Normally, articles are anonymous and do not identify primary sources for the information given.

Bible encyclopedias are multi-volume tools that provide much more extensive articles on biblical topics, giving information about key issues while mentioning significant details. More thorough encyclopedias provide an outline, a bibliography and each major entry carries the name of the author. Single-author encyclopedias are weaker tools.

General Topical Tools
• Bible Dictionary
• Bible Encyclopedia

Bible Survey Tools

Bible Survey Tools
- Bible Introduction
- Bible Survey

These tools provide overviews of the Bible, explaining the history and organization of the Bible, and the organization and background for each book.

Bible Introductions provide materials about the inspiration, canonicity, date, authorship, and transmission of the book of the Bible. Most Bible Introductions are either for the Old Testament or the New Testament.

Bible Surveys provide information about the historical setting, the purpose, and the plan of each book of the Bible. At times the introductory materials found in a Bible Introduction will also be included. At other times they will provide some commentary. Most Bible Surveys are either for the Old Testament or the New Testament.

Bible Commentaries

Bible Commentaries
- Expository Commentary
- Exegetical Commentary
- Background Commentary

These tools provide interpretive analysis of the books of the Bible. Commentaries are most useful to discover possible meanings of a passage and the support offered for those meanings. Some introductory materials about authorship, canonicity, purpose, and plan are available in more critical commentaries.

Expository commentaries emphasize applications and generally lack scholarly depth. They include little analysis of the text and often employ poor exegesis. Devotional commentaries should be avoided.

Exegetical commentaries provide an in-depth analysis of the text and are very helpful for gaining an awareness of interpretive problems and potential solutions. However, not all exegetical commentaries are as beneficial as others. Here are some suggestions for evaluating a commentary. A good exegetical commentary should include:

- An introduction discussing authorship, occasion for writing, purpose, and plan
- Analysis of passages with interpretive problems
- Analysis of the strength and weaknesses of various interpretations
- Comments based on the original languages
- Indexes of authors, scripture references, etc.
- Documentation of sources

Background commentaries provide historical and cultural information that is helpful to better understanding a passage. They rarely deal with exegetical questions. They are very helpful in gaining a better understanding of the text based on cultural analysis.

Word Study Tools

Word Study Tools
- Concordance
- Lexicon
- Theological Wordbook

These tools are used to research the meaning of specific words found in a passage. Word studies should be done in the original languages of the Bible - Greek, Hebrew, and Aramaic.

Concordances list the occurrences of words found in a translation of the Bible. They provide static indexes for words. Concordances exist for almost all English translations. Exhaustive concordances index every word while others index every significant word. Exhaustive concordances also provide a link between the original language words and their English translation. Bible software and online Bible study websites can be used in place of a concordance, and often provide more complex search engines that allows the user to search a Bible for individual words or groups of words.

Lexicons are one-volume dictionaries for Greek or Hebrew words. They provide a simple range of meaning for each word. The definitions tend to be short, often simple word substitutions. Scholarly lexicons also provide information about word origins. Since lexicons are designed for Bible study, they often include comments indicating how a word is used in a given passage.

Theological wordbooks provide articles on the meanings of words and are more extensive than lexicons. However, they include only theologically significant words. They are multi-volume and thus are significantly more expensive than are lexicons.

Historical Background Tools

These tools provide information on the history, geography, and culture of biblical books. We call this the historical background. Several types are books are available.

Historical Background Tools
• Atlas
• History
• Literature
• Religious Background
• Culture and Customs
• Archaeology

Atlases provide information on Bible geography and many include data on climate, trade routes and customs. The central feature of an atlas is its maps.

Historical Geographies provide much more extensive information on the geography of biblical locations. They include data on climate, trade routes and economics. They deal with the geography historically, distinguishing political boundaries and tying into the history presented in the Bible.

Histories of the ancient Near East and of Israel are excellent sources for chronological material and background details of a historical nature.

Literature contemporaneous to various Biblical periods can be found in works about each nation (i.e., Egypt, Assyria, etc.) or in anthologies which are collections of literature that parallel the Biblical material.

Religious background, including material on customs, deities and religious systems, are contained in books on ancient religions (i.e., Babylonian, Greek, Roman, etc.) or books on the religious background of the Bible.

Culture and customs are to be found in books that discuss the life and times of various Biblical periods. General works exist which cover all periods of the Bible and provide basic data on most of the customs, occupations and events of ancient times.

Archaeologies of the Bible tend to be technical works but can provide a wealth of data on the history, customs and material culture of the Bible. Some are arranged chronologically and discuss discoveries relevant for each period (i.e., Patriarchs, History, Gospels, etc.) while others are arranged by geographical area (i.e., Palestine, Egypt, etc.).

Periodicals and Abstracts

Periodicals are extremely important for solid research. Scholarly discussions of current topics are found in periodicals. Often classical or seminal articles on a given topic are published in periodicals. Several tools exist to help you research subjects in periodicals.

Periodicals & Abstracts
• Periodicals
• Abstracts

Abstracts provide a brief summary of the content of an article. Since you can list abstracts for a given search criteria, they are very helpful in determining how relevant an article is for one's research. In addition, articles written in a foreign language are summarized in English. You should first use a periodical index to locate titles relevant to your research. Then look these titles up in an abstract to see if there is a summary of the article. Especially helpful are Religion Indices and Religious & Theological Abstracts available online as a service of a library.

Unpublished Dissertations are also available on microfiche. These provide a wealth of research on biblical and theological issues.

Selected Bibliography

General Topical Tools

Achtemeier, Paul J., Publishers Harper & Row and Society of Biblical Literature. *Harper's Bible Dictionary*. 1st ed. San Francisco: Harper & Row, 1985.

Alexander, T. Desmond, eds. *Dictionary of the Old Testament: Pentateuch*. InterVarsity Press, 2002.

Arnold, Bill T., eds. *Dictionary of the Old Testament: Historical Books*. InterVarsity Press, 2005.

Bromiley, Geoffrey W., ed. *The International Standard Bible Encyclopedia*. Revised Edition. 5 Vols. Grand Rapids: Eerdmans Publishing Co., 1979.

Douglas, J. D., ed. *The Illustrated Bible Dictionary*. 3 Vols. Leicester, England: InterVarsity Press, 1980.

Douglas, J. D., ed. *The New Bible Dictionary*. Third Edition. Downers Grove: InterVarsity Press, 2002.

Easton, M.G. *Easton's Bible Dictionary*. c1897.

Elwell, Walter, ed. *The Baker Encyclopedia of the Bible*. Grand Rapids: Baker Book House, 1993.

Elwell, Walter A. and Philip Wesley Comfort. *Tyndale Bible Dictionary*. Tyndale reference library. Wheaton, Ill.: Tyndale House Publishers, 2001.

Freedman, David Noel, ed. *Anchor Yale Bible Dictionary*. 6 Vols. New York: Doubleday Publishing Company, 1993.

Tenney, Merrill, ed. *Zondervan Pictorial Bible Encyclopedia*. 5 Vols. Grand Rapids: Zondervan Publishing Company, 1976.

Wood, D. R. W. and I. Howard Marshall. *New Bible Dictionary*. 3rd ed. Leicester, England; Downers Grove, Ill.: InterVarsity Press, 1996.

The Essential IVP Reference Collection 3.0 - includes works from the best of today's biblical and theological scholars. The following volumes are included.

> *Dictionary of Jesus and the Gospels*
> *Dictionary of Paul and His Letters*
> *Dictionary of the Later New Testament and Its Developments*
> *Dictionary of New Testament Background*
> *IVP Bible Background Commentary: Old Testament*
> *IVP Bible Background Commentary: New Testament*
> *New Bible Dictionary*
> *New Bible Commentary*
> *Hard Sayings of the Bible*
> *The Dictionary of Biblical Imagery*
> *New Bible Atlas*
> *New Dictionary of Biblical Theology*
> *New Dictionary of Theology*
> *Pocket Dictionary for the Study of New Testament Greek*
> *Pocket Dictionary of Apologetics and Philosophy of Religion*
> *Pocket Dictionary of Biblical Studies*
> *Pocket Dictionary of Theological Terms*

Introductions & Surveys

Archer, Gleason Leonard. *A Survey of Old Testament Introduction*. 3rd. ed. Chicago: Moody Press, 1998, c1994.

deSilva, David Arthur. *An Introduction to the New Testament: Contexts, Methods and Ministry Formation*. Downers Grove, Ill.: InterVarsity Press, 2004.

Drane, John William. *Introducing the New Testament*. Completely rev. and updated. Oxford: Lion Publishing plc, 2000. [Limited scholarship]

Drane, John William. *Introducing the Old Testament*. Completely rev. and updated. Oxford: Lion Publishing plc, 2000. [Limited scholarship]

Geisler, Norman L. and William E. Nix. *A General Introduction to the Bible*. Rev. and expanded. Chicago: Moody Press, 1996, c1986.

Guthrie, Donald. *New Testament Introduction*. 4th ed. The master reference collection. Downers Grove, Ill. Inter-Varsity Press, 1996, c1990.

Smith, James E. *The Books of History*. Joplin, Mo.: College Press, 1995.

Smith, James E. *The Pentateuch*. Joplin, Mo.: College Press, 1993.

Smith, James E. *The Major Prophets*. Joplin, Mo.: College Press, 1992.

Smith, James E. *The Minor Prophets*. Joplin, Mo.: College Press, 1992.

Smith, James E. *The Wisdom Literature and Psalms*. Joplin, Mo.: College Press Pub. Co., 1996.

Commentaries

Background Commentaries

Matthews, Victor Harold, Mark W. Chavalas and John H. Walton. *The IVP Bible Background Commentary: Old Testament*. electronic ed. Downers Grove, IL: InterVarsity Press, 2000. [Excellent, scholarly, conservative]

Keener, Craig S. and InterVarsity Press. *The IVP Bible Background Commentary: New Testament*. Downers Grove, Ill.: InterVarsity Press, 1993. [Excellent, scholarly, conservative]

Exegetical Commentaries

_____. *New International Commentary on the Old Testament*, 22 Vols. 1976-2007. [Very scholarly, conservative, some vols. not completed]

_____. New *International Commentary on the New Testament*,18 Vols. 1978-2007. [Very scholarly, conservative, some vols. not completed]

_____. *New Testament Handbook Series* (20 Vols.), United Bible Society. [Valuable exegetical, historical, cultural, and linguistic information]

_____. *Old Testament Handbook Series* (21 Vols.), United Bible Society. [Valuable exegetical, historical, cultural, and linguistic information]

_____. Word *Biblical Commentary*, 59 Vols. Thomas Nelson, 1982-2007. [Scholarly, conservative]

_____. *Baker Exegetical Commentary on the New Testament*, 8 Vols. Baker Academic Publishing, 2004. [Scholarly, conservative, not all vols. completed]

_____. Expositor's Bible Commentary, 12 Vols. Zondervan Publishing. 1976-1982. [Moderate scholarship, conservative]

_____. NIV Application Commentary, 36 Vols. Zondervan Publishing. 1995-2004. [Moderate scholarship, incorporates application, conservative]

Carson, D. A. *New Bible Commentary: 21st Century Edition.* 4th ed. Leicester, England; Downers Grove, Ill., USA: Inter-Varsity Press, 1994. [Moderate depth, conservative]

Osborne, Grant R., ed. *The IVP New Testament Commentary Series*, Downers Grove, Ill.: InterVarsity Press, 1994-2004. [Moderate scholarly, conservative]

Keil, Carl Friedrich and Franz Delitzsch. *Commentary on the Old Testament.* Peabody, MA: Hendrickson, 2002. [Republished Classic, scholarly, very old (1866-91)]

Jamieson, Robert, A. R. Fausset, A. R. Fausset, David Brown and David Brown. *A Commentary, Critical and Explanatory, on the Old and New Testaments.* Oak Harbor, WA: Logos Research Systems, Inc., 1997. [Republished, moderate value, very old (1871), conservative]

Walvoord, John F., Roy B. Zuck and Dallas Theological Seminary. *The Bible Knowledge Commentary: An Exposition of the Scriptures.* Wheaton, IL: Victor Books, 1983-c1985. [Moderate value, conservative, 3 vols.]

_____. *The New American Commentary.* Nashville: Broadman & Holman Publishers, 1994-2007. [Moderately scholarly, conservative]

Marchall, I. Howard, Donald A. Hagner, eds. The New International Greek Testament Commentary. William B. Eerdmans, 1982-2005. [Scholarly, knowledge of Greek required, conservative]

Henry, Matthew. *Matthew Henry's Commentary on the Whole Bible: Complete and Unabridged in One Volume.* Peabody: Hendrickson, 1996, c1991. [Reproduced, very old (1706), conservative]

Hughes, Robert B. and J. Carl Laney. Tyndale *Concise Bible Commentary.* The Tyndale reference library. Wheaton, Ill.: Tyndale House Publishers, 2001. [Minimal depth, conservative]

Expository Commentaries

Spence, H. D. M., ed. *The Pulpit Commentary.* Bellingham, WA: Logos Research Systems, Inc., 2004. [Reproduced, very old (1800s), conservative]

Anders, Max ed. *Holman New Testament Commentary Series.* Holman Reference. Nashville, TN: Broadman & Holman Publishers, 1998. [Not scholarly, good for sermon preparation, conservative, NT only.]

Wiersbe, Warren W. *The Bible Exposition Commentary.* Wheaton, Ill.: Victor Books, 1996, c1989. [Not scholarly, good for sermon preparation, conservative, NT only.]

Geographical Backgrounds of Bible Times

Aharoni, Y & M. Avi-Yonah. *The Macmillan Bible Atlas.* New York: The Macmillan Co., 1967. Revised Edition, 1993.

Aharoni, Y. *The Land of the Bible.* Philadelphia: Westminster Press, 1967.

Kramer, Samuel Noah. *The Sumerians: Their History, Culture and Character.* Chicago: University of Chicago Press, 1963

Moscati, Sabatino. *The World of the Phoenicians.* Weidenfeld & Nicholson, 1968.

Pitard, Wayne T. *Ancient Damascus.* Winona Lake: Eisenbrauns, 1987.

Saggs, H. W. F. *Babylonians.* Norman: University of Oklahoma Press, 1995.

Unger, Merrill F. *Israel and the Arameans of Damascus.* Grand Rapids: Baker Book House, 1957.

Van Seters, John. *The Hyksos: A New Investigation.* New Haven: Yale University Press, 1966.

Yamauchi, Edwin M. *Persia and the Bible.* Grand Rapids: Baker Book House, 1990.

Cultural Backgrounds of the Bible

Borowski, Oded. *Agriculture in Iron Age Israel.* Winona Lake: Eisenbrauns, 1987.

Duckat, W. *Beggar to King; All the Occupations of Biblical Times.* New York: Doubleday, 1968.

Grant, Michael & Rachel Kitzinger. *Civilizations of the Ancient Mediterranean; Greece and Rome.* 3 Volumes. Scribners, 1988

Kitchen, Kenneth. *The Bible in its World.* Downers Grove: InterVarsity Press, 1978.

Livingston, G. Herbert. *The Pentateuch in Its Cultural Environment.* Grand Rapids: Baker Book House, 1974.

Matthews, Victor H. *Manners and Customs in the Bible.* Revised Edition. New York: Hendrickson, 1991.

Matthews, Victor H and Don C. Benjamin. *Social World of Ancient Israel 1250-587 BCE.* New York: Hendrickson, 1993.

Noth, Martin. *The Old Testament World.* Philadelphia: Fortress 1966.

Roaf, Michael. *Cultural Atlas of Mesopotamia and the Ancient Near East.* New York: Equinox Books, 1990.

Sasson, Jack, ed. *Civilizations of the Ancient Near East.* 4 volumes. Scribners, 1995.

Stephens, William. *The New Testament World in Pictures.* Nashville: Broadman, 1987.

Thompson, J. A. *Handbook of Life in Bible Times.* Downers Grove: InterVarsity, 1986.

Van Der Woude, A. S. ed. *The World of the Bible.* Grand Rapids: Eerdmans, 1986.

Vaux de, Roland. *Ancient Israel. Its Life and Institutions.* New York: McGraw-Hill Book Company, 1961.

Yadin, Y. *The Art of Warfare in Biblical Lands.* 2 vols. New York: McGraw-Hill, 1963.

Summary

The HGRT Methodology requires knowledge of the history of Bible times, familiarity with the original languages of the Bible, and an understanding of biblical genres. This can be gained only by research. Meaningful research requires a good research strategy that includes a proper order and the use of appropriate tools.

Key Terms

Bible Dictionary	Concordance	Archaeologies
Bible Encyclopedia	Lexicon	Periodical
Expository Commentary	Theological Wordbook	Abstract
Exegetical Commentary	Background Commentary	

Review Questions

1. Why is research necessary for good Bible study?
2. What suggestions can help you produce meaningful research?
3. What is the difference between a Bible Dictionary and a Bible Encyclopedia?
4. What is the difference between a Bible Introduction and a Bible Survey?
5. What is the difference between an expositional commentary and an exegetical commentary?
6. What features should you look for in a commentary?
7. What is the purpose of a concordance?
8. What is the difference between a lexicon and a theological wordbook?
9. What types of books can be used to research the historical background of Bible times?
10. What is the difference between a periodical and an abstract?
11. How can abstracts be helpful in research?

Chapter 4

The Historical Background
Considering the Historical & Cultural Context

Outline

Introduction 50

    Principle of Interpretation 50

    Definition of Historical Background 50

    Importance 50

    Goal 50

Major Areas of Historical Background 51

    History 51

    Geography 52

    Culture 53

Two Strategies for Studying the Historical Background 53

    Immediate Preparation for Exegesis of a Book 53

    Life-Long Inquiry 54

Sources for Studying the Historical Background 54

Summary 55

Review Questions 55

Learning Objectives

After completing this chapter, you should be able to

- ❑ Define Historical Background.
- ❑ Discuss the three major areas of historical background.
- ❑ List the basic guidelines in researching areas associated with historical background.
- ❑ Discuss the strategies for studying the historical background of the Bible.
- ❑ Discuss the sources that can be used for studying the historical background of the Bible.

Introduction

Principle of Interpretation

> **Principle**
> The most probable interpretation of a passage is the one that best harmonizes with the broad historical background of the people to whom the book was originally addressed or about whom the book was written

The most probable interpretation of a passage is the one that best harmonizes with the broad historical background of the people to whom the book was originally addressed or about whom the book was written.

Definition

> **Definition**
> The broad historical-cultural setting in which the author and his audience lived
>
> **Major Areas**
> - History
> - Geography
> - Culture

The **historical background** is the broad historical-cultural setting in which the author and his audience lived. This includes the historical, geographical, political, cultural, religious and literary background that influenced the thinking of the author and his audience. We can use the expression, "life and times in..." to express the idea. What was life and times in Egypt like when Moses delivered the children of Israel? What was life and times in Israel like when Jesus was born? Scholars also call this the **context of culture**. We will divide the historical background into three major areas:

- History
- Geography
- Culture

Importance

The biblical authors did not write in a vacuum, but in a specific historical context. The historical background colored the manner in which the authors expressed themselves and affected the issues they addressed. Unless we understand the historical setting, we may not fully appreciate or correctly understand the original historical meaning of the text.

Goal

> **Goal**
> To be able to read the biblical text from the historical viewpoint of the author's original audience

Our goal is to be able to read the biblical text from the historical viewpoint of the author's original audience. To do so, we must disengage ourselves from our own cultural context so we do not read our own contemporary culture into the biblical text and transport ourselves back into the original setting so we can perceive the biblical in the same way as the original readers.

Major Areas of Historical Background

History

Guidelines

Before we study a book of the Bible, we should first determine where the book fits into the basic flow of biblical history. Next, we should determine where the book fits into the broader secular history of that time, and finally, we should determine what nations and peoples are a part of that history.

History Guidelines
- Determine where book fits into biblical history
- Determine where book fits into secular history
- Determine what nations and peoples are a part of the history

Periods of Biblical History

The Pre-Hebraic Period	ca. 3200-2200 BC
Patriarchal Period	ca. 2200-1550 BC
Nation Building Period	ca. 1550-1400 BC
Judges Period	ca. 1400-1050 BC
United Kingdom Period	ca. 1050-930 BC
Divided Kingdom Period	ca. 930-586 BC
Babylonian Captivity	ca. 586-520 BC
Restoration Period	ca. 520-415 BC
The Intertestamental Period	ca. 415-168 BC
The New Testament Period	ca. 168 BC-100 AD

Ancient Near Eastern Empires

The most important empires include the Sumerians, Egyptians, Hittites, Babylonians, Assyrians, Chaldeans, Persians, Greeks, and Romans.

Ancient Near Eastern Neighbors

The most important countries and people groups in the Near East include the Amorites, Arameans, Arabs, Canaanites, Edomites, Moabites, Philistines, Phoenicians, and Samaritans.

Examples of the Historical Background

The significance of Ahab's sin against Naboth (1 Kings 21) can be fully understood only in the light of another important historical event that year, Ahab's well-known victory in the Battle of Qarqar in 853 BC.

The timing of the LORD's command to rebuild the temple (Haggai 1:1-2) can only be fully appreciated in the light of the campaign of Darius, the emperor of Persia, to put down rebellion in Syria-Palestine in 520 BC.

Geography

Guidelines

Geography Guidelines
- Locate countries, cities, and villages
- Study the topographic features of the land
- Study the climatic conditions of the land

Before we study a book of the Bible, we should become familiar with the geographical setting of the people to whom the book is addressed and about whom the book speaks. Begin by locating countries, cities, and villages on a map. Study the topographic features of the land. Finally, study the climatic conditions of the land.

Elements of the Geographic Background

National and tribal borders
Locations of cities and villages
International highways and internal roads
Mountain ranges and valleys
Rivers, lakes, seas, and oceans
Desert and fertile regions
Seasonal weather tendencies

Spheres of the Geographical Setting

Universal geography: The Near East and Mediterranean world
International geography: Syria-Palestine
National geography: Israel
Regional geography: Twelve tribes
Local geography: Specific cities

Examples of the Geographical Background

No matter what direction you come from, you always go up to Jerusalem (Matt. 20:17; Luke 9:51; Acts 11:2) since Jerusalem is located in the Judean mountains.

The brook Jesus crossed when He went to the Garden the night before He was crucified (Matt. 26:36; Mark 14:32; Luke 22:39).

Jesus called Hell "Gehenna" (Matt. 5:22,29-30; 18:9), which was a valley (the valley of Hinnoam) outside Jerusalem where its trash burned all day and night.

The citizens of the colony of Philippi had Roman citizenship; this is the picture describing our citizenship in heaven (Phil. 3:20).

The fact that there is no river in Jerusalem, yet Psalm 46:4 refers to a "river whose streams make glad the city of our God."

Culture

Guidelines

Many passages refer to ancient Near Eastern customs that are foreign to our contemporary Western way of acting and thinking. If we do not understand the cultural significance of a particular ancient custom, we will easily misinterpret the meaning of the passage. First, identify the unique cultural practices described in the passage. Next, determine how the practices fit into the broader culture of that period. Finally, determine how the practices affect the interpretation of the passage.

> **Culture Guidelines**
> - Identify the unique cultural practices
> - Determine how the practices fit into the broader culture
> - Determine how the practices affect the interpretation of the passage

Elements of Culture

Social customs	Political customs
Marriage and family customs	Religious customs
Economic customs	Architectural customs
Legal customs	Agricultural customs

Examples of the Cultural Background

Abraham's acceptance of Hagar, Sarah's hand-maiden, to father a child (Gen. 16) in light of the ancient Mesopotamian customs

The nature of slavery in Israel (Ex. 21:1-11; Deut. 15:12-18) in contrast to slavery in ancient Egypt and 19th century America

The significance of Christ saying, "It is finished!" (John 19:30) in the light of the use of this phrase in the Roman prison system

The significance of Christ's reference to "putting the hand to the plow and looking back" (Luke 9:62) in the light of farming techniques and the kind of plows used in first-century Palestine

Two Strategies for Studying the Historical Background

Immediate Preparation for Exegesis of a Book

Before you begin the actual exegesis of a book of the Bible, you should first study the historical background/setting behind that book. To familiarize yourself with the general historical, geographical, and cultural setting of the book, consult Bible Introductions, Bible Surveys, and commentaries. Read through the book, making a list of everything that you will need to study in relation to the historical background of the book. Research these items by consulting Bible encyclopedias and other research books dealing with its background.

> **Preparation for Exegesis**
> - Study historical background before exegesis
> - Familiarize yourself with historical setting
> - Research list of historical items in book you will study

As you study a passage, you should also consult a background commentary. This type of commentary is designed to provide important historical and cultural information verse by verse. So, instead of presenting exegetical comments, they present pertinent background information. Several of these commentaries are available.

Matthews, Victor Harold, Mark W. Chavalas and John H. Walton. *The IVP Bible Background Commentary: Old Testament.* Downers Grove, IL: InterVarsity Press, 2000.

Keener, Craig S. and InterVarsity Press. *The IVP Bible Background Commentary: New Testament.* Downers Grove, Ill.: InterVarsity Press, 1993.

Mare, Harold W. *New Testament Background Commentary: A New Dictionary of Words, Phrases, and Situations in Biblical Order.* Scotland, UK: Christian Focus Publications, 2004.

Life-Long Inquiry

Life-Long Inquiry
- Have systematic plan for continual study
- Build a library of resource books
- Read about history and culture of ancient Near East

Embark on a systematic study of the historical backgrounds of the Bible that you will carry out throughout your entire life. Set up a systematic study plan so that each year you are studying a new area, e.g., study the Egyptians this year, the Canaanites next year, and so on. Begin to build a personal library of resource books and journal articles of each area of historical backgrounds. Get in the habit of reading books on the history and culture of the ancient peoples of the Near East. One suggestion would be to read magazines such as *National Geographic.*

Sources for Studying Historical Backgrounds

Sources for Study
- Ancient Literature
- Archaeologies
- Histories of Israel
- Histories of Near East
- Bible Geography Texts
- Bible Culture Texts

In Chapter 3 we discussed the basic methods and tools for performing biblical research. To discover the historical backgrounds of the Bible, you must use the methods and tools outlined in that unit. Below is a brief review of the types of tools that you should use.

- Anthologies of Ancient Literature
- Old and New Testament Archaeologies
- Histories of Israel
- Histories of The Ancient Near East
- Books on Biblical Geography
- Books on Biblical Culture

Summary

One important principle of the HGRT Methodology is the Principle of Historical Background, which states that the most probable interpretation of a passage is the one that best harmonizes with the broad historical background of the people to whom the book was originally addressed or about whom the book was written. The historical background includes three major areas: history, geography, and culture. Each area has specific guidelines that should be followed when attempting to perform research in these areas. Before you begin the actual exegesis of a book of the Bible, you should first study the historical background behind that book. You should also make it a lifelong goal to study the historical background of the whole Bible. Sources for this study include ancient literature, archaeologies, and histories of Israel, histories of the ancient Near East, books on biblical geography, and books on biblical culture.

Key Terms

Cultural Context   Historical Background

Review Questions

1. What is the principle of interpretation that relates to the historical background of a book of the Bible?
2. What is meant by historical background?
3. What are the three major areas of historical background?
4. What guidelines should you use when you are studying the historical setting of a book of the Bible?
5. What guidelines should you use when you are studying the geographical setting of a book of the Bible?
6. What guidelines should you use to study the cultural practices mentioned in the Bible?
7. When should the historical background be studied for a book of the Bible you want to interpret?
8. What steps can you take to generally become more familiar with the historical backgrounds of the Bible?
9. What are some good sources for the study of historical backgrounds?

This page intentionally left blank.

Chapter 5

The Occasion for Writing
Considering the Situational Context

Outline

Principle of Interpretation 58

The Historical Occasion Defined 58

    Basic Definition 58

    Distinguished from Background and Purpose 58

    Nature of the Historical Occasion 59

    Examples of the Historical Occasion 59

Studying the Historical Occasion for Writing 60

    The Goal and Objectives 60

    Guidelines for Determining the Occasion 60

    Cautions and Suggestions 61

Summary 62

Review Questions 62

Learning Objectives

After completing this chapter, you should be able to

- ❑ Define the historical occasion for writing.
- ❑ Distinguish between the occasion for writing and the historical background or author's purpose.
- ❑ Discuss the nature of the occasion for writing.
- ❑ Identify the goals and objectives in studying the occasion for writing.
- ❑ List the basic guidelines in reconstructing the occasion for writing.

| **Principle** |
| The most probable interpretation of a passage is the one that best harmonizes with the situation of the original author and readers |

Principle of Interpretation

The most probable interpretation of a passage is the one that best harmonizes with the situation of the original author and readers.

The Scriptures were written for the benefit of all believers of all ages; however, each book was originally addressed to a specific historical audience. To interpret the meaning of the author properly, we must read from the viewpoint of the original audience. Thus, we must be aware of their situation, their feelings, and their perspectives.

| **Occasional Documents** |
| • Prophetic Books |
| • Psalms |
| • New Testament Epistles |

Understanding of the occasion is always beneficial but is often critical to understanding certain types of documents, called **occasional documents**. These include the Old Testament prophetic books, the Psalms, and the New Testament epistles.

The Historical Occasion for Writing Defined

Basic Definition

| **Definition of Historical Occasion** |
| The situation that motivated the author to address his audience about the issue that is the focus of the book |

The **historical occasion** is the situation that motivated the author to address his audience about the issue or issues that are the focus of the book. Scholars call this the **rhetorical situation** or **situational context** because it is the historical situation that motivated the author's message.

Distinguished from Background and Purpose

Historical Background

The historical occasion differs from the historical background of a book because it is not merely the cultural backdrop for the book but involves the specific issues that the author is addressing in the book. The historical background is general, while the historical occasion is specific. For instance, the general historical background of life in America during the Civil War would not reveal why Abraham Lincoln delivered his *Gettysburg Address*. The address was more specifically occasioned by the decision of Congress to turn the battleground in Gettysburg into a national cemetery and memorial park.

Author's Purpose

The historical occasion differs from the author's purpose in that the occasion involves historic facts, while the author's purpose involves his goal in writing. The two are related in the sense that the purpose naturally flows from the occasion. It is the historical occasion that determined the author's purpose for writing his book. The occasion involved people, places, and events. The purpose is the goal that the author has in mind. For instance, President Lincoln's purpose for giving the *Gettysburg Address* was to honor those soldiers that fought in the battle and to encourage his audience to continue the fight for national unity. The occasion was the decision of Congress to turn the battleground in Gettysburg into a national cemetery and memorial park.

Nature of the Historical Occasion

Though every book of the Bible was occasioned by some situation, it is not always possible to reconstruct that occasion in detail. Most authors assume that the readers are aware of the occasion. They rarely ever review or summarize the occasion. However, they often allude to the occasion throughout their writings. When attempting to reconstruct the occasion, we must observe the three major groups that are usually involved and the situations that prompted the author to write.

Nature of Historical Occasion
- Assumed by Author
- Alluded to by Author
- Includes Three Groups
- Involves Situations

Three Groups

Three groups are normally involved in the historical occasion: the author, the audience, and other individuals, third parties, who play a role in the situation. The relationships between these three groups are important. At times the relationship between author and his audience is tender and friendly, at other times the relationship is hostile. The same is true with the relationship between the author and others involved or between the audience and others involved.

Three Groups Involved
- Author
- Audience
- Other Third Party

Types of Situations

Often the occasion involves some kind of problem. This is by far the most common type of situation. Much of the Bible is addressed to deal with problems and negative situations. However, at other times the occasion is something positive. It is also common that the occasion involves multiple situations often mixed together. For instance, Paul wrote 1 Corinthians in response to several situations. The church was divided. Members were taking each other to court, were involved in immorality, were disruptive during church worship, and even were denying the resurrection of the dead. Additionally, the church had written to Paul, asking several questions.

Types of Situations
- Mostly Problems
- Sometimes Positive
- Multiple Situations

Examples of Historical Occasions

The historical occasion that motivated Lincoln's *Emancipation Proclamation* was the pressure for abolition of slavery mounted in Congress and the country during the Civil War.

The historical situation that motivated Peter to write 1 Peter was the persecution that Jewish believers were suffering, and the danger that some might give up under that pressure (1 Peter 1:6).

Studying the Historic Occasion for Writing

Goal and Objectives

The General Goal

General Goal
To read the Bible from the viewpoint of the original audience

Our general goal is to read the Bible from the viewpoint of the original audience. To do this we must disengage ourselves from our present situation and transport ourselves back into the historical situation of the biblical writer and his original audience.

The Specific Objectives

Specific Objectives
• Identify people involved
• Identify relationships between people
• Identify problems and situations

In attempting to reconstruct the occasion, we have three objectives:

- To identify the people involved in the occasion including: author, audience, and third-party participants.

- To identify the interpersonal relationships that existed among the three groups.

- To identify the problems or positive situations that prompted the author to write.

Guidelines for Determining the Occasion

Sources of Information
• The book of the Bible you are studying
• Historical books of the Bible
• Bible Surveys and commentaries

Normally, the book of the Bible you are studying is the only direct source for information about the situation. Sometimes material from the historical books of the Old or New Testaments can also be used. Some of this information is summarized in introductory sections of commentaries or Bible Surveys. However, it is always best to take the time to observe the occasion for yourself. This is especially true for the occasional documents, prophetic books, psalms, and New Testament epistles. Either way, it is important to identify the following items and ask the following questions.

Identify the Author and His Situation

Ask questions about:
• The author and his situation
• The recipients and their situation
• Others who were involved in the situation

- The identity of the author: Who was he?
- The time in which he wrote: When did he write?
- The place from which he wrote: Where was he?
- The circumstances he was in: What was going on?

Identify the Audience and Their Situation

- The identity of the audience: To whom was the book originally written?
- The place where they lived: Where did the readers live?
- The circumstances they were in: What was going on in the readers' lives that lead the author to write?
- What other events or actions played a role in the situation?

Identify Others Who Were Involved in the Situation

- What other individuals were involved in the situation?
- What were the personal relationships between the author, the audience, and other involved individuals?

Cautions and Suggestions

When attempting to reconstruct the historical occasion, keep the following cautions in mind:

- You need to recognize that reconstructing the historical occasion is somewhat a matter of informed guesswork.
- While you might be fairly certain about your reconstruction, you should avoid the foolish arrogance of absolute certainty.
- If the reconstruction is complex or extremely hypothetical, you should not use it as dogmatic proof for an interpretation.
- Reconstruct the historical occasion not only on the basis of what the biblical text states explicitly, but also on what the text implies indirectly.
- Sometimes the reconstruction of the occasion can only be general, while at other times it can be very specific.

Summary

One important principle of the HGRT Methodology is the Principle of the Occasion for Writing, which states the most probable interpretation of a passage is the one that best harmonizes with the situation of the original author and readers. The historical occasion, also called the rhetorical situation, is the situation that motivated the author to address his audience. Though the occasion is always beneficial, in occasional documents, such as the prophetic books, psalms, and the NT epistles, the occasion is critical. The historic occasion normally involves three groups, the author, the audience, and other individuals. The historic occasion also involves a situation that prompted the author to write. This situation is often a problem, though it can be more positive. The book of the Bible you are studying is the only direct source of information about the occasion. In reconstructing the occasion, identify the author and his situation, the audience and their situation, and others who are involved in the situation.

Key Terms

Historical Occasion   Occasional Document   Rhetorical Situation

Situational Context

Review Questions

1. What is the principle of interpretation that relates to the historical occasion of a book of the Bible?
2. What is meant by historical occasion?
3. What is meant by an occasional document?
4. How does the historical occasion differ from the historical background or the author's purpose?
5. What three groups of people are usually involved in the occasion for writing?
6. What kinds of situations are involved in the occasion for writing?
7. What are three objectives when reconstructing the occasion for writing?
8. What is the primary source of information about the occasion for writing?
9. What questions should be asked when attempting to reconstruct the occasion for writing?
10. What cautions and suggestions should be considered when reconstruction the occasion for writing?

Chapter 6

The Author's Purpose

Outline

Principle of Interpretation 64

The Author's Purpose for Writing Defined 64

    Basic Definition 64

    Relationship to the Occasion for Writing 65

    Nature of the Author's Purpose 65

    Categories of Purpose 66

    Example of Purpose 67

Discovering the Author's Purpose for Writing 67

    The Goal and Objectives 67

    Guidelines for Determining the Author's Purpose 68

Summary 69

Review Questions 69

Learning Objectives

After completing this chapter, you should be able to

- ❏ Define the author's purpose for writing.
- ❏ Distinguish between the author's purpose and the occasion for writing.
- ❏ List the basic categories of purpose.
- ❏ Identify the goals and objectives in discovering the author's purpose.
- ❏ List the basic guidelines for discovering the author's purpose.

Principle
The most probable interpretation of a passage is the one that best harmonizes with the author's purpose in writing

Principle of Interpretation

The most probable interpretation of a passage is the one that best harmonizes with the author's purpose in writing.

Individual statements ultimately get their meaning from their relationship to the whole message in which they are given. The purpose of the message clarifies statements and controls interpretation. Take for instance Paul's statement in Romans 2:6.

God "will give to each person according to what he has done."

Is Paul suggesting that salvation is based on our own works? Such an interpretation goes directly against his stated purpose in Romans 1:16-17, that righteousness is gained by faith alone. An understanding of Paul's purpose controls our interpretation of this passage and forces us to seek another explanation to Paul's words in Romans 2:6. Thus we see that to properly understand individual statements, we must interpret them within the context of the author's purpose.

The Author's Purpose for Writing Defined

Basic Definition

Definition of Author's Purpose
The specific goal that he seeks to achieve in his audience's response to his book

The **author's purpose** is the specific goal that the author seeks to achieve in his audience's response to his book. The biblical authors always wrote with the goal of influencing the understanding, feelings, convictions, attitudes and actions of their audience in a predetermined manner. The biblical author's general purpose may be to inform, to convince, to motivate, or to impress his audience.

In academic writing we are taught that we should begin the writing process by identifying a topic and writing a **thesis statement**. The thesis statement is a formal statement of our purpose for writing. Not all types of writing include a formal thesis statement. Poems normally do not state their purpose. However, the poem, like all other meaningful writing, does have a purpose that provides unity and coherence to the message.

Relationship to the Occasion for Writing

The reason that an author was motivated to write to begin with was because he had analyzed his audience and realized that he needed to address some situation that they had. When a biblical author wrote to a particular audience, he had a specific purpose in mind that addressed a particular situation. The situation existed before the author determined to write. So too, we must reconstruct the historical occasion before we can fully understand the author's purpose. Generally, statements and allusions to the situation and purpose will be scattered through the message.

Relationship to Occasion
- Addresses the occasion
- Occasion existed first
- Reconstruct occasion to understand purpose

Nature of the Author's Purpose

One of the distinctive characteristics of written communication is that it is purposeful. Biblical authors wrote their books with a specific purpose that they hoped to accomplish. This purpose determined the author's selectivity, what and how much he included in the message; the author's plan, the order in which materials are presented; and the author's literary genre, the kind of literature he uses to communicate his ideas. At times the author explicitly states his purpose while at other times he leaves it up to the reader to discover the purpose implicitly.

Nature of Author's Purpose
- All books have purpose
- Determines content
- Sometimes explicit, other times implicit

Controls the Content of the Book

The purpose of the author is the central and controlling factor of all that he says in his writing. It leads to three important characteristics in his writing.

Unity   Most books have one central purpose that encompasses all the parts. Each section in the book expands upon and develops this central purpose. As a result, the book has unity.

Selectivity Everything that an author chooses to include in his book should somehow develop or support his purpose. This concept is called **selectivity**. Therefore, we must ask, "Why did the author include this piece of material with respect to his purpose?"

Order   The material found in the book is arranged in a way that best develops the author's purpose. This concept is called **order**. In a five-paragraph theme, the three middle paragraphs compose the main content. The author may take some time thinking about the order of these paragraphs. The final decision about the order will be based on the purpose of the theme.

Purpose Controls Three Characteristics of Writing
- Unity
- Selectivity
- Order

Stated Explicitly or Implied

Sometimes the author will explicitly state his purpose for writing (Prov. 1:1-6). Most often explicit statements of purpose are found at the beginning (Luke 1:1-4) or near the end of the book (John 20:30-31). Sometimes the author will only state his purpose for individual sections within a book (1 John 2:1). Sometimes the author does not explicitly state his purpose. In this case, his purpose must be discerned from the content of the book. For instance, Matthew does not state his purpose but an examination of the content reveals that Matthew's purpose was to prove that Jesus was Israel's Messiah.

Stated Explicitly or Implied
- Sometimes states purpose explicitly at beginning or end of book
- Sometimes states purpose only for section
- Sometimes no statement of purpose

Categories of Purpose

Categories of Purpose
- To Inform
- To Persuade
- To Motivate
- To Impress

The biblical authors always wrote with the goal of influencing the understanding, feelings, convictions, attitudes and actions of their audience in a predetermined manner. The biblical author's general purpose may be to inform, to convince, to motivate, or to impress his audience. Several of these purposes might be present in a book, but only one will dominate and be the primary purpose. The others are merely subordinate purposes and often are limited in scope to a section of the book. Below are the major categories of purpose.

To Inform

To Inform
To teach, enlighten or educate his audience, so that it will understand a specific biblical concept

The author's purpose is to teach, enlighten or educate his audience, so that it will understand a specific biblical concept. Of course, once informed, the audience is expected to act upon the information; but the author's primary purpose aims at the audience's comprehension and retention of his teaching. The author presents his material so that the audience will understand and remember what he has written. The book that aims to inform will consist largely of cognitive material, e.g., explanations, analyses, descriptions, demonstrations, definitions, examples, illustrations, quotations, and narratives. Examples include Proverbs, Luke, and Leviticus.

To Persuade

To Persuade
To convince his audience to adopt beliefs or attitudes that are biblical or to reject beliefs or attitudes that are unbiblical

The author's purpose is to convince his audience to adopt beliefs or attitudes that are biblical or to reject beliefs or attitudes that are unbiblical. The author focuses on evaluating positions, challenging beliefs, and resolving doctrinal disputes. The book may take the form of a debate in which the author presents his case and appeals to expert testimony (quotations, examples from the OT). Examples include Romans 1-11 and John.

To Motivate

To Motivate
To move his audience to action either to do what is right or to stop doing what is wrong

The author's purpose is to move his audience to action either to do what is right or to stop doing what is wrong. When an author seeks to motivate, he is dealing with an audience that needs to be encouraged to repent from sin or an audience already committed to godliness that needs encouragement to persevere in righteous living. In a book designed to motivate, the author uses what will encourage his audience to trust and obey the Lord more than it already is doing. The author may appeal to positive motivation (e.g. offer of rewards in the future or benefits in the present) or negative motivation (e.g. threat of discipline in the present or loss of rewards in the future). In a book designed to motivate, the author will often use material that is designed to appeal to the emotions that will motivate the audience. Examples include Deuteronomy, Hebrews, and Romans 12-15.

To Impress

To Impress
To increase his audience's appreciation and respect for a person, group, cause, or object

The author's purpose is to increase his audience's appreciation and respect for a person, group, cause, or object. The emphasis is on changing or deepening the audience's feelings. An example is a psalm in which the author seeks to move his audience to worship the LORD by impressing it with His character and His deeds. Examples include various Psalms and Isaiah 40.

Other Categories

Often a single book will contain more than one category. For instance, Romans 1-11 is intended to persuade while Romans 12-15 is intended to motivate. Some sections in a book may have purposes not listed above, though rarely will a whole book reflect other purposes. For instance, Romans 1:1-15 constitutes a greeting and thus has an inter-personal purpose.

Example of Purpose

All four gospels deal with the life of Christ, and yet they are at times very different. Much of the difference relates to their different purposes. John and Luke explicitly state their purposes.

> Jesus did many other miraculous signs in the presence of his disciples, which are not recorded in this book. But these are written that you may believe that Jesus is the Christ, the Son of God, and that by believing you may have life in his name.
>
> John 20:30-31

> Therefore, since I myself have carefully investigated everything from the beginning, it seemed good also to me to write an orderly account for you, most excellent Theophilus, so that you may know the certainty of the things you have been taught.
>
> Luke 1:3-4

John's gospel is designed to convince his audience that Jesus is the Son of God. The purpose is evangelistic. Luke's gospel is designed to inform Christians of the historic accuracy of Christ's life. As a result of these differing purposes, the content and organization of the two gospels is somewhat different. John's gospel is organized around 7 great miracles, the last of which is the raising of Lazarus. John's gospel is the least chronological. On the other hand, Luke's gospel emphasizes detailed history. It is the only gospel to link the birth of Christ with secular events when he tells us that Christ was born while Quirinius was governor of Syria. Such details are common in Luke (Luke 3:1-2) and agree with his purpose. Whether in John or Luke, we see that the author's purpose affected the content and organization of the book.

Discovering the Author's Purpose

Goal and Objectives

The General Goal

Our goal in discovering the author's purpose is to become aware of the overall intent of the author in writing and to see how that intent affects the interpretation of individual passages.

General Goal
To become aware of the overall intent of the author in writing and to see how that intent affects the interpretation of individual passages

The Specific Objectives

In attempting to discover the author's purpose, we have these objectives:

- To identify any explicit statements of purpose found in the book.
- To identify the relationship between the occasion for writing and the author's purpose.
- To understand how the content of the book reveals the author's purpose.
- To determine the basic category of purpose.
- To state the author's purpose in a single sentence.

Guidelines for Determining the Author's Purpose

Normally, the book of the Bible you are studying is the only direct source for information about the author's purpose. However, the purpose may be summarized in introductory sections of commentaries or Bible Surveys. It is always best to take the time to observe the purpose for yourself by following the guidelines below.

Observe Whether the Author Explicitly States His Purpose

- Statements of purpose are often at the beginning or end of the book.
- Statements of purpose may be limited to one section of a book.
- Statements of purpose may be very general.

Relate the Purpose to the Historical Situation

- Reconstruct the occasion for writing before attempting to discover the author's purpose.
- Remember that the purpose for writing naturally flows out of the occasion for writing.
- Attempt to understand how the author's purpose relates to the occasion.

Look for Clues in the Content of the Book

- Identify the overall theme or topic of the book.
- Identify what content the author includes and excludes in the book.
- Identify the basic plan and order of the material in the book.

Construct a Purpose Statement for the Book

- Identify the overall category of purpose.
- Write the purpose of the book as a single sentence.
  You can use the following model:

  The author wrote the book to (inform, persuade, motivate, or impress) the readers that ...

  Example:

  Paul wrote Romans to persuade the church that righteousness is gained from God by faith in Christ, not from self-effort by the Law.

Summary

One important principle of the HGRT Methodology is the Principle of the Author's Purpose for Writing, which states that the most probable interpretation of a passage is the one that best harmonizes with the author's purpose in writing. The author's purpose is the goal that he seeks to achieve in his audience. Normally the purpose flows out of the occasion for writing. The purpose controls the unity, selectivity, and order of the material in the book. It may be explicitly stated or only implied. The major categories of purpose are: to inform, to persuade, to motivate, and to impress. The book of the Bible you are studying is the best source for discovering the author's purpose. Important guidelines for discovering the author's purpose are:

- Observe whether the author explicitly states his purpose
- Relate the purpose to the historical occasion for writing
- Look for clues in the content of the book
- Construct a purpose statement for the book

Key Terms

Author's Purpose   Thesis Statement   Selectivity   Order   Unity

Review Questions

1. What is the principle of interpretation that relates to the author's purpose for writing a book of the Bible?
2. What is meant by author's purpose?
3. How does the author's purpose relate to the historical occasion for writing?
4. What three characteristics of writing does the author's purpose control?
5. In what ways does an author reveal his purpose?
6. What are four broad categories of purpose?
7. What is the primary source of information about the author's purpose?
8. What guidelines should be used when attempting to discover the author's purpose?
9. What form should be used when attempting to state the author's purpose?

This page intentionally left blank.

Chapter 7

Discourse Analysis
Considering the Literary Context

Outline

Principle of Interpretation 72

Literary Context 72

    Literary Context Defined 72

    Nature of Literary Context 73

    Methods Employed in Analyzing Literary Context 77

Discourse Analysis 73

    Levels of Discourse 73

    Characteristics of Discourse 74

        Cohesion 74

        Connection 75

    Unit Boundaries 76

Performing Discourse Analysis 77

    Goals and Objectives 77

    Guidelines 77

        A General Sequence 77

        Top-Down Approach 78

        Bottom-Up Approach 78

Creating Models of the Discourse 79

    Guidelines for Creating an Outline 79

    Guidelines for Creating a Horizontal Chart 80

    Guidelines for Creating a Condensation 82

Summary 83

Review Questions 84

72

Learning Objectives

After completing this chapter, you should be able to

- ❑ State the principle of interpretation that relates to the literary context
- ❑ Define literary context
- ❑ Evaluate the methods used to analyze the literary context
- ❑ Define discourse analysis
- ❑ Describe the various levels of discourse
- ❑ Identify the characteristics of discourse
- ❑ Describe the various types of cohesion within a discourse
- ❑ Describe the various types of connection between discourse units.
- ❑ Apply appropriate guidelines in analyzing biblical discourse
- ❑ Model a discourse in the form of an outline, chart, and condensation

Principle of Interpretation

Principle
The most probable interpretation of a passage is the one that best agrees with the literary context of the book in which it is found

The most probable interpretation of a passage is the one that best agrees with the literary context of the book in which it is found.

To understand individual statements properly, we must not only interpret them in light of the purpose of the book in which they are found, but we must also interpret them in light of the materials that surround them. When we are aware of the plan and structure of the book, we will be in a better position to discern how surrounding materials clarify the meaning of individual statements. Thus, analysis of the structure and overall plan of the book is a very important step in the process of interpreting any statement within the book.

Literary Context

Literary Context Defined

Literary Context
The connection of thought that exits between the various sections of a composition

The **literary context** is the connection of thought that must exit between the various sections of a text in order to communicate the author's message. If a text has a unifying purpose, then it must have a discernable context. Each part of the text must have some connection with the other parts of the text.

A Discourse
A text that is characterized by unity, cohesion, and purpose

Such a text, characterized by unity, cohesion, and purpose, may be called a **discourse**. Though a discourse may be either spoken or written, for our purposes we will be considering the written discourses of the Bible. Such a discourse may encompass a complete book of the Bible, such as Romans; or it may encompass only a portion of a book of the Bible, such as a psalm.

Nature of Literary Context

Nature of Literary Context
- Sometimes highly unified
- Sometimes loosely connected
- Remote context valuable to identify shifts in near context

We assume that a connection of thought exists between all the materials in a discourse since the author wrote with a purpose that unifies the composition. This assumption is only partially true. Some books of the Bible have a very tightly focused purpose. Other books seem to have a more loosely connected set of purposes.

Biblical Hermeneutics: A Guide for Studying the Bible

The same is true with our own writing. When I write an academic theme, I have a tightly focused singular purpose and my theme is highly unified. However, when I write a personal letter, my purpose is mixed and the material in the letter is only loosely connected. As a result, the immediate context has a more direct bearing on a statement than does the remote context. This is also true in the Bible.

An understanding of the remote context helps us determine when there is a shift in context. That is, when the topic of discussion changes. This is very important for interpretation. The understanding of the literary context helps us determine how closely the parts of the message are connected.

Methods Employed in Analyzing Literary Context

The idea that literary context exists and that it needs to be understood is nothing new. However, in the past, biblical scholars have often minimized the analysis of the literary context in favor of grammatical analysis of the sentence and semantic understanding of the individual words.

This resulted in mostly **thematic analysis**, an approach that attempts to divide the text based on shifts in topic. A good example of this approach can be seen in the analysis of the plan of Romans 1-11. Most scholars understand these chapters to be a basic presentation of major theological themes (condemnation, justification, sanctification). This approach does not provide much analysis of how the sections work together or of changes in literary style. Discourse is not simply a string of propositions or theme statements.

Many scholars suggest that biblical authors employed rhetorical devices and models that were common within their culture. An approach to understand the broader literary context by using genres within the cultural context of the author is called **rhetorical analysis.** A good example of this is the application of Greco-Roman epistolary form to the epistles of the New Testament. The approach has been beneficial but is not without its problems. First, biblical writers did not limit themselves to the rhetorical forms found within their own culture. For instance, the Gospels are a rhetorical form with many unique features. Though they have some resemblance to Greco-Roman biography, they defy classification. Another problem with rhetorical analysis is that it fails to address the more universal aspect of language as text.

In the middle of the 20th century a new approach was suggested, **discourse analysis**. This approach attempts to understand the literary context by applying basic principles of human communication. This approach is still very much in its infancy but it provides so much benefit that we are presenting it as the major method for understanding the literary context.

Discourse Analysis

Discourse analysis is an attempt to understand the text beyond the level of the sentence through an analysis of its larger literary units and the connective relationships between those units. Simply put, discourse analysis applies literary principles in an attempt to understand the literary units of a discourse and how those units work together to develop the author's overall message.

Levels of Discourse

In one sense, a discourse could be thought of as a series of words. Yet, it is clear that words are grouped together into larger grammatical structures called sentences; and sentences are combined into paragraphs. Most scholars agree that analysis of the discourse goes beyond

Methods of Analysis
- Thematic Analysis
- Rhetorical Analysis
- Discourse Analysis

Thematic Analysis
Approach that attempts to divide the text based on shifts in topic

Rhetorical Analysis
Approach that uses genres within the cultural context to understand the literary context

Discourse Analysis
An attempt to understand the text beyond the level of the sentence through an analysis of its larger literary units and the connective relationships between those units

Levels of Discourse
- Paragraphs
- Embedded Discourse
- Larger Embedded Discourses
- Main Discourse

an analysis of the sentence and generally identify the paragraph as the base unit for analysis. In Chapter 8 you will learn how to analyze individual paragraphs.

Though paragraphs deal with a single narrowly focused topic, they cannot provide a full discussion of a broad topic. So, paragraphs are grouped together into what is called an **embedded discourse**. Such discourses provide a fuller discussion of a topic. In turn, these embedded discourses may be combined to form **larger embedded discourses.** This hierarchical structure will continue to grow into larger and larger levels. The number of levels within a discourse differs from discourse to discourse. So, generally speaking, the *main discourse* consists of larger embedded discourses which in turn consist of smaller embedded discourses.

Characteristics of Discourse

Characteristics of Discourse
• Cohesion
• Connection

Discourse units are characterized by cohesion and connection. **Cohesion** refers to the overall unity of the units and connection refers to the semantic relationships that exist between the units.

Cohesion

Cohesion
The semantic unity of the material found in the unit

A key characteristic of a discourse unit is cohesion. The unit has a central topic or primary message that the unit is attempting to communicate. All the parts of the unit are working together to develop this topic. The topic is very broad for the main discourse and is narrower for smaller embedded discourses. Yet, whether broad or narrow, all the subunits within the discourse unit are working together to develop this topic.

Types of Cohesion

Types of Cohesion
• Standard Genre Forms
• Lexical Cohesion
• Pronominal Cohesion
• Subject/Actor Cohesion
• Verbal Cohesion
• Temporal Cohesion
• Spatial Cohesion

The author can mark out this topic in several different ways. He can organize his material following the **form of a standard genre**. The individual units are discernable to those who are familiar with the genre. For instance, Rom. 1:1-7 forms the standard salutation for a Greco-Roman epistle. Knowing how such salutations were formed makes identification of the unit easier.

Another method of marking out the general topic of discussion is by **lexical cohesion**, the repetition of words with the same basic meaning. This includes the use of synonyms and antonyms. For instance, in Romans 8 the term, "spirit" occurs 21 times. This concentration helps to mark out the unit. In smaller embedded discourses there are normally high concentrations of similar words forming semantic threads. In larger discourses these words may be lightly sprinkled throughout the text.

The topic may also be marked out by a cluster of pronouns all referring to the same person or thing. This is called **pronominal cohesion**. For instance, the 2nd person singular pronoun clearly marks out Rom. 2:1-29 as a cohesive unit.

The topic of a unit is often seen in the common subject of many sentences spread across several paragraphs. What is important is to observe the unifying performer of the actions represented. Since in passive sentences the subject is not the performer of the action, it might be better to talk about a common actor. **Subject/actor cohesion** exists when a common performer of the action can be seen in the text. For instance, in Gal. 1:11-2:21 the subject/actor is Paul. This is seen in his constant use of "I" as the subject of the verbs.

Verbal cohesion exists when the major verbs within a discourse unit have the same verbal characteristics. For example, a hortatory unit will most likely have verbs that are imperatives. This is the case in Rom. 12-16 where the great majority of the imperative verbs are found in the book.

Another form of cohesion is called, **temporal cohesion**. This exists when a unit is united by a single timeframe. It is common to have all the verbs exhibiting the same timeframe (past, present, future). Temporal connectors may also help to identify this type of cohesion. For instance, in Gal. 1:11-2:21 Paul presents historical material in a chronological order. This chronological sequence marks out a major embedded discourse within the book.

Spatial cohesion exits when a discourse unit is marked out by a common location. A good example of this is found in the Gospel of John. John describes several visits of Jesus to Jerusalem. These shifts from Galilee to Jerusalem help to mark out the embedded discourses within the Gospel.

Connection

Along with cohesion, discourse units must also exhibit **connection**, that is, they must be related in some meaningful way to the surrounding units within an embedded discourse. Thus, connection refers to the interrelatedness of two or more discourse units. These connections can be classified as logical or rhetorical.

> **Connection**
> The interrelatedness of two or more discourse units

Logical Connections

Logical connections connect units by rational relationships. For instance, a unit may provide an explanation of something found in the prior unit. Logical connections include: contrast, comparison, conclusion, continuation, causation, explanation, and purpose.

> **Logical Connection**
> Connections that establish a rational relationship between units

Such connections are often marked out by means of **structure markers**. A structure marker is a word or phrase used by the writer to explicitly identify the type of relationship. For example, Paul uses "therefore" in Rom. 12:1 to establish a connection between Rom. 1-11 and Rom. 12-15. However, not all relationships are explicitly marked. In such cases, we must study the materials in each unit and draw conclusions about the relationships.

> **Structure Marker**
> Word or phrase used by the writer to explicitly identify the type of relationship

The following is a list of logical connections and the structure markers that mark them out.

Contrast	Comparison	Conclusion
On the other hand	Similarly	Therefore
Nevertheless	Like wise	Consequently
On the contrary	In like manner	So
However	So also	Finally
Conversely	In the same way	Then
Notwithstanding	Just as	Thus
Although	As an example	Hence
In contrast		As a result

Continuation	Causation & Substantiation	Explanation & Analysis
Furthermore	If.. then	For
Moreover	Even if	Indeed
Again	So then	You see
Next	Because	Now
First... Second	Since	
Also		
And then	**Purpose**	
In addition	In order that	
Likewise	For this cause	
	To this end	
	With this in view	

Rhetorical Connections

Rhetorical connections connect units at a macro level based on the overall design of a discourse. A quality discourse will include an introduction, a body that incorporates several main points, and a conclusion. For instance, the unit represented by Rom. 1:16-17 is the introduction or thesis for the larger embedded discourse in Rom. 1:16-11:36. The unit represented by Rom. 11:33-36 is the conclusion to the same embedded discourse.

Unit Boundaries

A **unit boundary** is the location in the text where one unit ends and another begins. Identification of these boundaries is a very important goal in discourse analysis. Keep in mind that these boundaries may mark the beginning of a new paragraph, a new smaller embedded discourse, or a new larger embedded discourse. Since the paragraph is the smallest discourse unit, all unit boundaries must also be boundaries between paragraphs. A unit boundary will never occur in the middle of a paragraph.

Several techniques can be used to identify unit boundaries. First, one must look for **shifts in cohesion**. This may be identified by a change in genre or form within a genre, by a shift in lexical cohesion, pronominal cohesion, verbal cohesion, temporal cohesion, spatial cohesion, or by a change in subject/actor cohesion.

Second, look for instances of **inclusio**, a technique in which the author marks the beginning and ending of an embedded discourse by the use of parallel lexical or grammatical forms. For instance, Romans 2 is marked off by the idea of judging others. In Rom. 2:1 Paul talks about "you (sg) who pass judgment" on the Gentiles. Then in Rom. 2:27 Paul concludes that the Gentile "judge you (sg)". This ironic statement creates an inclusio that marks out the unit.

Transitions can also be used to identify a unit boundary. A transition provides a smooth way to move from one unit to another by interspersing elements of both units.

A common word or concept at the end of one unit and in the beginning of the next is called a **hook word**. For instance, in Rom. 3:21 Paul repeats the word, "Law" from Rom 3:19-20 and repeats the concept of justification, "justify", *dikaioo* in Rom. 3:20 and "righteousness", *dikaiosune* in Rom. 3:21.

Rhetorical devices are often used in transitions. For instance, in 1 Corinthians Paul moves from one subject to the next using the express, "Now concerning..." (I Cor. 7:1, 1 Cor. 8:1, 1 Cor 12:1, 1 Cor. 16:1). Paul also commonly employs rhetorical questions to introduce a new topic or unit (Rom. 3:1, Rom. 3:9, Rom. 4:1). Conjunctions that link paragraphs are commonly employed as transitions as is the case with "then" in Rom. 4:1.

Introductions and **conclusions** may signal a unit boundary. 1 Cor. 1:10-17 is a good example of an introduction to the larger embedded discourse 1 Cor. 1:10-4:21. Paul introduces the problem of division and gives the primary exhortation to be united. The units that follow provide the causes and cures for division and encourage unity.

Rom. 3:9-20 is a good example of a conclusion. It forms the conclusion for the embedded discourse Rom. 1:18-3:20. The conclusion is introduced by the rhetorical question, "What then? Are we better than they?" This is followed by a summary conclusion concerning both Jews (Rom. 2:1-3:8) and Gentiles (Rom 1:18-32); an extensive list of supporting Scriptures (Rom. 3:10-18); and related implications (Rom. 3:19-20).

Performing Discourse Analysis

Goal and Objectives

The General Goal

The goal in performing discourse analysis is to understand the message of the text at a macro level through an awareness of how the author develops his argument and how he uses certain linguistic devices to achieve his ends.

General Goal
To understand the message at a macro level through awareness of how the author develops his argument and how he uses linguistic devices to achieve his ends

Specific Objectives

In attempting to understand the discourse, the analyst must:

- Identify cohesive units of differing size: paragraphs, embedded discourses, larger embedded discourses, and the main discourse
- Identify unit boundaries
- Determine the types of connections that exist between units
- Create a model of the discourse

Specific Objectives
- Identify cohesive units of differing size
- Identify unit boundaries
- Determine types of connections between units
- Create a model

Guidelines for Performing Discourse Analysis

A General Sequence

Discourse analysis must include three basic tasks. First, the analyst must identify types of cohesion that exit in the text. This includes the identification of:

General Sequence
- Identify Cohesion
- Identify Unit Boundaries
- Identify Connections

- Lexical threads   repeated words and concepts
- Pronoun threads   repeated pronouns with the same referent
- Subject/actor threads   repeated performer of main actions
- Verbal Cohesion   clusters of verbs with the same properties
- Temporal Cohesion   actions within the same timeframe
- Spatial Cohesion   actions at the same location

Second, the analyst must identify unit boundaries. These boundaries are identified by:

- Shifts in Cohesion
- Inclusio
- Transitions
- Rhetorical Devices
- Introductions
- Conclusions

Finally, the analyst must determine the types of connections that exist between the units. These connections may be logical or rhetorical. To aid in this identification, the analyst must observe structure markers and other rhetorical devices employed by the writer to relate units.

Top-Down Approach

Top-Down Approach
- Review Situational Context
- Perform Genre Analysis
- Identify Macro Structure
- Determine Connections
- Identify Embedded Discourse
- Divide down to the Paragraph

Scholars suggest both a bottom-up and a top-down approach to discourse analysis. In the top-down approach one begins with the **situational context** and author's purpose and then attempts to discover the top-level units that make up the macro discourse.

This should include **genre analysis**. An awareness of the genre provides an awareness of the typical forms employed by that genre. These forms can be used as a grid for understanding the macro structure. Typical features within the genre may include certain typical structural devices that reveal shifts in cohesion and types of connection. For instance, in Hebrew narrative the *waw* consecutive is commonly employed to link a series of past events. The absence of the *waw* may signal the beginning of the new narrative unit.

The analyst must identify the macro structure of the text. The macro structure consists of the top-level units of the main discourse. The analyst should begin by applying the typical form of the genre to the text. However, keep in mind that typical forms are not absolute guides. Authors will commonly alter such forms to meet their purposes. The analyst should also remember that discourses normally include an introduction, main body with several points, and a conclusion.

The analyst must also determine the types of connections that exist between the units. These connections may include both logical and rhetorical connections.

Each macro unit is then studied to see if it contains an embedded discourse. This is the case when a unit can be divided based on shifts in cohesion found within that unit. When this occurs, the analyst repeats the process given above with the embedded discourse, dividing the text further and further into smaller and smaller embedded discourses. This process continues until the analyst reaches the paragraph, the smallest discourse unit.

Bottom-Up Approach

Bottom-Up Approach
- Analyze Paragraphs
- Group Paragraphs into Embedded Discourse
- Determine Connections
- Group Embedded Discourses into Larger Discourse
- Repeat Process Unit Main Discourse is Reached

In the bottom-up approach one begins with the **individual paragraphs** and then attempts to discover how a group of paragraphs work together to form an embedded discourse. See Chapter 8 for information on analyzing individual paragraphs.

To identify which paragraphs should be grouped together to form an embedded discourse, the analyst must consider the cohesiveness and rhetorical nature of the paragraphs. The group of paragraphs should exhibit the following types of cohesiveness:

- Lexical threads   repeated words and concepts
- Pronoun threads   repeated pronouns with the same referent
- Subject/actor threads   repeated performer of main actions
- Verbal Cohesion   clusters of verbs with the same properties
- Temporal Cohesion   actions within the same timeframe
- Spatial Cohesion   actions at the same location

They should also exhibit the main rhetorical connections that typify any discourse:

- Introduction
- Body that incorporates several main points
- Conclusion.

Finally, the analyst must determine the types of connections that exist between the units. These connections may be logical or rhetorical. To aid in this identification, the analyst must observe structure markers and other rhetorical devices employed by the writer to relate units.

Once the lower levels of embedded discourses are discovered, the analyst seeks to determine if any of these discourses are working together to form a larger discourse. This is done by looking for high levels of cohesion and connection. This process continues until the main discourse is found.

Creating Models of the Discourse

Once the analysis is completed, the analyst must represent the conclusions. Outlining, charting, and condensations are ways of modeling or representing the structure of the discourse.

Guidelines for Creating an Outline

The classical way to present the plan of a book is by creating an outline. However, we need to distinguish between a topical outline and a rhetorical outline. **Topical outlines** of the Bible are designed for preaching and popular teaching. They tend to summarize major units with one or two words. They rarely attempt to reveal the fuller relationships of the sections. Though helpful for popular Bible study, they are not sufficient for scholarly exegesis. **Rhetorical outlines** are more complete, using full sentences to summarize sections. They reveal relationships and the author's fuller argument. You should create rhetorical outlines. Below are some suggestions for formatting rhetorical outlines.

- Stated all points with complete sentences.
- The smallest points on the outline should cover no less than a paragraph.
- Use standard outlining divisions and procedures.
  Divisions should include: Roman numerals, capital letters, Arabic numerals, and lower-case letters, indented appropriately. For every 1 there must be a 2, for every A there must be a B.
- Include the references for each point in a column at the far right. Take care that all verses from the text are referenced in the order in which they occur in the text.
- Include a thematic title for the book at the top of the outline. Do not use the title of the book as the theme. The theme may be stated as a thesis statement.

> **Rules for Outlining**
> - Stated all points with complete sentences
> - The smallest points cover no less than a paragraph
> - Use standard outlining divisions and procedures
> - Include the references in a column at the far right
> - Include a thematic title at the top of the outline

Outline of Embedded Discourse in Romans 1:18-3:20

B. **Refuting Jewish Superiority and Hope:** Jews have no superior position before God through the Law since they are sinners like the Gentiles and thus under the wrath of an impartial God.

                                              1:18-3:20

    1. **Gentile Sin and Condemnation Stated**: In spite of the Gentiles' original position, their sin leaves them inexcusably in a state of condemnation.   1:18-32

    2. **Jewish Sin and Condemnation Proven**: In spite of your position as a Jew, your sin leaves you in a state of condemnation.   2:1-3:8

        a) **General Statement of Jewish Condemnation and Divine Judgment:** Because you practice that which   2:1-16

you condemn in others, you stand condemned, since
God judges all impartially based on what they do.

b) **Specific Indictment of Jewish Sin and Explanation**   2:17-29
of Circumcision: Your position as a Jew is nullified
because you have broken the Law in which case
circumcision provides no benefit.

c) **Jewish Condemnation is Just:** In spite of the   3:1-8
advantages of Judaism and the glory God receives when
He judges, Jews are justly condemned.

3. **Conclusion:** The Jew has no advantage over the Gentiles   3:9-20
with respect to divine judgment since both are under sin's
condemnation against which the Law affords no help.

Guidelines for Creating a Horizontal Chart

Charts provide a method to represent visually the plan and structure of a passage or a book of the Bible. Generally, we use horizontal charts to represent larger sections and vertical charts to represent smaller sections such as a paragraph. Below is a list of guidelines for creating a horizontal chart.

- The progress of thought or plan always flows from left to right.
- Sections that are above or below other sections have reference to the same material in the text.
- Subsections are displayed below and within major sections.
- The starting verse of each section is placed at the far bottom left of the section.
- Words or short phrases are used as section titles.
- Key structure markers are placed between the sections they relate.
- Key words and verse references from the text may appear in a separate area of the chart.
- A theme for the whole passage or book is located at the top of the chart.

Rules for Developing Horizontal Charts
- Progress of plan flows from left to right
- Sections above or below refer to the same material
- Subsections display below and within major sections
- Starting verse of each section placed at the far bottom left
- Use words or short phrases
- Key words and verse references may appear in a separate area
- Theme is located at top

Sample Horizontal Chart[3]

Colossians: Christ is All and in All				
Mainly Personal	*Mainly Doctrinal*		*Mainly Practical*	*Mainly Personal*
Introduction	Doctrinal	Polemical	Hortatory	Closing
CHRIST YOUR INHERITANCE	CHRIST YOUR INDWELLER	CHRIST YOUR SUFFICIENCY	CHRIST YOUR MOTIVATION	CHRIST YOUR MASTER
1:1	1:13	2:6	3:5	4:7
Paul, to the saints at Colossae 1:1 We give thanks 1:3 We pray 1:9	Christ: image of God, first place 1:13 I proclaim Him 1:24 Christ: God's mystery 2:1	Walk in Him 2:6 In Him: fullness of deity 2:8 None: act as judge, defraud you 2:16 Why do you submit? 2:20 Seek what is above 3:1	Put on compassion, kindness... 3:5 Wives, husbands, children... 3:18 Prayer, conduct toward outsiders 4:2	Tychicus 4:7 Aristarcus, etc. send greetings 4:14 I, Paul write this greeting 4:18

Guidelines for Creating a Condensation

In a condensation each paragraph in the text is reduced to a single sentence. These sentences are then grouped together into paragraphs that represent smaller embedded discourses. High levels of discourse are identified through the use of center and left justified titles. Below are some guidelines for creating a condensation of a book of the Bible.

- Create a sentence synopsis for each paragraph in the book.
- Identify structure markers between paragraphs.
- Identify the type of relationship that the structure markers reveal.
- Use the structure markers and the relationships to smoothly join the sentences.
- Group your sentences into paragraphs to reflect the smaller embedded discourses.
- Use section titles within the condensation to reveal the larger embedded discourses.
- Place a title at the top of the condensation that summarizes the author's purpose.

Sample Condensation of Hebrews 1:1-4:16

Listen to the Son's Message that is greater than that of Angels

God, who in the past spoke through the prophets, has spoken to us a final message by His Divine Son who is even superior to the angels. For unlike the angels who are merely servants, God calls him his Son, God, and Lord. Therefore, we must pay attention to the Son's message because it is more binding than even the Law that came by angels.

You see, God has not subjected the future world to angels but to the man, Jesus who suffered for us all. To save mankind, Jesus was willing to identify with men as a brother. Therefore, he took on their complete humanity even to the point of mortality so that he could atone for their sins.

Don't miss the divine rest available in Jesus, the Son

Therefore, concentrate on Jesus who is God's faithful Son and our Lord, not merely a servant like Moses. As Scripture says, "don't harden your heart" and so lose out on God's rest. Rather, encourage each other to faithfulness. Remember that is was because of their unbelief that your fathers whom God delivered from Egypt were not allowed to enter God's rest.

Therefore, we must be careful that we don't like them miss God's rest. For, this rest is still available to those who believe. Now, God does not miss anything. So, hold firmly to your faith in Jesus, our high priest.

Summary

Principle of interpretation: The most probable interpretation of a passage is the one that best agrees with the literary context of the book in which it is found.

Literary context is the connection of thought that must exist between the various sections of a text. Such a text may be called a discourse. A discourse may encompass a complete book of the Bible or may encompass only a section of a book. This connection is sometimes highly unified and other times only loosely connected.

Three major methods have been employed in analyzing the literary context. Thematic analysis attempts to divide the text into units based on shifts in topic. Rhetorical analysis attempts to understand the literary context based on genres used with the author's culture. Discourse analysis attempts to understand the text beyond the level of the sentence through an analysis of the larger literary units and the connective relationships they exhibit.

In discourse analysis the paragraph is the smallest literary unit. Paragraphs work together to form embedded discourses. In turn, embedded discourses work together to form the main discourse of the text. This hierarchical structure can have any number of discourse levels.

Discourse is characterized by cohesion and connection. Cohesion refers to the semantic unity that exists within a unit. Several types of cohesion exist including Genre Form cohesion, lexical cohesion, pronominal cohesion, subject/actor cohesion, verbal cohesion, temporal cohesion, and spatial cohesion.

Connection is the interrelatedness of two or more discourse units. Connection can be logical or rhetorical. Logical connections establish a rational relationship between the units. There relationships are often marked out by the author using structure markers. Rhetorical connections connect units at a macro level based on the overall design of discourse: introduction, body, and conclusion.

A unit boundary is the location in the test where one unit ends and another begins. Unit boundaries can be identified by shifts in cohesion, inclusio, transitions, rhetorical devices, and the presence of introductions or conclusions.

The goal of discourse analysis is to understand the message of the text at a macro level through an awareness of how the author develops his argument and how he uses certain linguistic devices to achieve his ends.

The analysis must identify cohesive units of difference size, identify unit boundaries, determine types of connections, and create models of the text. This can be accomplished using top-down and bottom-up approaches. Modeling can be accomplished by outlining, charting, and condensations.

Key Terms

Cohesion	Lexical Cohesion	Spatial Cohesion
Connection	Literary Context	Structure Marker
Discourse	Logical Connection	Subject/actor Cohesion
Discourse Analysis	Pronominal Cohesion	Temporal Cohesion
Embedded Discourse	Rhetorical Analysis	Thematic Analysis
Genre Analysis	Rhetorical Connection	Unit Boundary
Hook Words	Rhetorical Devices	Verbal Cohesion
Inclusio	Shift on Cohesion	

Review Questions

1. What is meant by literary context and how does it differ from cultural context and situational context?
2. What are three different methods that can be used in analyzing literary context?
3. What are the limitation to thematic analysis and rhetorical analysis?
4. What is discourse analysis and how does it differ from thematic and rhetorical analysis?
5. What is the smallest base unit for analysis in discourse analysis?
6. What is meant by embedded discourse?
7. What are the two main characteristics of discourse?
8. What is meant by cohesion?
9. What are the different types of cohesion?
10. What is meant by connection?
11. What are the different types of connection?
12. What is meant by unit boundary?
13. What techniques can you use to discover unit boundaries?
14. What is the goal in performing discourse analysis?
15. What are the three main tasks in the general sequence of discourse analysis?
16. What is the difference between a top-down and a bottom-up approach to discourse analysis?
17. What modeling techniques can you use to represent a discourse's structure?

Chapter 8

Paragraph Analysis
Considering the Immediate Context

Outline

Principle of Interpretation 86

    Importance of the Paragraph 86

    Paragraph – The Basic Unit of Study 86

The Nature of Paragraphs 87

    Paragraph Defined 87

    Elements of the Paragraph 87

        The Topic of the Paragraph 87

        The Development of the Paragraph 88

        The Arrangement of the Paragraph 89

        The Internal Structural Devices 89

Analyzing a Paragraph 91

    Goal and Objectives 91

    Guidelines for Analyzing a Paragraph 92

    Guidelines for Creating a Sentence Synopsis 93

    Guidelines for Creating a Vertical Chart 93

Summary 95

Review Questions 95

References 96

86

Learning Objectives

After completing this chapter, you should be able to

- ❑ State the principle of interpretation that relates to the immediate context.
- ❑ Define terms related to the paragraph.
- ❑ List and explain the basic elements of the paragraph.
- ❑ Identify the goals and objectives in studying a paragraph.
- ❑ List the basic guidelines for analyzing a paragraph.
- ❑ Create a synopsis and vertical chart for a paragraph in the Bible.

Principle of Interpretation

Principle
The most probable interpretation of a passage is the one that best agrees with the immediate context in which it is found

The most probable interpretation of a passage is the one that best agrees with the immediate context in which it is found.

In prose, the immediate context is equated with the paragraph; while in poetry, the immediate context is equated with a stanza. In this chapter, we will assume that we are working in prose. Later in Chapter 20, we will discuss stanzas.

Importance of the Paragraph

The paragraph is the basic and most important literary unit used for communicating in writing. A.T. Robertson notes, "The paragraph was to the ancients the most important item of punctuation."[1] In the same vein Fee writes, "We simply cannot stress enough the importance of your learning to think paragraphs, and not just as natural units of thought, but as the absolute necessary key to understanding the argument in the various epistles."[2]

It is ironic that the paragraph is the most important unit of thought, yet it often receives the least amount of attention by Bible students.

The Paragraph as the Basic Unit of Study

Paragraph Basic Unit of Study
- Not chapter or verse divisions
- Not sentences

The chapter and verse divisions of the Bible, added in 1227 AD, tend to obscure the author's flow of thought. Paragraph divisions, on the other hand, reflect the author's flow of thought. Therefore, the paragraph should be used as the basic unit of study in Scripture, not the chapters and verses. Although an individual sentence provides a complete thought, that thought remains undeveloped. It is the paragraph that fully develops the thought. Therefore, the paragraph should be used as the basic unit of study in Scripture, not the sentence.

Unfortunately, some fairly recent translations such as the New American Standard Bible continue to format their translations in columns of verses. Readers should pick a translation that is formatted in standard paragraph format.

The Nature of Paragraphs

Paragraph Defined

Basic Definition

A **paragraph** is a series of sentences that develop a single topic. Thus, paragraphs like discourse units exhibit cohesion. All the sentences in the paragraph work together and develop the topic. The topic of a paragraph is normally very narrow and is often stated in a single sentence. The additional sentences within the paragraph develop the topic by filling out the topic.

> **Paragraph**
> A series of sentences that develop a single topic

The defining characteristic of the paragraph is not its length, but the existence of a central topic. The average paragraph can range from a few sentences in popular literature to numerous sentences in technical literature. Sometimes short paragraphs are used for dialogue in novels and can actually be as short as one sentence.

Differences in Translations

At times translations of the Bible will disagree as to the size of paragraphs. For instance, the NIV tends to have very short paragraphs while the NASB often combines two or three NIV paragraphs into one. Generally speaking, it is best to use a more literal translation when attempting to identify the paragraphs.

Elements of the Paragraph

Paragraphs contain some basic elements that are important to observe. These are a topic, development, order or arrangement, and the use of structural devices.

> **Elements of the Paragraph**
> - Topic
> - Development
> - Arrangement
> - Structural Devices

The Topic of the Paragraph

The **topic** is the main idea discussed in the paragraph. It tends to be general and undeveloped. The topic of the paragraph is often expressed in a single sentence that may appear anywhere in the paragraph. This sentence is called the **topic sentence**. The topic sentence normally is the first sentence in a paragraph; but can occur anywhere, at the beginning, middle, or end of the paragraph.

> **Topic**
> - The main idea discussed in the paragraph
> - General and undeveloped
> - Explicitly stated in topic sentence
> - Topic sentence often at beginning
> - Topic sentence can be anywhere
> - Topic sentence not required.

While every paragraph has a topic, a formal topic sentence is not always found. In such cases the topic may be implied throughout the paragraph rather than being explicitly stated in one sentence. If the topic is not stated explicitly in a concrete topic sentence, the student must identify the implicit and abstract topic idea.

Example Revealing the Topic

In the following example, the topic sentence is underlined. Notice that the topic sentence is the most general and undeveloped thought in the paragraph.

> To study the Bible effectively, you will need a few basic books. Of course, you will need one or more Bibles. Pick a modern literal translation to use as your main study Bible, and then a few other translations for survey reading. In addition, you should have a Bible dictionary so that you can research various topics, a concordance to find various passages, and a good one-volume commentary to assist you in interpretation. If you can afford it, you might also purchase lexicons or theological wordbooks for both the Old and New Testaments.

The Development of the Topic

Development
Additional detailed information given to support the topic

The **development** refers to the additional detailed information given to support the idea expressed in the topic idea or topic sentence. This information gives content to the author's generalities about the topic by using relevant details and illustrations.

It is important to identify the manner in which the supporting sentences develop the topic. No sentence can be interpreted correctly without an understanding of its role within the paragraph. The supporting sentences may develop the topic sentence in several different ways.

Types of Development
- Explanations
- Specification
- Support
- Examples & Illustrations
- Comparison & Contrast
- Cause & Effect

Explanation. The author may explain or clarify anything vague or ambiguous in the topic sentence by using definitions or explanations. 1 Corinthians 13:4-7 is a paragraph that explains and clarifies the meaning of love.

Specification. The author provides specifics or descriptions of what is only identified in general in the topic. Philippians 2:6-8 provides specific details about the attitude that was in Christ introduced in 2:5.

Support. The author may select specific facts to support or defend a claim made in the topic sentence. In Romans 3: 9-18 Paul provides Scriptural support for his claim in 3:9 that all are under sin.

Example/Illustration. The author may provide extended examples to illustrate the topic sentence. The illustrations are used to teach the unknown in the light of the known. James 3:1-13 uses illustrations to emphasize the need to control the tongue.

Comparison/Contrast. The author may clarify certain ideas in the topic sentence by comparing or contrasting them with other well-known ideas, in order to highlight the similarities or differences. Romans 5:15-17 contrasts the sin imputed through Adam to clarify the righteousness imputed through Christ.

Cause/Effect. The author may discuss the cause/effect relationships between the topic idea and other issues. 1 Corinthians 15:12-19 develops the topic of the resurrection by stating the hypothetical effects if there were no resurrection.

Example Revealing the Development

In the following example, the paragraph is developed through specification. The topic, books needed for Bible study, is in bold. The development, the underlined material, gives us the specific books that are needed.

> **To study the Bible effectively, you will need a few basic books**. Of course, you will need <u>one or more Bibles</u>. Pick a modern literal translation to use as your main study Bible, and then a few other translations for survey reading. In addition, you should have a <u>Bible dictionary</u> so that you can research various topics, a <u>concordance</u> to find various passages, and a <u>good one-volume commentary</u> to assist you in interpretation. If you can afford it, you might also purchase <u>lexicons or theological wordbooks</u> for both the Old and New Testaments.

The Arrangement of Sentences in the Paragraph

The arrangement is the order of the sentences in the paragraph. The arrangement is purposeful and may follow several standard patterns.

Chronological Arrangement. Narrative accounts commonly arrange the material in their paragraphs in chronological order. The paragraph simply traces the events in the order in which they occurred. The topic sentence may summarize the events presented in the paragraph or may be unstated.

Spatial Arrangement. Paragraphs that provide visual descriptions of something or someone usually order the material in a spatial manner, that is, the order may be from top to bottom, left to right, north to south, and so on. An example of spatial arrangement is John's description of the New Jerusalem in Revelation 21:9-27.

Psychological Arrangement. The arrangement may be more psychological than spatial if the author stresses what impressed him the most. Normally the paragraph is descriptive with the order moving from most impressive to least impressive. An example of psychological arrangement is John's description of his vision of Christ in Revelation 1:12-16.

Deductive Arrangement. The topic sentence functions as a thesis or proposal, and it appears near the beginning of the paragraph. The rest of the paragraph develops or supports the introductory thesis. The deductive arrangement often begins with a general topic statement and then provides particulars about the topic. Examples of deductive arrangement include Romans 1:18-32 and Romans 3:9-18.

Inductive Arrangement. The paragraph begins with a series of sentences that are designed to lead up to the concluding and climactic topic sentence. Inductive arrangements begin with a series of particulars and then conclude with a general statement related to the particulars. An example can be found in Hebrews 1:5-14.

Combination of Deductive and Inductive Arrangements. Paragraphs can begin inductively in that they begin with particulars that lead up to the general topic sentence in the middle of the paragraph. The second half of the paragraph then develops deductively in that the following material develops out of the topic. The author moves from particular to general and then moves back to particular again. Romans 6:1-14 is a good example.

Example Revealing the Arrangement

In the following example, the arrangement of the sentences is deductive. The topic sentence is first and is printed in bold. The remaining sentences give the particulars.

> **To study the Bible effectively you will need a few basic books**. Of course, you will need one or more Bibles. Pick a modern literal translation to use as your main study Bible, and then a few other translations for survey reading. In addition, you should have a Bible dictionary so that you can research various topics, a concordance to find various passages, and a good one-volume commentary to assist you in interpretation. If you can afford it, you might also purchase lexicons or theological wordbooks for both the Old and New Testaments.

Arrangement
The order of the sentences in the paragraph

Types of Arrangement
- Chronological
- Spatial
- Psychological
- Deductive
- Inductive
- Combined Deductive & Inductive

The Internal Structural Devices

Writers use several common techniques within the paragraph to reveal the topic and development of a paragraph. We call these **internal structural devices**.

Structural Devices Revealing the Topic

Topic Sentence. The author often states the topic in an explicit sentence. This sentence reveals the basic idea in the paragraph. It tends to be general in nature, needing expansion and clarification.

Example. In Hebrews 3:1-6, the first sentence is the topic sentence, urging the reader to think about Jesus. The remaining sentences describe Jesus in more detail.

Linking Pronouns. Topical ideas are often expressed as nouns early in the paragraph. However, it is common to refer back to these nouns by using pronouns. Several pronouns that point back to a common antecedent are called linking pronouns. In discourse analysis this is called **pronominal cohesion**. A pronoun string helps to reveal key ideas related to the topic. Linking pronouns may be personal pronouns, relative pronouns, possessive pronouns, or reflexive pronouns. Some of the most common linking pronouns are: I, me, you, he, him, his, she, her, hers, it, its, they, them, their, these, that, who, whose. What is important is that all of the pronouns have the same referent or antecedent.

Example. Note the linking pronoun, "they" in Romans 1:21-23, and the linking pronoun "you" in Romans 2:1-4.

Repetition of Key Words between Sentences. Ideas that are a part of the topic are often repeated throughout the paragraph. In discourse analysis this is called **lexical cohesion**. Words are repeated or synonyms are substituted. It is also helpful to identify antonyms, hyponyms, and meronyms. Hyponyms are words where one of the words is included within the other word. For instance, tulip is a hyponym of flower. Meronyms are words where one of the words is a part of the other word. For instance, leg is a meronym of body.

Example. Note the repetition of the key word "circumcised" in Romans 4:9-12 and "one" in Ephesians 4:4-6.

Structural Devices Revealing the Development

Explicit Transitional Words between Sentences. Sentences are often linked together by grammatical connectives that reveal the progression of thought. It is important to note that these words and phrases link the sentences within the paragraph. As such, they help to reveal the development and arrangement of the paragraph. Some of the most common transitional words between sentences are: "Therefore," "For this reason," "As a result," "For," "However," "So," "Consequently," etc.

Example. In Galatians 5:2-6, notice the use of "again" (5:3), "but" (5:5), and "for" (5:6) to link the sentences within the paragraph together.

Parallel Sentence Structure. Parallel structure involves putting elements of like meaning into like grammatical constructions, making it easy to follow the train of thought. Each parallel is not merely repetitive; rather, it tends to add some new additional idea to the topic idea of the paragraph. The presence of parallel structure often reveals the development of the paragraph.

Example. Note the parallel sentence structure in Romans 1:8-14 that develops the topic of Paul's desire to minister to the Romans:

I	thank my God	for you
I	make mention	of you
I	long to see	you
I	may impart some gift	to you
I	might obtain fruit	among you

Example Revealing the Internal Structural Devices

In the following example, the writer used several structural devices to reveal the subject and the development. First, the topic sentence printed in bold reveals the topic. Second, several hyponyms are used to link with the topical idea of books, including Bible, dictionary, commentary, and wordbook. Third, the linking pronoun, "you", printed in caps, links the development back to the subject. Fourth, parallel structures printed in italics help to reveal the development. The author also uses a few key transitional words, underlined below, to reveal the progression of thought.

> **To study the Bible effectively** *YOU will need a few basic books*. Of course, YOU *will need one or more Bibles*. Pick a modern literal translation to use as YOUR main study Bible, and then a few other translations for survey reading. <u>In addition,</u> YOU *should have a Bible dictionary* so that YOU can research various topics, a concordance to find various passages, and a good one-volume commentary to assist YOU in interpretation. If YOU can afford it, YOU *might* <u>also</u> *purchase lexicons or theological wordbooks* for both the Old and New Testaments.

Analyzing a Paragraph

Goal and Objectives

The General Goal

Our goal in analyzing the paragraph is to understand how all the sentences within the paragraph reveal and develop the basic topic, and then to use this understanding when attempting to interpret individual statements.

General Goal
To understand how all the sentences within the paragraph reveal and develop the basic topic, and then to use this understanding when attempting to interpret

Specific Objectives

In attempting to analyze a paragraph, we have these objectives:

- To identify the topic of the paragraph.
- To understand how the sentences develop the topic.
- To identify the overall arrangement of the sentences in the paragraph.
- To understand how each sentence fits into the paragraph.
- To create a visual representation of the paragraph.

Specific Objectives
- Identify the topic
- Understand the development
- Identify the arrangement
- Understand how sentences fit together
- Create a visual representation

Source of Information
- The book of the Bible you are studying
- Commentaries not very helpful
- English Grammar and Composition textbook

Guidelines for Analyzing a Paragraph
- Identify the paragraph
- Identify the topic
- Analyze the development
- Determine the sentence arrangement
- Summarize the paragraph

Guidelines for Analyzing a Paragraph

The book of the Bible you are studying is the only direct source for information about its paragraphs. Indeed, you will find little help in most commentaries, which tend to focus more on the meaning of individual words or the broader context. Consulting an English Grammar and Composition textbook can be helpful for reviewing details about the basic nature of paragraphs.

Identify the Paragraph Divisions

- The original Hebrew and Greek texts do not indicate the starting and ending points of paragraphs. However, they also do not necessarily indicate the beginning and ending of sentences. In fact, the earlier Greek manuscripts did not even place spaces between words. *The student must determine the paragraph divisions.*

- Not all translations agree on the paragraph divisions. At times the differences are based on translation theory and conception of paragraph length. For instance, the NIV, seeking to provide an easy to read translation, normally keeps paragraphs short. The NASB, on the other hand, tends to have longer paragraphs. *The student should compare the paragraph divisions of several translations.*

- To be more certain, *the student should consult the paragraph divisions found in the editions of the Greek New Testament and the Hebrew Old Testament.*

Identify the Topic of the Paragraph

- Look for a topic sentence.
- Look for repeated words and synonym.
- Look for linking pronouns.

Analyze the Development

- Look for parallel structures.
- Look for transitional words and phrases between sentences.
- Identify the type of development from the suggested list on page 88.

Determine the Arrangement of the Sentences

- Note the position of the topic sentence.
- Look for transitional words and phrases that reveal the arrangement.
- Identify the type of arrangement from the suggested list on page 89.

Summarize the Paragraph

- Create a sentence synopsis of the paragraph.
- Create a vertical chart of the paragraph.

Guidelines for Creating a Sentence Synopsis

The sentence **synopsis** is a condensation of a paragraph into a single sentence. This sentence identifies the topic of the paragraph and summarizes the development. Below are some helpful guidelines for creating a sentence synopsis.

- Write from the point of view of the author (a condensation), not from the point of view of the reader (a summary).

- Keep the synopsis to twenty words or less.

- Use nouns rather than verbs to reduce the length of your sentence. (e.g. "resurrection" rather than "He was raised.")

- Avoid parroting the words of the text. Use your own vocabulary.

- Avoid vagueness. Synopses should retain meaningful content and description.

- Avoid particularization, that is, choosing one particular idea in the paragraph rather than summarizing the whole paragraph.

- Avoid mentioning the author unless the author speaks of himself in the paragraph (e.g. "Paul says that ...").

Below are good and bad examples of sentence synopses for Romans 2:1-5. Read the passage and then study the synopses below.

Good: Because you practice what you condemn in others, you stand condemned.

Bad: Paul talks about sin. (Topic with no development. Refers to author.)

Bad: You are storing up wrath. (Particular statement from 2:5, not summary of the topic and its development.)

Sentence Synopsis
Sentence that identifies the topic of the paragraph and summarizes the development

Rules for Creating A Sentence Synopsis
• Write from author's point of view
• Keep the synopsis to twenty words
• Avoid parroting the text
• Avoid vagueness
• Avoid particularization
• Avoid mention of author

Guidelines for Creating a Vertical Chart

Vertical charts provide a method to represent visually the flow of thought within a paragraph. Below is a list of guidelines for creating a vertical chart.

- The flow of thought always moves from top to bottom.

- Lines in the chart indicate only one level of sectioning. These sections are based on the relationships of the sentences within the paragraph.

- Actual words from the text in the chart are usually displayed in the form of a mechanical layout. (See *Guidelines for Creating A Mechanical Layout* in Chapter 9). Not every word from the text must be included.

- The starting verse reference of each section is placed at the top left corner of the section.

- Key words are often in all caps or bold.

- Arrows and circles are commonly used to reveal parallels and development.

- The topic of the paragraph is located at the top of the chart with the verses covered in the chart.

Rules for Developing Vertical Charts
• Flow of thought moves from top to bottom
• Only one level of sectioning
• Print words from text within chart.
• Print starting verse of each section at top left
• Print keys words in bold
• Arrows and circles to reveal development
• Print topic at top of chart

Sample Vertical Chart

I Peter 3:8-12
Giving a Blessing

	3:8	

Bless, and not Curse	To Sum Up:
	Let all be
	    Harmonious
	    Sympathetic
	    Brotherly,
	    Kindhearted
	    Humble in spirit;
	NOT: returning
	        Evil for evil
	        Insult for insult
	BUT: **giving a blessing**
		Main Exhortation

The Lord Rewards Righteous	3:10
	
	FOR [Psalm 34:12-16]
	    (he who loves life)
	    Let him … Refrain … from evil & guile
	    Let him … do good
	    Let him … seek peace
	
	FOR: Eyes of the Lord on the righteous
	          Ears attend to their prayer
	BUT: Face of the Lord against … evil
		Support

Summary

One important principle of the HGRT Methodology is the Principle of the Immediate Context, which states that the most probable interpretation of a passage is the one that best agrees with the immediate context of the book in which it is found. The immediate context is equated with the paragraph in prose writing and with the stanza in poetic writing.

The paragraph is the basic unit of thought and the most important focus of Bible study. The paragraph is a series of sentences that develop a single topic. The topic is the general idea presented in the paragraph and is often indicated by a topic sentence. The development refers to the additional detailed information given to support the topic. The paragraph can be developed by explanation, specification, support, example/illustration, comparison/contrast, and cause/effect. The sentences in the paragraph can be arranged in chronological, spatial, psychological, deductive, or inductive order. The writer reveals the topic and development through internal structural devices, such as topic sentences, linking pronouns, repeated words, parallel structures, and transitional words.

Important guidelines for analyzing a paragraph are:

- Identify the paragraph divisions.
- Identify the topic of the paragraph.
- Analyze the development.
- Determine the arrangement of the sentences
- Summarize the paragraph in a synopsis or vertical chart.

Key Terms

Immediate Context	Paragraph	Topic of Paragraph
Paragraph Development	Internal Structural Device	Topic Sentence
Linking Pronoun	Parallel Structure	Paragraph Synopsis
Vertical Chart		

Review Questions

1. What is the principle of interpretation that relates to the immediate context of a book of the Bible?
2. What is the basic unit of study in Scripture?
3. What is meant by a paragraph?
4. What are the key elements of a paragraph?
5. In what ways might the topic of a paragraph be developed?
6. In what ways might the sentences of a paragraph be arranged?
7. What is meant by internal structural device?
8. What internal structural devices help to reveal the topic of a paragraph?
9. What internal structural devices help to reveal the development of a paragraph?
10. What guidelines should be used when attempting to analyze a paragraph?
11. What are the rules for creating a synopsis of a paragraph?
12. In what two ways can you summarize a paragraph?
13. What are the rules for creating a synopsis of a paragraph?
14. What are the rules for creating a vertical chart for a paragraph?

References

[1] Robertson, *A. T. A Grammar of the Greek New Testament in the Light of Historical Research*. Nashville: Broadman Press, 1934. pp. 241.

[2] Fee, Gordon D. and Douglas Stuart. *How to Read The Bible For All Its Worth*. Grand Rapids: Zondervan Publishing House, 1993. pp. 54-55.

[3]Jensen, Irving L. *1 & 2 Thessalonians*. Chicago: Moody Bible Institute, 1974. pp. 38.

Chapter 9

Grammatical Analysis
Considering the Sentence

Outline

Principle of Interpretation 98

    Importance of Grammatical Analysis 98

Nature of Grammatical Analysis 99

    Basic Definitions 99

    Translations and Grammatical Analysis 99

    Basic Components of the Sentence 100

    Parts of the Sentence 102

Analyzing Sentences 104

    Goal and Objectives 104

    Guidelines for Analyzing Sentences 104

    Guidelines for Creating a Mechanical Layout 105

Summary 108

Review Questions 108

Learning Objectives

After completing this chapter, you should be able to

- ❑ State the principle of interpretation that relates to grammar.
- ❑ Define grammar and grammatical analysis.
- ❑ Classify words by their part of speech or linguistic function.
- ❑ Describe the basic components of the sentence.
- ❑ Describe the subject and predicate parts of the sentence.
- ❑ Analyze a sentence to determine how each word relates.
- ❑ Create a mechanical layout for the sentences in the Bible.

Principle
The most probable interpretation of a passage is the one that best agrees with the grammar of the individual sentences in the passage

Principle of Interpretation

The most probable interpretation of a passage is the one that best agrees with the grammar of the individual sentences in the passage.

Importance of Grammatical Analysis

Words are the building blocks of language. However, it is possible to know the meanings of words and still not understand what is being said. This is true because language combines words together to form more extensive thoughts using specific rules to relate words. Without knowledge of these rules, understanding is impossible.

An example from Greek might be helpful. Below is a word for word rendering of John 3:16 from the Greek.

> So for loved the God the world that the son the only-begotten gave that all the believing into him not perish but have life eternal.

A few conclusions should be obvious. First, not all languages form relationships between words in the same way. Second, to understand the meaning of a message, one must understand how words are combined to form fuller thoughts. Finally, the knowledge and skills needed to analyze sentences differ from the skills needed to discover the meanings of words and the skills needed to discover the author's plan and argument.

Nature of Grammatical Analysis

Basic Definitions

Grammatical Analysis

Grammar refers to the rules within a language for relating words to create meaning. Thus, the process of analyzing the relationships between words is called **grammatical analysis**.

> **Grammatical Analysis**
> The process of analyzing the relationships between words

Two Categories: Morphology and Syntax

Morphology. Morphology deals with the rules that govern the forms of words. For instance, in English many verbs add the suffix, '-ed', to form the past tense. The past tense of call is called. We will not deal with morphology in this chapter.

> **Morphology**
> The rules that govern the forms of words

Syntax. Syntax deals with the rules that govern the positioning of words in the sentence to form word clusters, phrases, clauses, and sentences. For instance, English always places the adjective between the definite article and the noun it modifies, as in the noun cluster, "the little boy." Syntax will be the focus of discussion in this chapter.

> **Syntax**
> The rules that govern the positioning of words in the sentence

Scope of Grammatical Analysis

Grammatical analysis does not deal with isolated words but with groups of words. The sentence is the basic unit of analysis in grammatical analysis. Sentences often include smaller groups of words: clusters, phrases, and clauses. These too are important to study and analyze.

> **Scope of Grammatical Analysis**
> The sentence is the basic unit of analysis in grammatical analysis

Translations and Grammatical Analysis

Grammatical Analysis is *best accomplished using the original language* text (Hebrew, Aramaic, or Greek). This is true because:

- Some nuances are hard to capture in another language.

- Sometimes translators are forced to choose between different interpretations based on the original structure.

- Sometimes language forces a translation to be more or less exacting than the original.

> **Translations to Use**
> - Best done in original language
> - Better done in literal translation

Grammatical Analysis is *better accomplished using a more literal English translation that employ formal equivalency*. This is true because:

- Less literal translations often break up longer complex sentences into several shorter sentences. Though the translation is easier to read, it often makes implicit relationships that are explicit in the original.

- Less literal translations, which use dynamic equivalency, often abandon the original structure altogether and re-couch the text in a very different grammatical structure.

Basic Components of the Sentence

Individual Words

Parts of Speech. Words have both semantic and functional meaning. The semantic meanings of a word include the thoughts that are associated with the word. The functional meanings of a word refer to the ways in which a word can be used within a sentence. The *eight traditional functions of words* form the parts of speech. They are as follows:

Noun	Pronoun	Adjective	Article
Preposition	Verb	Adverb	Conjunction

A given form may function as more than one part of speech. For instance, the form, 'fish', can be both noun and verb.

Linguistic Structuralism. Modern linguistics has developed new ways of describing the functions of words. These new paradigms are attempts to simplify grammatical analysis. One such attempt reduces the functions of words to *four basic types: substantives, assertives, modifiers, and connectives.*

- **Substantives** are used to name things. In English, nouns, pronouns, gerunds, and noun clauses are considered substantives.

- **Assertives** are used to make an assertion. In English, finite verbs are considered assertives.

- **Modifiers** are used to limit, describe, or explain. In English, articles, adjectives, adverbs, prepositional phrases, infinitive phrases, and participle phrases are considered modifiers.

- **Connectives** are used to join words and groups of words. In English, conjunctions and prepositions are considered connectives.

Word Groups

Words are related to form fuller ideas. Four basic groups exist: *clusters, phrases, clauses, and sentences.*

Word Clusters. Though nouns and verbs can be used alone in a sentence, most often they are found with modifiers. A noun or verb with all its modifiers is called a word cluster. In the following examples the noun or verb that is central to the cluster is underlined. The additional words are modifiers.

Noun cluster	the purple <u>ribbon</u>
Noun cluster	a beautiful <u>tree</u> swaying in the breeze
Verb cluster	<u>ran</u> quickly
Verb cluster	fortunately <u>was found</u> under the seat.

Traditional Parts of Speech
- Noun
- Pronoun
- Adjective
- Article
- Preposition
- Verb
- Adverb
- Conjunction

Linguistic Classification of Word Functions
- Substantive
- Assertive
- Modifier
- Connectives

Word Groups
- Word Clusters
- Phrases
- Clauses
- Sentences

Word Cluster
A noun or verb with all its modifiers

Phrases. A phrase is a group of words having the same function as a single word yet lacking either a subject or a predicate. Phrases are classified as prepositional phrases, verbal phrases, or appositive phrases.

- **Prepositional phrases** consist of a preposition and a noun or noun cluster. For instance, "in the house" is a prepositional phrase. Such phrases are either adjectival or adverbial modifiers. In the following sentences, the prepositional phrases are underlined.

> The boy with the large hat laughed wildly.   (Adjectival)
> The soldiers huddled in the foxhole.   (Adverbial)

- **Verbal phrases** consist of a verbal (participle, gerund, or infinitive) and may include any additional components of a predicate (modifiers, complements, etc.). In the following sentences, the verbal phrases are underlined.

> The man speaking to the audience gestured often.   (Participle phrase)
> Many people need to love God.   (Infinitive phrase)
> Swimming in the ocean alone is dangerous.   (Gerund phrase)

- An **appositive** is a substantive used to describe an already mentioned substantive. Appositives with their modifiers may be regarded as phrases since they function as a modifier. In the following examples, the appositive phrases are underlined.

> The man, a teacher at the college, walked into the room.
> Paul, an apostle of Jesus Christ, wrote many epistles.
> They appointed Mr. Jones, a friend of my father, to head the team.

Clauses. A clause is a group of words containing a complete subject and predicate. The subject refers to that about which the author is writing, and the predicate makes some assertion about the subject. Clauses are classified as being independent or dependent (subordinate).

Types of Clauses
• Independent Clauses
• Dependent Clauses
• Noun Clause
• Adverb Clause
• Adjective Clause

- Independent clauses can stand by themselves as sentences. Note the following examples:

> I will help the teacher.
> Sally and Tom ate fish for dinner.
> The men sat on the bench and talked about the game.

- Dependent clauses cannot stand-alone. They function as substantives (noun replacements), or modifiers (adjective or adverb replacements). Study the following examples. The dependent clauses are underlined.

Noun Clause	I will help whoever comes to me.
Adverb Clause	I can see where no one else sees.
Adjective Clause	The man who comes to me will live.

Sentence. A sentence consists of one or more independent clauses and its modifier. There are four basic types of sentences

- **Simple.** A sentence having only one clause.
- **Compound.** A sentence having two or more independent clauses.
- **Complex.** A sentence having at least one dependent clause.
- **Compound-Complex.** A sentence having two or more independent clauses and one or more dependent clauses.

Parts of the Sentence

Subject and Predicate

Subject
Something about which a statement is made

Predicate
That which is asserted about something

A sentence or clause makes a statement about something, and to make a statement you must name what it is you are talking about and assert something about it. Thus, a sentence or clause must include both a substantive (noun or pronoun) and an assertive (verb). The substantive is called the **subject**, and the assertive is called the **predicate**. Let's look at a few simple sentences that include only a simple substantive as subject, and a simple verb as predicate.

Subject	Predicate
Men	love.
Dogs	ate.
People	will hear.

Modifiers

Both the subject and the predicate can be expanded through the use of modifiers. In the following sentences, the subject is expanded with modifiers that are underlined. The substantive (noun) is called the simple subject. The substantive with all its modifiers is called the complete subject.

Subject	Predicate	Modifier
Men with big hearts	love.	Prepositional phrase
The large dogs	ate.	Article and adjective
People living in Florida	heard.	Participle phrase

In the following sentences, the assertive is expanded with modifiers that are underlined. The assertive (verb) is called the simple predicate. The assertive with all its modifiers is called the complete predicate.

Subject	Predicate	Modifier
Men with big hearts	love completely.	Adverb
The large dogs	ate to keep from dying.	Infinitive phrase
People living in Florida	heard in time.	Prepositional phrase

Complements

Some verbs express a general action that needs to be completed through the use of a substantive, called a **complement**. These complements expand the predicate. There are five types of complements: direct object, indirect object, subject complement, object complement, and retained object.

Direct Object. The direct object indicates what or who receives the action of the verb.

Subject	Verb	Direct Object
Boys	love	baseball.
The good student	reads	the book.
People living in Florida	heard	the explosion.

Indirect Object. The indirect object indicates, without the use of a preposition, to or for whom the action of the verb is performed.

Subject	Verb	Indirect Object	Direct Object
The boys	gave	their teacher	the book.
The teacher	taught	the students	English.
He	told	me	the story.

Subject Complement. The subject complement is a substantive or substantive modifier that refers to the subject and describes or limits it. The subject complement is used with the verb, to be, and other state-of-being verbs such as: seem, become, and remain; and verbs of sense such as: feel, look, smell, sound, taste.

Subject	Verb	Subject Complement
The boys	are	friends.
The teacher	became	sick.
The flowers	smell	lovely.

Object Complement. The object complement, used with verbs such as elect, choose, make, call, and appoint, etc. refers to or describes the direct object.

Subject	Verb	Direct Object	Object Complement
The committee	appointed	Bill	chairperson.
The teacher	made	Sally	group leader.
The people	elected	him	mayor.

Retained Object. The retained object is used with verbs in the passive voice.

Subject	Verb	Retained Object
They	were given	food.
The students	were taught	a good lesson.
The family	was shown	the house.

Analyzing Sentences

Goal and Objectives

General Goal
To understand the relationship between every word, phrase, and clause in the sentence

The General Goal

Our goal in analyzing sentences is to understand the relationship between every word, phrase, and clause in the sentence.

Specific Objectives

Specific Objectives
• To identify the clauses in the sentence
• To identify the subject and predicate of each clause
• To distinguish between the independent and dependent clauses
• To identify how the simple subject and simple predicate are modified

In attempting to analyze a sentence we have these objectives:

- To identify the clauses in the sentence.
- To identify the subject and predicate of each clause.
- To distinguish between the independent and dependent clauses.
- To identify how the simple subject and simple predicate are modified.

Guidelines for Analyzing Sentences

Source of Information
• The book of the Bible you are studying
• Original Language Commentaries
• Literal English Translation

The book of the Bible you are studying is the only direct source for grammatical analysis. It is best if you can study using the Hebrew or Greek text. Commentaries of the original Greek or Hebrew text can be very helpful. If you are studying in English, use a very literal translation. Below are the guidelines you should follow.

Divide the Sentence into Clauses

- Look for finite verbs (not participles, gerunds, or infinitives).
- Look for the subjects of these verbs.
- Each subject-verb pair should be a clause.
- Some clauses are embedded within other clauses.

Identify the Independent Clauses

Guidelines for Analyzing a Sentence
• Divide sentence into clauses
• Identify the independent clauses
• Determine how subject and predicate are modified
• Create a mechanical layout

- See if the clause could be a sentence if written alone.
- Clauses that begin with who, which, what, or that are not independent clauses unless the sentence ends with a question mark.
- Clauses that begin with the conjunctions such as since, because, why, where, when, while, after, before, if, although, as, in order that, that, and so that are not independent clauses. (Some of these words are not always conjunctions.)

Determine How the Simple Subject and Simple Predicate Are Modified.

- Determine what each simple modifier (adjectives, adverbs) modifies.
- Determine what each phrase (prepositional, verbal, and appositional) modifies.
- Determine how each dependent clause (noun, adverb, adjective) is used.

Create A Mechanical Layout.

- See guidelines below on creating a mechanical layout.

Guidelines for Creating a Mechanical Layout

Definition of Mechanical Layout

The mechanical layout is an analytical and visual method that is helpful in the process of understanding the structure of a sentence or a related group of sentences. In the mechanical layout, the analyst identifies the various clauses and phrases in the sentence, and then displays them in a visual format that draws attention to the structure of the sentence.

> **Mechanical Layout**
> An analytical and visual method that is helpful in the process of understanding the structure of a sentence

Benefits of Mechanical Layout

Creating a mechanical layout has benefits both during and after sentence analysis.

- The process of constructing a mechanical layout forces the interpreter to observe and interact with the structure of the sentence.

- The finished mechanical layout can be used as an interpretive tool during the process of interpretation.

- The mechanical layout can help identify the central idea and the structure of the sentence by allowing the student to locate and identify the main clause and any subordinate clauses or phrases.

- Constructing a mechanical layout is easier than the more traditional sentence diagram.

Guidelines for Creating

- Place each clause on a separate line.

- Place independent clauses (subject, main verb, and complements) on a line at the left-hand margin of the page.

- Place dependent clauses indented on a line directly under or above the part of the independent clause that they modify or represent.

- When a dependent clause precedes the independent clause, it may be placed either above or below the independent clause.

- Place embedded dependent clauses on a line under the clause split, re-uniting the split clause on one line.

- Place single modifiers and modifying phrases on the line with what they modify unless they precede the subject and verb, in case they should be indented on a separate line.

- If there are two or more modifiers that modify the same word, they should be placed in a parallel column directly below the word. Any grammatically parallel structures should be aligned vertically in a column.

- Place conjunctions to the left of the items they connect.

> **Guidelines for Analyzing A Sentence**
> - Each clause on separate line
> - Independent clause at far left
> - Dependent clauses indented above or below what they modify
> - Single modifiers on line with what they modify
> - Multiple modifiers in column under what they modify
> - Place conjunctions to left of items they connect

Sample Mechanical Layouts

The following examples are good illustrations of mechanical layouts in a variety of syntactical constructions. The mechanical layout in Example One corresponds to the exact order of the text. Example Two illustrates how to display a dependent phrase ("By His great mercy") that precedes the independent clause ("He has given us new birth"). Example Three shows a different way to display a long dependent clause ("Although He existed in the form of God...") that precedes the independent clause ("He did not regard...").

Example One:

2 Timothy 3:16-17

All Scripture is inspired and is useful for teaching, for rebuking, for correcting, and for training in righteousness, so that the man of God may be fully equipped for every good work.

```
All Scripture    is inspired
           and   is useful        for teaching,
                                  for rebuking,
                                  for correcting,
                         and      for training in righteousness,
           so that the man of God may be fully equipped for every good work.
```

Example Two:

1 Peter 1:3-5

By His great mercy He has given us new birth into a living hope through the resurrection of Jesus Christ from the dead, and into an inheritance which can never perish, spoil or fade, and is kept in heaven for you who are shielded through faith by God's power.

```
He has given us new birth
     By His great mercy
     into a living hope
                    through the resurrection of Jesus Christ from the dead,
 and into an inheritance
                which    can never    perish,
                                      spoil
                            or   fade,
           and  is kept
                in heaven
                for you
                        who are shielded
                              through faith
                              by God's power.
```

Example Three:

Philippians 2:6-11

Although He existed in the form of God, He did not regard equality with God a thing to be grasped, but He emptied Himself taking the form of a bond-servant, being made in the likeness of men, and being found in appearance as a man, He humbled himself becoming obedient to the point of death, even death on a cross. Therefore, God highly exalted Him and bestowed on Him the name which is above every name that at the name of Jesus every knee should bow those who are in heaven, and on earth, and under the earth, and that every tongue should confess that Jesus Christ is Lord to the glory of God, the Father.

Although He existed in the form of God,
He   did not regard equality with God a thing to be grasped,
but **He   emptied Himself**
taking the form of a bond-servant,
being made in the likeness of men,
and
being found in appearance as a man,
He   humbled himself
becoming obedient to the point of death,
even death on a cross.
Therefore
God   highly exalted Him
and **bestowed on Him the name**
which is above every name
that at the name of Jesus every knee should bow
those who are in heaven,
and on earth,
and under the earth,
and that every tongue should confess
that Jesus Christ is Lord
to the glory of God, the Father.

Summary

One important principle of the HGRT Methodology is the Principle of Grammar, which states that the most probable interpretation of a passage is the one that best agrees with the grammar of the individual sentences in the passage. Grammatical analysis is the process of analyzing the relationships between words in a sentence. It is best done in the original languages. If done in English, use a very literal translation.

Grammatical analysis involves an understanding of the individual function of words; how words are combined to form clusters, phrases, and clauses; and how sentences are composed of subjects and predicates.

Important guidelines for analyzing sentences are:

- Divide the sentence into clauses.
- Identify the independent clauses.
- Determine how the simple subject and simple predicate are modified.
- Create a mechanical layout of the sentence.

Key Terms

Grammar	Grammatical Analysis	Morphology
Syntax	Substantive	Assertive
Preposition	Appositive	Phrase
Subject	Predicate	Clause

Review Questions

1. What is the principle of interpretation that relates to the grammar of a passage?
2. What is meant by grammatical analysis?
3. What is the best text or translation for performing grammatical analysis?
4. What are the eight parts of speech?
5. What are the four functions of words based on linguistic structuralism?
6. What does word cluster mean?
7. What are the three basic types of phrases?
8. What is the difference between an independent and dependent clause?
9. What are the four basic types of sentences?
10. What is the subject and predicate of a sentence?
11. What are the five types of predicate complements?
12. What are the guidelines for analyzing a sentence?
13. What are the guidelines for creating a mechanical layout?

Chapter 10

The Meaning of Words

Outline

Principle of Interpretation 110

    The Importance of Studying the Meaning of Words 110

The Nature of Words 111

    Words and Their Meanings 111

    Principles Related to Words and Meanings 112

    Sources for Discovering Word Meanings 115

    Word Study Fallacies 116

    How to Write Definitions 117

Performing Word Studies 118

    Tools for Performing a Word Study 118

    Goal and Objectives 121

    Guidelines for Performing a Word Study 121

    Special Considerations 124

        Hebrew Word Studies 124

        Greek Word Study Tools 127

Final Word of Caution 129

Bibliography of Word Study Tools 129

Summary 132

Review Questions 134

Learning Objectives

After completing this chapter, you should be able to

- ❏ State the principle of interpretation that relates to words and their meaning.
- ❏ Define word, meaning, and definition.
- ❏ Explain the six different types of meaning.
- ❏ Discuss the implications of the principles of words and their meaning.
- ❏ Evaluate the three basic sources for discovering the meanings of words.
- ❏ Explain and apply a specific process for determining the meanings of words.
- ❏ Write definitions using extensional and intentional approaches.
- ❏ Identify important tools used in performing word studies of biblical words.

Principle of Interpretation

> **Principle**
> The most probable interpretation of a passage is the one that best harmonizes with the normal meanings of every word in the passage

The most probable interpretation of a passage is the one that best harmonizes with the normal meanings of every word in the passage.

Importance of Studying the Meaning of Words

Words are the building blocks of language. As such no possible understanding of a passage can occur without knowledge of their meaning. Consider the following lines from the poem *Through the Looking-Glass* by Lewis Carroll.

> "Twas brillig, and the slithy toves
> Did gyre and gimble in the wabe.
> All mimsy were the borogroves,
> And the mame raths outgrabe."

The poem has perfect grammatical structure and poetic form. Yet, we still cannot understand it because we do not know the meaning of the words.

This is compounded by the fact that the meanings of words are not always obvious. Take for example, the term, asleep, used in 1 Thessalonians 5:10.

> He died for us so that, whether we are awake or asleep, we may live
> together with him.

In 4:13-18 Paul describes those who have died in Christ as being asleep. Then in 5:4-7 Paul describes those who walk in the darkness of sin as being asleep. Which idea does Paul mean in 5:10? The answer is not obvious. It requires a thorough study of the terms and their context.

The Nature of Words

Words and Their Meanings

Word

A **word** is a linguistic sound or form with which are associated thoughts, feelings, and functions. As such, a word is a written or spoken symbol.

Word Linguistic form with which are associated thoughts, feelings, and functions

Meaning

The **meaning** of a word consists of the thoughts, feelings, and functions that are associated with the word. The meaning of the word is what is symbolized. Several different types of meanings need to be distinguished.

Meaning The thoughts, feelings, and functions associated with a word

Semantic Meaning (Denotation). The thoughts associated with a word, the mental pictures that a word produces when we see or hear it, are called the word's semantic meaning or denotation. This is the most common idea associated with word meanings. Normally, when we go to a dictionary our purpose is to look up a word's semantic meaning.

Connotation. The feelings associated with a word are called the word's connotation. Some words have very similar semantic meaning but very different connotations. For instance, the word, mother, and the word, mom, are identical in denotation but have different connotations. To completely grasp meaning, we need to be familiar with a word's connotation as well as its denotation. Every word has a denotation, however, not every word has a connotation.

Syntactical Function. The functions associated with a word are called the word's syntactical function and are related to the word's grammatical usage. For instance, the word, cat, is a noun and the word, run, is a verb. Some words can have more than one function, as does the word, fish, which can be either a noun or a verb.

Referent Meaning. The sense of a term is the general idea that a word conveys. It is equal to the semantic meaning. However, when words are actually used, they often represent something more specific. The **referent** of a word is the concrete object or abstract concept to which the word is referring. For instance, if I state that your mother is looking for you, you immediately have a picture in your mind on *your* mother. You can see her. Thus, the word in my sentence not only has the general denotation of a mother but more specifically the referent meaning of *your* mother.

Types of Meaning • **Semantic Meaning** or **Denotation**: thoughts associated with word • **Connotation**: feelings associated with word • **Syntactic Function**: grammatical function. • **Referent Meaning**: concrete object or abstract concept to which the word is referring • **Contextual Meaning**: single meaning in a context • **Figurative Meaning**: when the referent does not correspond to the normal semantic meaning

Contextual Meaning. Words often have more than one semantic meaning. Because of this, we say their meaning is only potential. Thus, definitions found in a dictionary only tell us what a word might mean. The actual meaning can only be discovered within the context in which it is used. For instance, the word, fair, has many potential meanings. However, when I say, "The decision of the judge was fair", it has only one meaning, its contextual meaning. The contextual meaning of a word changes from context to context.

Referent The concrete object or abstract concept to which the word is referring

Figurative Meaning. The meaning of a word is figurative when it refers to a referent that does not correspond to the normal semantic meaning of that word. For instance, when the word, pig, is used to refer to an untidy person, we are using the word figuratively. In Chapter 11 we will discuss the figurative meanings of words in detail.

Principles Related to Words and Their Meanings

Principles Related to Words and Their Meaning

- Meanings are conventional not appropriate
- Meanings change with time
- Words in different languages do not fully correlate
- Meanings change from person to person
- Words have a broad range of meaning
- Words in use have only one meaning
- Meaning of a word in use is determined by context

Onomatopoeia
The sound of a word imitates the sound of the action it represents

Several important principles about the nature of words and their meanings affect how we study words. We will look at the principles and draw some implications about how to study words found in the Bible.

The meanings of words are conventional and not appropriate.

By this we mean that there is no necessary connection between a word and the meanings associated with that word. We might ask the question, "Why is a pig called a pig?" It is not because a pig looks like a pig or eats like a pig! We just agree that this animal is called a pig. There is nothing about the English word, pig that makes it more appropriate to stand for this farm animal than the Greek word for pig, *choiros*.

The only exception to this rule is **onomatopoeia**, a figure of speech in which the sound of the spoken word is designed to imitate the sound of the action that is represented by the word. For example, the English word for a dog's bark is woof, which sounds like the very thing that it represents.

Implication: We must be careful not to be fooled by the look or sound of words when we work in other languages. The looks and sounds of English words are no more appropriate for their meanings than are the looks and sounds of words in other languages.

The meanings of words change with time.

Language is not static. It is constantly changing and so are the meanings that we associate with words. New meanings appear and old meanings disappear. Take for instance, the word, rocket, as used in the *Star-Spangled Banner*. In 1814, the year in which Francis Scott Key penned the poem, rockets were very different from what they are today. The word had a different meaning.

Implication: Since the Bible is an ancient book, we need to perform word studies in the ancient Hebrew, Greek, and Aramaic languages. We should not use modern language dictionaries to determine the meaning of biblical words.

The meanings of words in different languages do not fully correlate.

One language may use one single word to represent a broad range of various meanings, while another language may use many different words or synonyms to express this range of various meanings. For example, the English language has only one word for snow while the Eskimo language has over a dozen different words that are used to distinguish the various kinds of snow.

Implication: Since the Bible was written in Hebrew, Greek, and Aramaic, we must not attempt to discover the range of meaning for a word in a passage by using the range of meaning of a translated English word. The meanings of words in Hebrew, Aramaic and Greek differ from the meanings of parallel English words. We must get the range of meaning of the Hebrew or Greek word that underlies our English translation.

The meanings of words change from person to person.

While most words have a broad range of meanings, different individuals sometimes have a tendency to use the same word in different ways. For example, in some areas of the country, the term, dinner, refers to the noon meal, but in other regions it refers to the evening meal. In America, the word, pants, refers to a pair of slacks, but in England, the same word is used to refer to underwear.

One person can consistently use a particular word to denote one specific category of meaning, while another person may use the same word to denote a different category of meaning. For example, Paul always uses the term, justification in reference to positional righteousness (Rom. 3:20, 24; Rom. 5:1) but James often uses it in reference to practical righteousness (Jas. 2:21, 24).

Implication: Since different people use words differently, it is very important to study how the same author uses a word on different occasions. That does not mean that we limit the possible meaning to those used by the author elsewhere, but it does mean that we give special consideration to those meanings that are commonly used by that author.

Normally, a word has a broad range of semantic meaning.

Most words have a broad range of meaning and some of those meanings may be totally different. This is called the **semantic range**. The semantic range of a word consists of all its different meanings found within the language.

> **Semantic Range**
> All the different meanings of a word found within the language

Many commonly used words have several meanings that are well known, but they can also have additional meanings that are not very well known to most people. For example, the word "trunk" is very familiar, but it has a very broad range of meaning, some of which are not known to most people.

>   The main stem of a tree
>   The torso of a human body
>   The proboscis of an elephant
>   A large box or chest for carrying clothes
>   The storage compartment of an automobile
>   Short trousers or breeches for swimming
>   The main line of something that has branches
>   A transportation line for long distance through traffic
>   A supply line or the main line
>   A direct link between two telephone offices or switchboards
>   A mast line on a sailboat
>   A central line on a ship

Implication: To ensure that we properly understand the meaning of a word in a passage, we must first discover the full semantic range of meaning. If we fail to discover all the potential meanings, we may miss the correct meaning in a passage.

A word in use can have only one meaning.

When we use words in sentences within a context, words normally only have one meaning. Let's consider the word, trunk. We noted above that the word has many potential meanings, its semantic range. However, in the following sentences, it has only one meaning per sentence.

114

The elephant picked up the peanut with its trunk.
My car has a smaller trunk than your car has.
Cutting the tree was difficult since its trunk was over 40 inches in diameter.

Only on rare occasions will an author attempt to convey two different meanings for a word in the same statement. When done, this subtle play on meaning is normally humorous. Note the play on meaning in the following sentence.

Bill always dreamed of having a hot car, but he never dreamed that he would get it through a gas line leak that led to the explosion.

Implication: It is usually incorrect to attach several meanings to a word in use. Though a word has many potential meanings, we must determine which meaning is the one intended by the author in a given passage.

The meaning of a word in use is determined by its context.

The meaning of a word in actual usage is determined by the context in which it is used. In order to determine the meaning of the usage of a word in a specific context, it is necessary to study the context in which it appears. The ideas expressed in the larger message of the literary context almost always clarify the intended meaning of the word.

The term, **collocates,** refers to any significant terms used in the context of the sentence that can affect the meaning of a word. For example, the contextual meaning of the verb, to dress, is affected by the collocated direct object as illustrated below.

> **Collocates**
> Any significant terms used in the context of the sentence that can affect the meaning of a word

To dress a <u>person</u>	= to put clothes on
To dress a <u>chicken</u>	= to pluck and clean to prepare for cooking
To dress a <u>wound</u>	= to clean and bandage
To dress a <u>salad</u>	= to add seasonings and spices
To dress one's <u>hair</u>	= to comb and stylize
To dress <u>army</u> <u>ranks</u>	= to organize and arrange for marching
To dress <u>timber</u>	= to prepare for cutting
To dress a shop <u>window</u>	= to arrange in an attractive manner

Implication: Word study requires a careful examination of the context before one can make a decision about the proper meaning of a word. The final determination about the meaning of a word in a passage must be the context. Part of the work in discovering the meaning is to gain an understanding of collocates associated with the various potential meanings of a word.

Sources for Discovering Word Meanings

How can we discover what words mean? One answer is to look in a dictionary. But we might ask, how do the authors of the dictionary know what the words mean? Lexicographers, the writers of dictionaries, use three techniques for discovering the meanings of words, *etymology, comparative philology,* and *usus loquendi.*

Etymology

Definition
Etymology attempts to determine the meaning of words through a study of the historic roots of the word. For example, the etymology of the English word butterfly consists of the two roots, butter and fly. The etymology of the Greek word *hupomenō* is the preposition *hupo* (under) and the verb *menō* (remain).

The Relation between the Roots and the Meaning

Sometimes, the actual meaning of a word is closely related to the roots that are combined. In this case, the meaning is discernable from the roots. For instance, the English word, absentminded, comes from absent and minded; and it means to be forgetful. The root meanings work together to form the new meaning in an understandable way.

On the other hand, the root elements of some words are misleading and the meaning is not discernable from the roots. The meaning of the English adverb, aboveboard, means without deceit and has nothing to do with the words, above (a location higher than another object) and board (a wooden plank). Similarly, the Greek word *anaginōskō* comes from two roots: *ana* (up) and *ginōskō* (to know). Therefore, one might expect that *anaginōskō* would mean to know up, but it actually means to read.

The Role of the Root Etymology in Determining Meaning

We must be very careful that we do not place undue emphasis on the root components of compound words. The root components are often not related at all to the actual meaning of the word. Therefore, etymology is not a reliable guide to the actual meaning of a word. In fact, many scholars question whether it is even legitimate to talk about the root meaning of a word.

Comparative Philology

Definition
Comparative Philology is the study of related words across a family of languages. Many languages have common origins. For instance, French, Spanish, and Italian are called Romantic languages because they all originated from ancient Latin. We might expect that many of the words in these languages will be similar.

The Role of Comparative Philology in Determining Meaning

Comparative philology is used to help determine the meaning of certain rare Hebrew words. By studying similar words in other Semitic languages, some meanings can be discovered. However, the science is subjective and makes many assumptions about the development of words. Therefore, we should accept the conclusions of comparative philology with some reservation. We should limit the use of comparative philology to rare words in Hebrew and Greek where there is little help elsewhere.

Usus Loquendi

Usus Loquendi
The common usage of a word within a language at a particular time

Usus Loquendi refers to the common usage of a word within a language at a particular time. Linguists who study the languages of remote tribal peoples must establish a working vocabulary. To do so, they listen and observe people as they speak the language. With time, they discover what words mean based on the usages that they observe. Their understanding is based on the actual usage of words, the *usus loquendi*.

The Role of *Usus Loquendi* in Determining Meaning

Value of Usus Loquendi
The best approach for determining the meanings of words

Usus Loquendi is by far the best approach for determining the meanings of words. For the most part the definitions found in our dictionaries represent meanings based on common usage. We can use these definitions but we must understand that such an approach is deductive. We are relying on the conclusions of others. Therefore, we must be careful to use only the most scholarly dictionaries.

Another approach is for us to do the work of the linguist or lexicographer. We can observe how biblical writers and their contemporaries used words and from these observations, draw our own conclusions about the meaning of words. This second approach is more inductive but also more time consuming and requires more knowledge of the original languages.

At this level of study, we will mainly be relying on the conclusions of the scholars concerning *usus loquendi* and will only modestly introduce the idea of discovering the *usus loquendi* for ourselves.

Word Study Fallacies

Word Study Fallacies

- Root Fallacy
- Temporal Semantic Fallacies
- Basic Meaning Fallacy
- Unwarranted Adoption Fallacy

When people, in attempting to explain the meaning of a word in the Bible, violate one of the principles related to the meanings of words or do not determine word meanings based primarily on *usus loquendi*, they enter into word study fallacies and their conclusions are most likely incorrect. D. A. Carson describes sixteen different word study fallacies.[1] Here are some of the most common fallacies that you should avoid.

English Only Fallacy

This occurs when the meanings associated with the English word used in a translation are used to determine meaning rather than the original language word from which the English word was translated. For example, Galatians 3:24 states, "the Law was our guardian" (ESV). According to the Merriam Webster's Collegiate Dictionary, a guardian is either one that guards, a superior of a Franciscan monastery, or one who has the care of the person or property of another.[2] Yet, the Greek word translated guardian, παιδαγωγός (*paidagogos*), refers to a slave, whose duty it was to conduct a boy to and from school and to superintend his conduct.[3] Clearly the semantic range of the English word does include the meaning of the Greek word.

Root Fallacy

This occurs when the meaning of a word is assumed to be based on etymology. As mentioned above, rarely can the meaning of a word be determined through a study of its roots. A mentioned above, one cannot get a good sense of the meaning of the English word, aboveboard, by simply thinking about the meaning of above and the meaning of board. This fallacy is also called the **etymological fallacy**.

Temporal Semantic Fallacies

Temporal fallacies occur when people assume that the meaning of a word in the Bible is the same as the meaning of that word in either an earlier timeframe or later timeframe. If the meaning is based on an earlier usage, it is called **semantic obsolescence**. If the meaning is based on a later usage, it is called **semantic anachronism**. To illustrated this, we will look at the Greek word, ἀρραβών found in Ephesians 1:30. In modern Greek, αρραβωνον means engagement or betrothal, and so a popular understanding of this verse is that the Holy Spirit is our engagement ring! Yet in biblical Greek, the word had no such idea. Rather, ἀρραβών refers to a down payment or guarantee.

Basic Meaning Fallacy

This fallacy assumes that every word has a basic meaning that can be seen each time it is used. This fallacy fails to understand the principle that words have a range of meaning. A version of this fallacy is found in the supposed **Law of First Mention**. This principle states that the first mention of a term or concept in the Bible provides a basic sense that can be applied to all other instances of the same word. The problem with this approach can be illustrated with the Hebrew word, כָּפַר (kapar), first mentioned in Genesis 6:14 when God told Noah to **cover** the ark inside and out with pitch. Later, this same verb root is found throughout Exodus and Leviticus to refer to the atoning of sin. In these passages, it is not merely the covering of sin that is meant, but the removal of sin through an atoning sacrifice.

Unwarranted Adoption Fallacy

This fallacy, also called the **Totality Transfer Fallacy**, is in some ways the opposite of the Basic Meaning Fallacy in that it assumes that most if not all of a word's semantic range are to be applied to the interpretation of a single passage. This violates the principle that a word in use normally has one meaning and that the meaning is determined by the context. Take for instance the Greek word, λόγος (logos). *A Greek-English Lexicon of the New Testament and Other Early Christian Literature* gives a range of meaning for *logos* to be: 1) a communication such as a word, a statement, a report or a speech; 2) a computation such as a formal accounting, a settlement, or a reason; 3) the personified expression of God.[4] Of these three potential meanings, only one is appropriate in John 1:1, "In the beginning was the Word (*logos*), and the Word (*logos*) was with God, and the Word (*logos*) was God."

How to Write Definitions

Definition Defined

A **definition** is an attempt to describe the meaning of a word. Definitions are a bit circular in that they use words to describe the meanings of other words. They can be as simple as word-substitution or as complex and exhaustive as large articles. We need to understand the two basic approaches to definitions and the various types of definitions we can create.

Definition
An attempt to describe the meaning of a word

Two Basic Approaches to Definitions

Extensional Definitions

The extensional approach tries to clarify the meaning of a word by citing examples of the general class to which the word belongs. An extensional definition consists of one or more examples that illustrate the meaning. For instance, in some dictionaries, under the definition of aardvark, you might find a picture of an aardvark. If a foreigner asked you, "What is a

Two Types of Definitions
- Extensional
- Intentional

Extensional Definition
Tries to clarify meaning by citing examples

tree?" you might point to a tree. Jesus gave an extensional definition of a neighbor in the parable of the Good Samaritan.

Extensional definitions are helpful in taking abstract ideas and making them concrete. They are easy to see and understand. However, they are limited since they only provide a few examples which normally do not include all the characteristics of the more general idea expressed in the word. This limitation is overcome through the use of intentional definitions.

Intentional Definition

Intentional definitions try to explain the meaning of a word by giving abstract descriptions. The simplest intentional definition is word substitution. For instance, a simple definition of friend might be companion. Two better types of intentional definitions are lexical definitions, and genus and differentia.

Lexical Definition

A lexical definition reports the meanings of a word as it is used within a particular language. Lexical definitions are used in dictionaries to report all of the categories of meaning (the semantic range) throughout that language. A lexical definition does not attempt to identify the manner in which a word is used in a particular context. It merely reports how it is used as a whole throughout an entire language during a particular time.

In terms of their form, lexical definitions usually do not consist of a complete sentence. They are short phrases or single word identifications. The typical lexical definition is simply a matter of word substitution, that is, one word is defined by close synonyms.

Genus and Differentia

Genus and Differentia is a sentence definition that has two elements: a generic element called the *genus* and a differentiating element called the *differentia*. The *genus* identifies the broad generic class to which the term belongs and the *differentia* distinguishes the term from other ideas in the same generic class.

For example, the term, house can be defined as, "A building (*genus*) designed to be used as a family dwelling (*differentia*).

Note: One of the foundational steps in theology is to define the major theological terms. The best way to define theological terms is with intentional definitions using genus and differentia.

Good Definitions both Intentional and Extensional

The best approach to writing your own definitions is to use a combination of the intentional and extensional approaches. Create an abstract conceptual definition of the term using genus and differentia and then provide concrete examples.

Performing Word Studies

Tools for Performing a Word Study

Before we consider the guidelines for performing word studies, we need to have a general understanding of the tools we will use. They include *concordances, lexicons, word study books* and *Hebrew and Greek interlinear Bibles*.

Concordance

A **concordance** is a book that lists occurrences of a word in the Bible. The words are listed in alphabetical order and their occurrences in biblical occurrence order. A concordance will include the word, and then for each occurrence a short phrase from the verse and the Scripture reference. Scholarly English concordances will also identify the original Greek or Hebrew term underlying the English translation. This is most often done through a numbering system. Scholarly English concordances will also include modest dictionaries of original Greek or Hebrew words in the rear of the concordance.

Concordances are always compiled from a specific Bible translation or from an original language text. For instance, *The Strong's Exhaustive Concordance* is compiled from the *King James Version* of the Bible. It is important to use a concordance that was compiled from the translation you used when you selected a word for study. See the *Bibliography of Word Study Tools* at the end of this chapter for specific concordances.

Concordances that list every occurrence of every word in a Bible are called **exhaustive concordances**. These are the types of concordances that you should use when performing word studies. Often Bibles will have concordances in the back. These are not exhaustive and should not be used to perform word studies. The major purpose for using an exhaustive English concordance is to discover every occurrence of a particular Greek or Hebrew word in the Bible.

English concordances in the main body of the concordance list alphabetically the English words found in the translation from which the concordance was compiled and the verse references where these words are found in the translation. However, our ultimate goal is not to discover the occurrences for a given English word but the occurrences of the underlying Greek or Hebrew words. These two will not be the same, since Greek and Hebrew words are commonly translated by more than one English word. To get a list of occurrences for the Greek and Hebrew words, we must use concordances that are compiled from the Hebrew and Greek texts. These concordances in the main body of the concordance list alphabetically the Hebrew or Greek words found in the Hebrew or Greek texts. The most popular of these concordances are the Englishman's Hebrew Concordance and the Englishman's Greek Concordance.

Bible Software and Bible study web sites d not always include concordances in the traditional sense. Instead the software provides search engines for searching for particular words, combinations of words, and phrases. You will find these tools to be more powerful and more flexible than traditional printed concordances. We will discuss some of these computerized tools later in the chapter.

> **Concordance**
> Lists occurrences of a word in the Bible
>
> Exhaustive concordances list every occurrence for every word.

Two Number Systems for Greek And Hebrew Words

Many word study tools designed for English students employ a numbering system that identifies each of the Greek and Hebrew word by giving it a different number. Two numbering systems are in use today; the older *Strong's numbers* and the newer *Goodrich-Koehlenberger numbers*. For example, the Greek word, ἀγαπη *(agape)* is assigned the numeric code 26 in the Strong's system and code 27 in the Goodrich-Koehlenberger system.

> **Numbering Systems**
> • Strong's Numbers
> • Goodrich-Koehlenberger Numbers

Strong's Numbers. James Strong developed the older and more traditional numbering system for *The Strong's Exhaustive Concordance*. This numbering system is used in most older word study tools. It has two major limitations. First, it uses the same set of numbers for both Hebrew and Greek words. This duplication of numbers has caused students some confusion. Second, some Greek and Hebrew words, not known to Strong at the time he created the system, are not included. This makes working with modern translations based on newer Hebrew and Greek texts difficult. To deal with the first problem, some systems adds a letter G before Greek codes and the letter H before Hebrew codes. Thus, the Strong's code 26 for the Greek word, ἀγαπη *(agape)* is G26 in The Logos Bible Software. The Strong's code 26 for the Hebrew word, אֲבִיגַיִל is H26.

Goodrich-Koehlenberger Numbers. Goodrich and Koehlenberger developed a newer numbering system for *The NIV Exhaustive Concordance* that addressed these limitations. This numbering system has a unique number for each word and includes the Hebrew and Greek words missing in the Strong's Numbering System. However, there is one limitation. The numbering system is used in only a few tools published since 1990.

The Problem. Some tools use the Strong's numbers and other tools use the Goodrich-Koehlenberger numbers, and still other tools do not use either. Though indexes exist to convert from one system to another, using these numbering systems is at best time consuming and at worst a total frustration. The best solution is to *learn the Hebrew and Greek alphabets* or to use software that links directly to the Greek and Hebrew sources. This eliminates the problem.

Lexicons

Lexicon
Dictionary of the Hebrew and Greek words

A **lexicon** is essentially a dictionary with English definitions of the Hebrew and Greek words used in the Bible. Like a typical dictionary, lexicons provide the basic range of meaning and definitions of words. The major purpose for using a lexicon is to discover the range of meaning that a Greek or Hebrew word can have.

Unlike a typical dictionary, lexicons provide examples of usage of the words in the Bible. In this sense, they are part commentary. Often you will be able to find the exact reference you are studying in the lexicon with some comment about the meaning of the word in that passage. You should remember that at this point the lexicon is functioning like a commentary. You should reserve judgment about the specific meaning in a passage until we have done a thorough study of the potential meanings and the context.

Lexicons list words in Greek or Hebrew and normally do not provide much help to English students who do not know the original languages. The key to quick and efficient use of lexicons is to learn the Greek and Hebrew alphabets. The alternative is to use the numbering systems described above and a complex system of indexes. Though both approaches will work, a little time invested in learning the Greek and Hebrew alphabets will pay off in the long run with great time savings.

Theological Wordbooks

Theological Wordbooks
Collection of articles written by scholars, discussing the meaning and usage of Greek and Hebrew terms

A **theological wordbook** is a single or multiple volume set that contains a collection of articles written by scholars, discussing the meaning and usage of Greek and Hebrew terms. These articles are much longer and extensive than the definitions found in lexicons. However, not every Greek or Hebrew word will be discussed. The purpose is not to give basic definitions to all words, but rather to give extensive discussions of important words.

Some provide articles on specific Greek or Hebrew words. Others provide articles on theological topics and then discuss the various words under the topic. Most provide indexes that help the reader find the material they need. Like lexicons, the assumption is that you are familiar with Greek and Hebrew. To get the most from these tools you need to know the Greek and Hebrew alphabets or you must use the numbering systems described above and complex indexes to find what you need.

Hebrew and Greek Interlinear Bibles

An **interlinear Bible** is a Bible that includes either the Hebrew or Greek text along with an English translation on separate lines. The Hebrew or Greek text is given and on a line under it, an English word equivalent is given. The words appear in the order of the original language, not in the order of the English translation. This makes it more difficult to use for those who can only read the English. Some interlinear Bibles include additional lines that include such things as the Strong's number, a transliteration (the word spelled with English letters), and parsing information. Below is an example from the Bible Hub website.

Interlinear Bible
A Bible containing both the original Hebrew or Greek and an English translation on alternate lines.

◀ John 1:1 ▶

John 1 Interlinear

1722 (e)	746 (e)	1510 (e)	3588 (e)	3056 (e)	2532 (e)	3588 (e)	3056 (e)	1510 (e)	4314 (e)
En	archē	ēn	ho	Logos	kai	ho	Logos	ēn	pros
Ἐν	ἀρχῇ	ἦν	ὁ	Λόγος	καὶ	ὁ	Λόγος	ἦν	πρὸς
in (the)	beginning	was	the	Word	and	the	Word	was	with
Prep	N-DFS	V-BA-3S	Art-NMS	N-NMS	Conj	Ar-NMS	N-NMS	V-SA-3S	Prep

Figure 10.1
Bible Hub Greek Interlinear

The advantage of using an electronic interlinear is that hyperlinks provide direct access to other tools such as lexicons and concordances.

Goal and Objectives

The General Goal

The goal in performing word studies is to determine the contextual meaning of the Greek or Hebrew words in a passage and to use those meanings to better understand the passage as a whole.

General Goal
To determine the contextual meaning of the Greek or Hebrew words in a passage and to use those meanings to better understand the passage as a whole

Specific Objectives

When performing a word study, the student must:

- Select a meaningful word to study.
- Identify the underlying Greek, Hebrew, or Aramaic word.
- Discover the range of meaning for the word.
- Observe how the word is used on other occasions, especially by the same author.
- Determine the single intended meaning of the word in the context.
- Write a contextual definition for the word that clarifies the meaning of the passage.

Specific Objectives
- Select a word to study
- Identify the underlying Greek, Hebrew, or Aramaic word
- Discover the range of meaning
- Discover how used on other occasions
- Determine meaning of the word in the context
- Write a contextual definition

Guidelines for Performing a Word Study

Below are the guidelines you should follow when performing a word study using either printed books or Bible Software whether the underlying word is Hebrew, Greek, or Aramaic. Though some of the actual tools will differ, the approach is the same for all three languages. See the later section on *Special Considerations* for help with unique features and specific tools for each language.

It is important that we use the right tool for each guideline. The following chart summaries the guidelines and the tools to use.

The guidelines will be illustrated using the Bible Hub website (www.biblehub.com). The site includes tools for performing topical studies, Greek and Hebrew study tools, concordances, commentaries, and dictionaries. There is also a Bible Hub app that can be used on mobile devices.

Word Study Guidelines and Tools

Guidelines for Performing Word Studies
- Determine which word to study
- Identify the underlying Hebrew or Greek word
- Determine the range of meaning
- Observe how the word is used in Scripture
- Study the context for clues
- Write a definition of the contextual meaning.

Guidelines	Tools
Determine which word to study	Passage being studied
Identify the underlying Hebrew or Greek word	Hebrew or Greek Interlinear Bible
Determine the range of meaning	Lexicons and Theological Wordbooks
Observe how the word is used in Scripture	Englishman's Hebrew or Greek Concordance
Study the context for clues	Context of passage being studied
Write a definition of the contextual meaning	Use intentional and extensional definitions

Determine Which Word to Study

It is not necessary, practical or efficient to conduct a word study on every word in a particular passage. However, you should perform a word study if the word is:

- Difficult to understand or unfamiliar to you.
- Ambiguous, vague or unclear in meaning.
- Theologically significant.
- Crucial to the interpretation of the passage.
- Central to the overall message of the context.
- Repeated in the immediate context or book as a whole.

In the illustration below we will be studying the word, "word" found in John 1:1 in the expression, "In the beginning was the word." If you were studying a Hebrew word from the Old Testament, the same procedures would be used.

Identify the Underlying Hebrew or Greek Word

Our goal is to discover the meaning of the original Greek or Hebrew word that underlies the English word. The basic challenge for students who cannot read Greek or Hebrew is to identify the Greek or Hebrew word that underlies the English translations. We will use the tools found on the Bible Hub website to assist us.

- Open your internet browser and enter the address **www.biblehub.com**.
- In the search bar at the top of the display type in John 1:1 and click on the magnifying glass.
- In the menu bar, click on **Interlinear**. You should see a display similar to the one in Figure 10.1 above.

- The top line contains the Strong's number for each word; the second line contains the transliterated dictionary form of the Greek word; the third line is the Greek text; the fourth line contains an English translation for the Greek word; and the bottom line contains information about the particular form.
- Scan over in the English line until you find the word you want to study. For this illustration, we will study the word, **word**. The Greek word is Λόγος and is transliterated, Logos.

Determine the Semantic Range of Meaning

- Click on the transliterated Greek word, Logos to access tools for studying this Greek word.
- The menu bar provides several tools. For now, we want to use a lexicon to determine the range of meaning for this Greek word. Bible Hub includes the Thayer's Greek Lexicon. Click on **Thayer's** to access the definitions for the word, Logos. [If you were performing a Hebrew word study, the lexicon would be the Brown-Driver-Briggs Hebrew lexicon.]
- Lexicons commonly mark the various possible meanings using numbers and/or letters. The Thayer's lexicon uses Roman numerals for very broad classifications of definitions and then specifies meanings within these broad classifications using number and further specification using lower-case letters.
- Clearly the word, Logos has a very broad range of meaning.
- You should also notice that along with definitions, Thayer's Lexicon, like most lexicons, identifies specific passages where the word takes on a particular meaning. this can be helpful but remember that when lexicographers suggest particular meanings for particular passages, they have moved from being lexicographers to being commentators. Be aware of this.

Observe How the Word Is Used Elsewhere in Scripture

- A Greek concordance is needed to identify where the same Greek word is used elsewhere in the Bible. Bible Hub provides the Englishman's Greek Concordance for this purpose.
- Click on **Englishman's** on the Menu bar. The concordance page will appear.
- The left column displays the occurrences of the Greek word. At the top of the column is a summary indicating that the word, Logos occurs 331 times in the Greek New Testament. This is followed by a listing of occurrences that include the Scripture reference for the occurrence, a portion of the Greek text, and then the same text as it appears in three different English translations.
- You can scroll the listing up and down to see each instance. You should take special notice of those occurrences where the word is translated similarly to its translation in the passage you are studying

Study the Context for Clues

- Look for collocates.
- Look for synonyms or antonyms.
- Look for definitions of the term by the author.
- Consider the overall thought of the immediate and near context.

Write a Definition of the Contextual Meaning

- Use Genus and Differentia.
- Give examples and illustrations.
- Cite parallel usages in other passages.

Special Considerations

Hebrew Word Studies

Table of Suggested Tools

Name	Comments
The Enhanced Brown-Driver-Griggs Hebrew and English Lexicon, 2000 (BDB)	This is an update of the 1951 reprint of the original 1906 lexicon. It is not *The New Brown-Driver-Briggs Hebrew-English Lexicon* published in 1977.
Gesenius' Hebrew-Chaldee Lexicon to the Old Testament	Older lexicon (1857) Predecessor of Brown-Driver-Briggs
Hebrew and Aramaic Lexicon of the Old Testament	The standard modern lexicon in English, 5 vols.
A Concise Hebrew and Aramaic Lexicon of the Old Testament	Modest Value Designed for translating by Hebrew students, it provides basic word substitution for definitions. Can be used for a quick overview of a word's range of meaning.
Enhanced Strong's Lexicon	Minimal Value This is essentially the dictionary found in the back of the concordance. It is very limited and uses the definitions found in BDB.
New American Standard Hebrew-Aramaic and Greek Dictionaries: Updated Edition	Minimal Value This is essentially the dictionary found in the back of the concordance for the NASB. It is very limited and uses the definitions found in BDB.
Dictionary of Biblical Languages with Semantic Domains: Hebrew (Old Testament)	Moderate Value Entries are listed in domain order, not in alphabetical order. Used the Louw-Nida semantic domain numbers. Caution: Links to LN are to Greek words, not Hebrew
Theological Wordbook of the Old Testament	Good theological wordbook The 1980 printed edition.
New International Dictionary of Old Testament Theology and Exegesis	Excellent theological wordbook

Verb Stems

Hebrew verbs have stems that greatly affect the meaning of the voice and intensity of the verb's action. The following chart for the Hebrew verb, to kill, illustrates how the stem can affect meaning.

	Simple	Intensive	Causative
Active	QAL קָטַל he killed	PIEL קִטֵּל he brutally killed	HIPHIL הִקְטִיל he made someone kill
Passive	NIPHAL נִקְטַל he was killed	PUAL קֻטַּל he was brutally killed	HOPHAL הָקְטַל he was made to killed
Reflexive	NIPHAL נִקְטַל he killed himself	HITHPAEL הִתְקַטֵּל he brutally killed himself	HISHTAPHEL הִישְׁתַּקְטֵל he made himself killed

When performing word studies of Hebrew verbs, you need to know not only the name of the verb but also the stem used in the passage you are studying. Bible Hub does not give this information and without it, you cannot perform an accurate word study. So, unless you know Hebrew or have a tool that can assist you in determining what verb stem is being using in the passage you are studying, you should not attempt to perform word studies on Hebrew verbs.

The Hebrew Alphabet

Name	Sign		Transliteration	Pronunciation
	Medial	*Final*		
Álep	א		'	a glottal stop
Bêt	בּ		b	b, as in ban
	ב		bh	v as in van
Gîmel	גּ		g	g as in god
	ג		gh	g as in dog
Dálet	דּ		d	d as in day
	ד		dh	th, as in they
He	ה		h	h as in hay
Waw	ו		w or v	w as in way
Záyin	ז		z	z as in zion
Het	ח		h or ch	ch as in loch
Tet	ט		t	t as in bet
Yod	י		y	y as in yet
Kap	כ	ך	k	k as in king
	כ		kh	ch as in Bach
Lámed	ל		l	l as in lake
Mêm	מ	ם	m	m as in mother
Nûn	נ	ן	n	n as in neck
Sámek	ס		s	s as in sack
`Áyin	ע		ʻ	a peculiar guttural
Pe(h)	פ		p	p as in pat
	פ		ph	f as in fat
Sade	צ	ץ	s or ts	ts as in bets
Qôp	ק		q	q as in plaque
Rês	ר		r	r as in rash
Sîn	שׂ		ś	s as in seen
Shîn	שׁ		š or sh	sh as in sheen
Taw	תּ		t	t as in tank
	ת		th	th as in thank

Hebrew reads right-to-left and Hebrew books read from our English perspective back-to-front. The Hebrew alphabet does not have vowels. After the destruction of Jerusalem in 70 A.D. and the collapse of Israel, the Hebrew language stopped being used except by religious scholars. Fearing that the pronunciation might be lost, they developed a system of vowel signs, called vowel *pointings*. Most of these pointings are placed under vowels. Only rarely will the vowels make a difference in the meaning of words. So, we will not be learning the vowel system.

Greek Word Studies

Chart of Suggested Tools

Name	Comment
Greek-English Lexicon of the New Testament and Other Early Christian Literature (DBAG)	Best Scholarly lexicon in English
Greek-English Lexicon Based on Semantic Domains (Louw-Nida)	Good Lexicon Entries are listed by semantic domains. Good for study of synonyms.
New International Dictionary of New Testament Theology (NIDNTT)	Good Wordbook
Exegetical Dictionary of the New Testament	Good Wordbook
Theological Dictionary of the New Testament (Kittle)	Good Wordbook Very extensive. Liberal theological bias
Dictionary of Biblical Languages with Semantic Domains: Greek (New Testament)	Moderate Value Entries are listed in domain order, not in alphabetical order. Uses the Louw-Nida semantic domain numbers.
Intermediate Greek-English Lexicon (Liddell & Scott)	Fair Lexicon Definitions cover classical Greek to the Patristics.
The Complete Word Study Dictionary: New Testament (Zodhiastes)	Popular Work Not appropriate for scholarly use but good for ministry use.
Concise Greek-English Dictionary of the New Testament	Minimal Value Provides short word substitutions for translating
Enhanced Strong's Lexicon	Minimal Value This is essentially the dictionary found in the back of the concordance. It is very limited and uses the definitions found in BDB.
New American Standard Hebrew-Aramaic and Greek Dictionaries: Updated Edition	Minimal Value This is essentially the dictionary found in the back of the concordance for the NASB. It is very limited and uses the definitions found in BDB.

The Greek Alphabet

Lower Case	Upper Case	Letter Name	Transliteration	Pronunciation
α	A	Alpha	a	a as in father
β	B	Beta	b	b as in boy
γ	Γ	Gamma	g	g as in gag
δ	Δ	Delta	d	d as in dad
ε	E	Epsilon	e	e as in egg
ζ	Z	Zeta	z	z as in zoo
η	H	Eta	e	e as in weight
θ	Θ	Theta	th	th as in think
ι	I	Iota	i	i as in picnic
κ	K	Kappa	k	k as in kick
λ	Λ	Lamda	l	l as in look
μ	M	Mu	m	m as in mud
ν	N	Nu	n	n as in none
ξ	Ξ	Xi	x	x as in box
ο	O	Omicron	o	o as in ought
π	Π	Pi	p	p as in paper
ρ	P	Rho	r	r as in right
σ	Σ	Sigma	s	s as in sign
τ	T	Tau	t	t as in time
υ	Υ	Upsilon	u	u as in duke
φ	Φ	Phi	ph	ph as in phone
χ	X	Chi	ch	ch as in Bach
ψ	Ψ	Psi	ps	ps as in Pepsi
ω	Ω	Omega	o	o as in tone

Begin by learning the lower-case forms. When written as the last letter in a word, the sigma has the form, ς. When a gamma precedes a kappa, gamma, or xi, it is pronounced like N (γκ as in sink, γγ as in sing, and γξ as in sinks). At times the iota is written as a subscript with the following vowels: α η ω. If a vowel is the first letter in a word, a breathing mark will appear over it. If the mark tails to the right, it is breathed, or rough (like putting an H on the front). If it tails to the left, it is not breathed or smooth ἀββα = *abba*, ἁγιος = *hagios*). Words often have accent marks. The type and position of the accent marks changes as words are used in sentences. Normally accent marks do not affect the semantic meaning of words, so they can be ignored.

A Final Word of Caution

Understanding the subtle nuances of words requires years of language study. Words take on meaning as they are used with other words and thus, it requires a thorough knowledge of a language to master word usage. For this reason, those who have not mastered the original Hebrew and Greek languages, should be cautious when making claims about the meanings of Hebrew and Greek words. Rather, English Bible students should rely on scholarly commentaries that are the products of biblical language scholars for understanding of original language words. The principles and procedures found in the chapter should be used as a means to critique the methods used by others.

The most important concepts that the reader should take away are those found under *The Nature of Words*. Most word study fallacies involve violating these concepts. For instance, the etymological fallacy of assuming that a word's meaning is equal to the sum of the meanings of its root is very common. If you become aware of these concepts, you will be able to discern word study fallacies when you see them.

Bibliography of Word Study Tools

English Word Study Tools: Concordances

English Version Concordances

Strong, James, ed. *The Strong's Exhaustive Concordance: King James Version.* Peabody, MA: Hendrickson's Publishers, 1993.

Strong, James, ed. *The New Strong's Exhaustive Concordance: King James Version.* Revised Edition. Nashville: Nelson, 1992.

Kohlenberger, John R., III, ed. *The NRSV Concordance.* Grand Rapids: Zondervan, 1990.

Kohlenberger, John R. III and Edward Goodrick, eds. *The NIV Exhaustive Concordance.* Grand Rapids: Zondervan, 1990.

Metzger, Bruce K., ed. *The NRSV Exhaustive Concordance.* Grand Rapids: Baker Book House, 1992.

Thomas, Robert L., ed. *New American Standard Exhaustive Concordance.* Nashville, Holman Press/Lockman Foundation, 1981.

Greek-English Word Study Tools

Greek-English Lexicons

Bauer, Walter. *A Greek-English Lexicon of the New Testament and Other Early Christian Literature.* Revised by Arndt and Gingrich. Chicago: University of Chicago, 1979. (Abbreviation: BAGD)

Bullinger, E.W. *A Critical Lexicon and Concordance to the English and Greek New Testament.* Grand Rapids: Zondervan, 1971.

Gingrich, Friedrich W., ed. *Shorter Lexicon of the Greek New Testament.* Chicago: University of Chicago Press, 1965. (Abbreviation: Little BAGD)

130

Liddell, H. G. and R. Scott, eds. *A Greek English Lexicon*. Ninth Edition. Oxford: Claredon Press, 1940.

Louw, Johannes P. And Eugene A. Nida. *Greek-English Lexicon of the New Testament Based on Semantic Domains*. 2 volumes. New York: United Bible Societies, 1988-89.

Moulton, J.H. and G. Milligan. *Vocabulary of the Greek Testament*. Peabody, MA: Hendrickson Publishers, 1998.

Thayer, Joseph Henry. *New Thayer's Greek-English Lexicon*. Wilmington, DE: Associated Publishers & Authors, 1977.

Greek Word Study Books

Balz, Horst and Gerhard Schneider, eds. *Exegetical Dictionary of the New Testament*. 3 volumes. Grand Rapids: Wm. B. Eerdmans, 1993. (Abbreviation: EDNT)

Brown, Colin, ed. *The New International Dictionary of New Testament Theology*. 4 volumes. Grand Rapids: Zondervan, 1975-85. (Abbreviation: NIDNTT)

Spicq, Ceslas. *Theological Lexicon of the New Testament*. 3 volumes. Translated by James D. Ernest. Peabody, MA: Hendrickson Publishers, 1998.

Friedrich, Gerhard, ed. *Theological Dictionary of the New Testament*. Abridged One-volume Edition. Grand Rapids: Eerdmans, 1981. (Abbreviation: Little Kittel).

Kittel, Gerhard and Gerhard Freidrich, eds. *Theological Dictionary of the New Testament*. 10 volumes. Grand Rapids: Eerdmans, 1964-1976. (Abbreviation: TDNT.)

Popular Level Greek Word Books

Barclay, William. *New Testament Words*. Philadelphia: Westminster Press, 1974.

Berry, George Ricker. A Dictionary of New Testament Greek Synonyms. Grand Rapids: Zondervan Publishing House, 1979.

Custer, Stewart. *A Treasury of New Testament Synonyms*. Greenville, SC: Bob Jones University Press, Inc., 1975.

Trench, Richard C. *Synonyms of the New Testament*. Grand Rapids: William B. Eerdmans, 1978 (originally published in 1880).

Vine, E.W. *An Expository Dictionary of New Testament Words*. Old Tappan: Fleming H. Revell Company, 1973.

Vine, E.W. *The Expanded Vine's Expository Dictionary of New Testament Words*. Edited by John R. Kohlenberger III. Minneapolis: Bethany House Publishers, 1984.

Vine, W. E., Merril F. Unger and William White, Jr. *Vine's Complete Expository Dictionary of the Old and New Testament Words*. Revised Edition. Nashville: Thomas Nelson, 1994.

Zodhiastes, Spiros. *The Complete Word Study Dictionary: New Testament*. World Bible Publishers, 1991.

Zodhiastes, Spiros, ed. *The Complete Word Study New Testament*. World Bible Publishers, 1991.

Biblical Hermeneutics: A Guide for Studying the Bible

Greek-English Concordances

Kohlenberger, John R. III, Edward W. Goodrick and James A. Swanson. *The Greek-English Concordance to the New Testament.* Grand Rapids: Zondervan, 1997.

Wigram, George. *New Englishman's Greek Concordance of the New Testament.* Grand Rapids: Zondervan, 1976.

Greek-English Interlinear

Berry, George R. *The Interlinear KJV Parallel New Testament in Greek and English: Based on the Majority Text with Lexicon and Synonyms.* Grand Rapids: Zondervan, 1958.

Green, Jay P., ed. *The Interlinear Bible: Greek-English New Testament.* Peabody, MA: Hendrickson, 1990.

Marshall, Alfred. *The Interlinear KJV-NIV Parallel New Testament in Greek and English.* Grand Rapids: Zondervan, 1988.

Marshall, Alfred. *The Interlinear NASB-NIV Parallel New Testament in Greek and English.* Grand Rapids: Zondervan, 1988.

Marshall, Alfred. *The Interlinear NRSV-NIV Parallel New Testament in Greek and English.* Grand Rapids: Zondervan, 1988.

Marshall, Alfred. *The NIV Interlinear Greek-English New Testament.* Grand Rapids: Zondervan, 1988.

Hebrew-English Word Study Tools

Hebrew-English Lexicons

Brown, Francis, S.R. Driver and Charles A. Briggs, ed. *The New Brown-Driver-Briggs Hebrew-English Lexicon.* Wilmington, DE: Associated Publishers and Authors, 1977.

Cline, David J. A., Editor. *The Dictionary of Classical Hebrew.* 5 volumes. Sheffield: Sheffield Academic Press, 1993-2001.

Holladay, William L. A Concise Hebrew and Aramaic Lexicon of the Old Testament. Grand Rapids: William B. Eerdmans, 1982.

Koehler, Ludwig and Walter Baumgartner. *The Hebrew Aramaic Lexicon of the Old Testament.* 5 volumes. Leiden: E.J. Brill, 1994-2000. (Available of CDROM)

Hebrew-English Word Study Books

Botterweck, G. Johanes and Helmer Ringgren, eds. *Theological Dictionary of the Old Testament.* 7 volumes. Grand Rapids: Eerdmans, 1974-1997.

Harris, R. L., G. Archer and B. K. Waltke. *Theological Wordbook of the Old Testament.* 2 volumes. Chicago: Moody, 1979.

Jenni, Ernst and Claus Westermann, eds. *Theological Lexicon of the Old Testament.* 3 volumes. Translated by Mark E. Biddle. Peabody, MA: Hendrickson Publishers, 1998.

VanGemeren, Willem A., et. al. *The New International Dictionary of Old Testament Theology and Exegesis.* 2 volumes. Grand Rapids: Zondervan, 1997.

Popular Level Hebrew Word Books

Girdlestone, Robert B. *Synonyms of the Old Testament*. Grand Rapids: William B. Eerdmans, 1978 (originally published in 1897).

Vine, E.W. *An Expository Dictionary of Old Testament Words*. Old Tappan: Fleming H. Revell Company, 1978.

Vine, W. E., Merrill F. Unger and William White, Jr. *Vine's Complete Expository Dictionary of Old and New Testament Words*. Revised Edition. Nashville, Thomas Nelson, 1994.

Wilson, William. *Old Testament Word Studies*. Grand Rapids: Kregel Publications, 1978 (originally published in 1870).

Hebrew-English Concordances

Kohlenberger, John R. III and James A. Swanson. *The Hebrew-English Concordance to the New Testament*. Grand Rapids: Zondervan, 1997.

Wigram, George. *New Englishman's Hebrew-Chaldee Concordance of the Old Testament*. Grand Rapids: Zondervan, 1976.

Hebrew-English Interlinears

Green, Jay P., ed. *The Interlinear Bible: Hebrew-English Old Testament*. Peabody, MA: Hendrickson, 1990.

Kohlenberger, John R. III. *The Interlinear NIV Hebrew-English Old Testament*. Grand Rapids: Zondervan, 1987.

Summary

One important principle of the HGRT Methodology is the Principle of Word Meaning, which states that the most probable interpretation of a passage is the one that best harmonizes with the normal meanings of every word in the passage. Words are the building blocks of language and understanding their meanings is crucial to correct interpretation. Several different types of meanings need to be distinguished.

Semantic Meaning	The thoughts that are associated with words
Connotation	The feelings that are associated with words
Syntactical Function	The grammatical usage of words
Referent Meaning	The concrete object the word refers to when used
Contextual Meaning	The single intended meaning of the word in use
Figurative Meaning	A meaning where the referent does not correspond with the normal semantic meaning.

The relationships between words and meaning affect how we study words. The following principles and implications impact our approach to word study.

Principle	Implication
The meanings of words are conventional and not appropriate.	The look and sounds of English words are no more appropriate to their meaning than are the looks and sounds of words in other languages.
The meanings of words change with time.	We should not use modern language dictionaries to study the ancient words of the Bible.
The meanings of words in different languages do not fully correlate.	We must study the underlying Greek and Hebrew words, not English words.
The meanings of words change from person to person.	We must give special attention to how the author used the same word elsewhere.
Words have a broad range of meaning.	We must first discover the broad range of meaning before we attempt to assign a meaning in a given passage.
A word in use can have only one meaning.	We must determine which potential meaning is correct in a given passage.
The meaning of a word in use is determined by its context.	We must carefully examine the context of the passage to determine which potential meaning is the intended meaning.

Word Study fallacies occur when you violate one of the principles related to the meanings of words or do not determine word meanings based primarily on usus loquendi. The most common fallacies are:

Root Fallacy	When the meaning of a word is assumed to be based on etymology.
Temporal Semantic Fallacies	When people assume that the meaning of a word in the Bible is the same as the mean of that word in either an earlier timeframe (obsolescence) or a later timeframe (anachronism).
Basic Meaning Fallacy	When people assume that every word has a basic meaning that can be seen each time it is used. This is the basis of the supposed Law of First Mention.
Unwarranted Adoption Fallacy	When people assume that most if not all of word's semantic range are to be applied to the interpretation of a single passage

Lexicographers research the meanings or words, using three sources. Etymology attempts to determine the meaning of words through a study of the historic roots of the word. It is an unreliable source for discovering meaning. Comparative Philology is the study of related words across a family of languages. It is used to establish the meaning of rare words but should be used with caution. *Usus Loquendi* refers to the common usage of words within a language. This is the best approach to determining meaning.

A definition is an attempt to describe the meaning of a word. There are two approached to writing definitions. Extensional definitions attempt to define words by citing examples but are limited to the examples given. Intentional definitions attempt to define words by giving their abstract qualities. Scholarly intentional definitions are either lexical definitions, the type found in dictionaries, or definitions using genus and differentia.

To perform word studies, we need to use concordances, lexicons, word study books, and interlinear Bibles. Concordances list the biblical occurrences of words. Lexicons give the basic range of meaning for words. Wordbooks give fuller articles discussing meaning. Interlinear Bibles provide a way to discover the Hebrew or Greek words that were the source of the English translation.

Important guidelines for performing word studies are:

- Determine which word to study.
- Identify the underlying Hebrew or Greek word.
- Determine the range of meaning.
- Observe how the word is used in Scripture.
- Study the context for clues.
- Write a definition of the contextual meaning.

Key Terms

Word	Meaning	Definition	Lexicon
Denotation	Connotation	Referent	Word Study Book
Semantic Range	Collocates	Etymology	
Comparative Philology	*Usus Loquendi*	Concordance	

Review Questions

1. What is the principle of interpretation that relates to the meaning of words?
2. What is meant by word, meaning, and definition?
3. What are the different types of meaning a word can have?
4. Why is it not valid to perform word studies in English?
5. What is meant by range of meaning?
6. What ultimately determines the meaning of a word?
7. What are the three sources for discovering the meanings of words?
8. What is the purpose of an interlinear Bible?
9. Why is etymology a poor source for determining the meanings of words?
10. When is comparative philology useful for determining the meanings of words?
11. What are the most common word study fallacies?
12. What is the difference between extensional and intentional definitions?
13. How do you write a definition using genus and differentia?
14. What is the basic purpose of a concordance, a lexicon, a wordbook, an interlinear Bible?
15. What are the two numbering systems for the coding of Hebrew and Greek words?
16. What are the guidelines for studying the meaning of a word?
17. Why is it more difficult to study the meanings for Hebrew verbs?

References

[1] Carson, D. A. *Exegetical Fallacies*. 2nd ed. Carlisle, U.K.; Grand Rapids, MI: Paternoster; Baker Books, 1996. pp. 28-64

[2] Merriam-Webster, *Inc. Merriam-Webster's Collegiate Dictionary, 11th Edition*. 2003.

[3] Bauer, Walter. *A Greek-English Lexicon of the New Testament and Other Early Christian Literature*. Chicago: University of Chicago, 1979. p. 748.

[4] Bauer, Walter. *A Greek-English Lexicon of the New Testament and Other Early Christian Literature*. Chicago: University of Chicago, 1979. pp. 599-601

Chapter 11

Figures of Speech
Interpreting Figurative Language

Outline

Introduction 136

    Definition of Figure of Speech 136

    Relationship to Normal Interpretation 136

    Purpose of Figurative Language 136

    Four Basic Elements 137

Specific Figures of Speech 138

    Figures of Comparison 138

    Figures of Representation 138

    Figures of Inclusion 138

    Figures of Substitution 139

    Figures of Understatement or Overstatement 139

    Figures of Suppression or Omission 139

    Figures of Rhetorical Opposites 139

How to Identify a Figure of Speech 140

    When to Adopt a Literal Sense 140

    When to Adopt a Figurative Sense 140

Guidelines for Interpreting Figures of Speech 141

Summary 142

Review Questions 143

Learning Objectives

After completing this chapter, you should be able to

- ❑ Distinguish between the literal and figurative use of words and phrases.
- ❑ Identify the four basic elements in a figurative expression.
- ❑ Identify a figure of speech by relationship and form.
- ❑ Interpret a figure of speech following appropriate guidelines.

Introduction

In Chapter 10 we discussed the meanings of words and learned the process for discovering the contextual meaning of a word. However, words are not always used in their usual sense. At times, they refer to items that do not correspond to the normal semantic meaning of the word. We say that they have a figurative meaning. Often, the figurative meaning cannot be discovered using the techniques for discovering the usual meaning. Our goal in this unit is to learn how to determine if words are being used in a figurative way and if so, how to discover their meaning.

Definition of Figure of Speech

Figure of Speech
Word or phrase that is used to mean something other than its normal, ordinary meaning

A figure of speech is a word or phrase that is used to mean something other than its normal, ordinary meaning. The meaning of a word is figurative when it refers to a referent that does not correspond to the normal semantic meaning of that word. Figures of speech are picturesque, out-of-the-ordinary ways of stating something that might otherwise be stated in a normal, plain, ordinary way.

Relationship to Normal Interpretation

Figures of speech are part of normal communication and therefore, any normal hermeneutical method must allow for figurative interpretation of them. It is better not to speak of figurative versus literal interpretation. Though we normally understand much of language literally, clearly, we must understand some language figuratively.

Purpose of Figurative Language

All languages include a wealth of figures of speech. There are several reasons why we use figurative language.

- It adds color and vividness.
- It attracts attention and adds emphasis.
- It communicates emotion.
- It makes difficult ideas easy to understand.
- It is efficient.
- It aids in retention.

Four Basic Elements

Figurative expressions involve four elements that work together to create the figurative meaning. They include the *literal expression*, the *type of figure of speech*, the *point of contact* between the literal and figurative meanings, and the *relationship* between the two meanings. The process of interpreting a figurative expression involves using these four elements to discover the meaning.

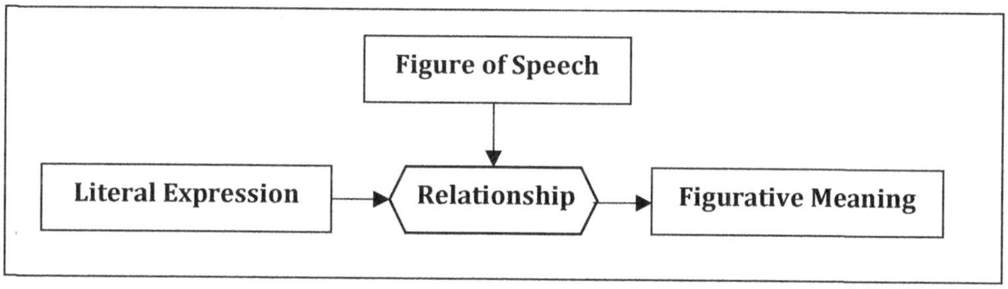

Four Basic Elements
- Literal Expression
- Relationship
- Figure of Speech
- Point of Contact

Figure 26.1
Four Basic Elements of Figurative Expressions

The Literal Expression

To understand a figure of speech, we must first know as much as possible about the literal expression. We must know the physical characteristics, associated activities, and connotations. The latter idea is very important, especially since modern feelings and relationships with objects are often quite different today than in biblical times.

Take, for example, the italicized figure of speech, "mighty men of valor...whose faces were *like the faces of lions*" (1 Chronicles 12:8). To modern western readers, the face of a lion is a beautify thing which brings pleasure to those who see it. However, to the ancient Middle Eastern reader, the face of a lion was the face of a serious predator and brought fear to those who saw it.

The Relationship between the Two Meanings

Some relationship exists between the literal expression and the figurative meaning. Some of the more important relationships include comparison, representation, substitution, inclusion, understatement, overstatement, opposites, and suppression. An understanding of the relationship is crucial to getting at the figurative meaning.

The Type of the Figure of Speech

The relationships that can exist between the literal and figurative meanings have been identified and named. We will be discussing 20 different figures of speech. Each has unique characteristics and a relationship. At times we identify the figure of speech and then use the relationship to understand the meaning. At other times, we identify the relationship and then recognize the type of figure. It is important to do both.

The Point of Contact

Normally only one of the characteristics of the literal expression is related in the figurative meaning. We call this the point of contact. It is important to properly identify the point of contact. For instance, Satan is compared to a lion in 1 Peter 5:8. Is the point of contact the fact that at a lion is beautiful, kingly, or noble? No, it is the fact that the lion is a vicious predator. Studying the context is the key to identifying the point of contact.

Specific Figures of Speech

Specific Figures of Speech

Comparison
- Simile
- Metaphor
- Hypocatastasis

Representation
- Personification
- Anthropomorphism
- Zoomorphism
- Symbol

Inclusions
- Merism
- Hendiadys

Substitution
- Metonymy
- Synecdoche

Under - Overstatement
- Hyperbole
- Meiosis
- Tapeinosis

Suppression – Omission
- Euphemism
- Apostrophe

Rhetorical Opposites
- Irony
- Paradox
- Oxymoron

Below are descriptions and examples of twenty figures of speech, grouped by the type of relationship they create between the literal expression and the figurative meaning. It is best to learn them in groups with the relationship they create. Study the examples closely. Try to distinguish between figures in the same group.

Figures of Comparison

Type	Definition	Example
Simile	An explicit comparison between two things using "like" or "as."	"He will be *like a tree planted by streams of water* (Ps. 1:3)."
Metaphor	An implicit comparison between two things by means of a direct assertion. Often introduced by a form of the verb, "to be."	"The LORD is my *shepherd* (Ps. 23:1.)"
Hypocatastasis	An implicit comparison in the form of a direct naming.	"Go and tell that *fox*" (Luke 13:32).

Figures of Representation

Type	Definition	Example
Personification	Gives human characteristics or human actions to inanimate objects, in appearance, attributes or actions.	"The *land mourns* and the *olive-oil laments*" (Joel 1:10).
Anthropomorphism	Describes God in human form.	"Let Your *ears* be attentive to my prayers" (Ps. 130:2).
Zoomorphism	Describes God or man in the form of animals, in appearance or action.	"Hide me, O LORD, under the shadow of Your *wings*" (Ps. 17:8).
Symbol	A literal object that stands both for itself and something else.	"And Jeshua was clothed with *filthy garments*... And He said, `Remove the *filthy garments* from him... Behold, I have taken away your *iniquity*'" (Zech. 3:1-5).

Figures of Inclusion

Type	Definition	Example
Merism	The use of two contrasting or opposite poles to indicate the whole. Two contrasting parts or two opposite extremes express totality.	"You know when I *sit down* and when I *get up*" (Ps. 139:2) – The LORD knows all of our daily actions.
Hendiadys	Two parallel nouns are used to express a single concept. One of the nouns is actually used in an adjectival sense to describe the other noun.	"I will multiply your *pains* and your *child-conceptions*" (Gen. 3:16) – I will make child conception painful for you.

Figures of Substitution

Type	Definition	Example
Metonymy	The substitution of a closely associated word or idea: the cause for the effect or vice versa, or the concrete for the abstract or vice versa.	Cause for Effect: "They have *Moses* and *the prophets*" (Luke 16:29). Concrete for Abstract: "God tests the *hearts* and *minds*" (Ps. 7:9).
Synecdoche	The substitution of one quantity for another quantity: the general for the specific or the specific for the general; the part for the whole or the whole for the part.	General for Specific: "Preach the gospel to *every creature*" (Mark 16:15) – to all human beings. Whole for Part: "God so loved *the world* that whosoever" (John 3:16) – the individual within the world.

Figures of Understatements and Overstatements

Type	Definition	Example
Hyperbole	An intentional exaggeration for the sake of emphasis that is not an intentional misrepresentation of the fact	"Their cities are walled up *to heaven!*" (Duet. 1:28).
Meiosis	An intentional belittling of a person or thing to express humility or to emphasize the grandeur of another person by comparison.	"I am only *dust and ashes* before You" (Gen. 18:27).
Tapeinosis	An intentional lessening of something by which the same thing is actually increased or intensified often using the negative of the opposite	"A broken and a contrite heart, O God, you *will not despise*" (Ps. 51:17) "We are *not ignorant* of Satan's schemes" – we are actually very well aware of Satan's schemes (2 Cor. 2:11).

Figures of Suppression or Omission

Type	Definition	Example
Euphemism	The use of a polite, mild or non-offensive expression in place of an impolite, embarrassing or offensive expression.	"Adam *knew* his wife Eve and she conceived and gave birth to a son" (Gen. 4:1). - They had sexual relations.
Apostrophe	Addressing a thing as if it were a person or addressing an absent or imaginary person as if he/she were present or alive.	"O *Absalom, Absalom*! Would that I had died instead of you. O *Absalom*, my son, my son!" (2 Sam. 18:38).

Figures of Rhetorical Opposites

Type	Definition	Example
Irony	An expression of thought in a form that conveys its opposite. The ironic statement usually contains a note of sarcasm or mockery.	"My, my! How the king has *distinguished* himself today!" (2 Sam. 6:20) – the king has made a complete fool of himself today.

| Paradox | A statement that seems absurd, self-contradictory or contrary to logical thought on the surface, but actually reflects a profound idea. | "Whoever *loses* his life for My sake will *save* it; but whoever *saves* his life will *lose* it" (Mark 8:35). |
| Oxymoron | The use of two words or statements that seem to contradict one another, but actually create a strong rhetorical contrast from what is expected. | "Offer your bodies as *living sacrifices*" (Rom. 12:1) – sacrifices are normally killed when they are offered and do not remain alive. |

How to Identify a Figure of Speech

When to Adopt a Literal Sense

Always assume the literal sense unless there is some good reason to prefer the figurative sense.

Example: There is no contextual justification to take the 144,000 of the 12 tribes of Israel in Revelation 7:1-8 as symbolic of Gentile believers (Jehovah's Witnesses). It refers to a literal group of Israelites. Also, there is no contextual justification to take the "1000 years" in Revelation 20:1-3 as symbolic. It refers to a literal 1000 years.

When to Adopt a Figurative Sense

Adopt a figurative sense when the literal sense is:

- Disavowed by the author. John clearly stated that Jesus meant his body when he spoke of raising the temple (John 2:19-21).

- Out of character with the subject. God is described as having "wings" in Psalm 91:4. This is obviously out of character with what we know about God, thus, it is figurative.

- Contrary to fact, experience, doctrine, context, or observation. "You have become kings" (1 Cor. 4:8) is contrary to fact as suggested in the context. For Paul continues, "I wish you had become kings."

- Impossible or absurd. God tells Jeremiah that He has made him "a fortified city, a pillar of iron and walls of bronze" (Jer. 1:18).

- Immoral. Jesus informs the crowd that they must "eat" His "flesh" and "drink" His "blood" to be saved (John 6:53). Taken literally, this would be cannibalism.

- Contrary to the general character and style of the book. Given the poetic nature of the Song of Songs, the request, "Catch the little foxes" (Song Sol. 2:15), probably does not refer to hunting.

How to Identify Figure

Adopt Literal Sense
- Unless some good reason not to do so.

Adopt Figurative Sense
When literal senses is:
- Disavowed by author
- Out of character
- Contrary to fact
- Impossible or absurd
- Immoral
- Contrary to character of book

Guidelines for Interpreting Figures

- Determine if the expression should be understood literally or figuratively using the suggestions above.

If the expression is figurative:

- Study the literal expression to discover as many characteristics about it as possible.

- Identify the type of figure and the relationship that exists between the literal expression and the figure.

- Research the expression to see if the expression has taken on a common usage.

- Study the context to determine what aspect of the literal meaning is being transferred in the figure of speech.

- Express the figurative meaning in literal terms.

Guidelines for Study
- Determine if the expression is literal or figurative

If a figure of speech:
- Study the literal expression
- Identify the type of figure and relationship
- See if figure has common usage
- Study context for clues
- Express meaning in literal terms

Example - "The Lord is my shepherd"

- Study all that you can about shepherds. The more you know about shepherds, the more likely that you will begin to understand the figure.

- The figure is metaphor, and the relationship is comparison. The Lord is being compared to a shepherd.

- Though both the OT and NT use the idea of God being a shepherd elsewhere, there does not seem to be a clear common usage.

- The context describes the shepherd in great detail. He provides rest, he leads, he protects, he prepares food, and he anoints. These aspects of shepherding seem to be the relevant characteristics.

- Based on the ideas above, it seems that the major point of comparison is that of the care given by the shepherd. The LORD is my caregiver.

Cautions and Suggestions

- Be careful that you do not assume that a figure of speech always means the same thing in every place. Example: The "dove" imagery is used to depict innocence (Matt. 10:16), stupidity (Hos. 7:11), flightiness (Hos. 11:11), beauty (Song Sol. 1:15), timidity (Song Sol. 2:14), speed (Ps. 55:6) and sorrow (Nah. 2:7).

- Be careful that you do not ignore the historical-cultural setting of the original author and superimpose contemporary concepts into the figure. Example: In our society, dogs are beloved household pets, but in the ancient world they were despised mongrels (Matt. 7:6; Phil. 3:2; Rev. 22:15).

142

Summary

A figure of speech is a word or phrase that is used to mean something other than its normal, ordinary meaning. All languages include figurative expressions, so a proper method of interpretation must take into consideration the possibility of figurative meanings.

A figurative expression involves four elements that work together to create the figurative meaning. They include the *literal expression*, the *type of figure of speech*, the *point of contact* between the literal and figurative meanings, and the *relationship* between the two meanings. The process of interpreting figurative expressions involves using these four elements to discover the meaning.

Types of Figures of Speech

Simile	An explicit comparison using "like" or "as."
Metaphor	An implicit comparison by means of a direct assertion.
Hypocatastasis	An implicit comparison in the form of a direct naming.
Personification	Gives human characteristics or human actions to inanimate objects.
Anthropomorphism	Describes God in human form.
Zoomorphism	Describes God or man in the form of animals, in appearance or action.
Symbol	A literal object that stands both for itself and something else.
Merism	The use of two opposite poles to indicate the whole.
Hendiadys	Two parallel nouns are used to express a single concept.
Metonymy	The substitution of a closely associated word or idea.
Synecdoche	The substitution of one quantity for another quantity.
Hyperbole	An intentional exaggeration for the sake of emphasis.
Meiosis	An intentional belittling of one person to aggrandize another
Tapeinosis	An intentional lessening of something when heightening is intended
Euphemism	The use of a non-offensive expression in place of an offensive one.
Apostrophe	Addressing a thing as a person, or an absent as if present or alive.
Irony	An expression of thought that sarcastically conveys its opposite.
Paradox	A statement that seems self-contradictory but reflects a profound idea.
Oxymoron	The use of two words or statements that seems contradictory.

Use the following guidelines when studying figures of speech.

- Determine if the expression should be understood literally or figuratively.

If the expression is figurative:

- Study the literal expression to discover as many characteristics about it as possible.
- Identify the type of figure and the relationship that exists between the literal expression and the figure.
- Research the expression to see if it has taken on a common usage.
- Study the context to determine what aspect of the literal meaning is being transferred in the figure of speech.
- Express the figurative meaning in literal terms.

Key Terms

Figure of Speech   Point of Contact   (See list of figures above)

Review Questions

1. What is a figure of speech?
2. What are the four basic elements in a figurative expression?
3. How do simile and metaphor differ?
4. How do anthropomorphism and zoomorphism differ?
5. How do merism and hendiadys differ?
6. How do metonymy and synecdoche differ?
7. How do meiosis and tapeinosis differ?
8. How do paradox and oxymoron differ?
9. When should you adopt the literal sense of an expression?
10. When should you adopt a figurative sense of an expression?
11. What are the guidelines for interpreting figures of speech?
12. What are some cautions you should consider when interpreting figures of speech?

This page intentionally left blank.

Chapter 12

GENRE ANALYSIS
Considering the Literary Genre

Outline

Principle of Interpretation 146

    The Importance of Studying Genre.. 146

Basic Terminology... 147

    Literary Genre 147

    Genre Dependence... 147

    Genre Analysis... 147

    Genre Competence.. 147

Three Elements of a Literary Genre 148

    Typical Form.. 148

    Typical Features 148

    Typical Function 148

Genre Analysis and Interpretation 149

    Relation to General Hermeneutics.. 149

    Genre Analysis Provides an Interpretive Grid...................................... 149

    Place of Genre Analysis in the Interpretive Process............................. 149

Overview of Biblical Genres 150

    Old Testament.. 150

    New Testament... 152

Summary 153

Review Questions.. 153

Learning Objectives

After completing this chapter, you should be able to

- ❑ State the principle of interpretation that relates to literary genre.
- ❑ Define literary genre, genre dependence, genre analysis, and genre competence.
- ❑ Explain the three typical characteristics of a genre.
- ❑ Discuss the relationship between genre analysis and general hermeneutics.

Principle
The most probable interpretation of a passage is the one that best harmonizes with the genre in which it was written

Principle of Interpretation

The most probable interpretation of a passage is the one that best harmonizes with the literary genre in which it was written.

Importance of Studying Genre

The Bible is literature, and literature follows established patterns and exhibits typical characteristics. Great mistakes in understanding can occur if we fail to take into consideration the type of literature we are reading. For instance, if we use the same interpretive approach when reading a science fiction novel that we do when reading a history book, we would conclude that aliens exist in outer space and time travel is possible.

On the other hand, the more we are aware of the unique features of the literary genre, the better we will understand what we read. For instance, knowing that *Pilgrim's Progress* is an allegory on Christian living opens our understanding and focuses our attention on descriptions in the story that might otherwise be overlooked.

So too, an awareness of the genres of the Bible help enhance our ability to understand the Bible and a lack of awareness will hamper our ability to understand. Klein writes,

> "Each kind of literature has its own frame of reference, ground rules, strategy, and purpose... The Bible student who knows the formation and function of each literary type is in the best position to interpret correctly and to avoid serious misunderstandings."[1]

Basic Terminology

Literary Genre

The term genre means type, variety, form, or kind. It is used in reference to the classification of objects into a specific category. The term, **literary genre**, refers to the different kinds of literary compositions that are distinguished by their unique forms. Each literary genre has unique characteristics, typical to that particular genre in respect to its form, features and function.

Some common literary genres in secular English literature include: novel, short story, poem, textbook, encyclopedia, professional journal, and business contract. The literary genres in Scripture include: narrative, laws, poetry, proverbs, prophetic speech, gospel account, and epistle.

Literary Genre
The different kinds of literary compositions that are distinguished by their unique forms

Genre Dependence

The proper interpretation of any text is **genre dependent**; that is, a passage must be interpreted in the light of its literary genre. If the literary genre is not properly understood or appreciated, the passage or book as a whole can be misinterpreted. Distinguishing the various literary genres will help us interpret the various portions of Scriptures more accurately by enabling us to recognize the distinctive characteristics of the various genres.

Genre Dependence
A passage must be interpreted in the light of its literary genre

Genre Analysis

Genre analysis is the process of identifying the specific literary genre of a biblical passage or book. Genre analysis pays special attention to the three basic elements of genre: the literary form, features, and function of a book.

Genre Analysis
The process of identifying the specific literary genre of a biblical passage or book

Genre Competence

Genre competence is the ability of an interpreter to recognize the literary genre (form, features, and function) of a biblical book and to use this awareness to better interpret that book. You can develop genre competence by learning the typical elements that are common to the distinct literary genres. For example, to gain genre competence in the basic forms of biblical poetry, the interpreter should become familiar with the forms, features, and functions of biblical poetry.

Genre Competence
The ability to recognize the literary genre of a book and to use this awareness to better interpret

Three Elements of Genre
- Typical Form
- Typical Features
- Typical Functions

Three Elements of a Literary Genre

Three elements, *a typical form, typical features, and typical functions* characterize a literary genre. Below is a description of each.

Typical Form

Typical Form
Recurring pattern that is characteristic of that particular genre

Each literary genre has a recurring pattern that is characteristic of that particular genre. This is called the typical literary form.

For example, modern letters typically begin with a greeting, move into the main body of material, and conclude with a salutation. The typical murder mystery has the following standard form.

- Murder of victim by an unknown assailant
- Investigation by the detective and discovery of clues
- Identification of the murderer
- Concluding explanation of how the murderer did the crime

Our analysis of the structure of a book should be based upon and informed by the typical literary form of its particular genre. Often the typical form will provide an important guide to uncovering the author's plan for the book or a section within the book.

Typical Features

Typical Features
Unique characteristics of language, style, structure, and even tone particular to that genre

Each literary genre tends to exhibit unique characteristics of language, style, structure, and even tone that are particular to that genre. These similarities constitute the genre's features.

For example, legal material tends to use precise language for the sake of clarity while poetry uses more figurative language to express a wide range of emotions. Narrative, on the other hand, tends to use dialogue and descriptive language.

Typical Function

Typical Function
Unique types of author's purpose common to a genre

Certain literary genres are more often associated with certain types of author's purposes. Thus, certain genres tend to have typical functions.

For example, poetry is called the language of love. That is because poetry, as a genre, tends to be used to express emotion. On the other hand, legal contracts are purposed to express precision in agreements. If your purpose is to express tender love to a friend, it is best done with a poem, not with a legal contract.

Genre Analysis and Interpretation

Relationship to General Hermeneutics

Genre analysis relates to the third aspect of the HGRT method of interpretation. It is important because full and complete interpretation is genre dependent. However, we must not isolate our analysis of genre from the general principles and guidelines we have already learned. Indeed, genre analysis simply helps us to refine and focus these principles and guidelines.

Genre involves *typical* forms, features, and functions. Each author applies and indeed even alters these characteristics to suit his purposes. We must be careful not to force the text into the typical elements of a genre. To do so would be to introduce another error of eisegesis. We must apply the general principles of hermeneutics that we have already learned and use our understanding of genre to enhance our understanding without controlling it.

Relationship to General Hermeneutics
- Important for complete interpretation
- Not isolated from general hermeneutical principles
- Do not force genre into the text

Genre Analysis Provides an Interpretive Grid

The literary genre of a biblical text provides an **interpretive grid** or the literary lens through which to interpret a passage. If you do not recognize the genre of a biblical passage, you will not have the proper interpretive grid through which to read the text. The literary genre provides the literary context necessary to correctly understand the author's original rhetorical meaning.

Interpretive Grid
A literary lens through which to interpret

Place of Genre Analysis in the Interpretive Process

Genre analysis should be one of the first things that a student does in the interpretive process. It should occur after you analyze the historical features: historical background, occasion for writing, and author's purpose; but before you analyze structural and grammatical features: literary and immediate context, sentences, and words.

When you study a book of the Bible, you should study the following eight aspects in the order listed below.

- Historical-Cultural Background (Cultural Context)
- Occasion for Writing (Situational Context)
- Author's Purpose
- Literary Genre of the Book (Genre Analysis)
- Literary Context of the Book (Discourse Analysis)
- Immediate Context (Paragraph Analysis)
- Individual Sentences (Grammatical Analysis)
- Meaning of Words (Lexical Analysis)

Overview of Biblical Genres

Old Testament Genres

Old Testament Genres
- Biblical Narrative
- Legal Genre
- Hebrew Poetry
- Psalms
- Wisdom Literature
- Prophetic Discourse
- Apocalyptic Literature

Biblical Narrative

Biblical narratives are *prose accounts that dramatically chronicle the unfolding of God's mighty deeds in the history of redemption.* They are historical-rhetorical-theological accounts that have theological and practical significance for the people of God throughout all ages. Biblical narratives contain both history and theology and are designed to teach us about God and his ways. As such they are ethical stories that we are to understand and apply.

Legal Genre

The literary genre known as legal genre encompasses the many commandments, prohibitions and case laws found in Scriptures. This not only includes the Old Testament commands and prohibitions, but also the New Testament commands and prohibitions. In the Old Testament, this genre is composed of the material that constitutes the Law of Moses while in the New Testament it is composed of the material that constitutes the Law of Christ (e.g., 1 Cor. 9:21; Gal. 6:2).

Hebrew Poetry

Hebrew poetry is a poetic form that is characterized by parallel structures, concise language, and figures of speech. Like most western poetry, Hebrew poetry employs a wealth of figures of speech and is highly structured. Unlike most western poetry, Hebrew poetry rarely employs parallels of sound, but rather employs parallels of thought and structure, called **poetic parallelisms**.

Hebrew poetry occurs throughout Psalms, Proverbs, Job, Song of Songs, Lamentations and parts of Ecclesiastes. These are known as the poetic books. The Hebrew prophets also employed poetic forms throughout their prophetic speeches. The prophetic books are composed largely of poetic material. Poetry also occurs within some Old Testament narratives (e.g., Gen. 2:23; Exod. 15:1-18). Poetry even occurs in the New Testament (e.g., Luke 1:46-55; 68-79).

Psalms

Basic Types
- Lament Psalms
- Declarative Praise Psalms
- Descriptive Praise Psalms
- Royal/Messianic Psalms
- Wisdom Psalm

The book of Psalms is a collection of psalms. The term, psalm, comes from the Greek word, ψαλμος (*psalmos*), meaning a poem that was sung to the accompaniment of music played on strings. The Old Testament equivalent word is *mizmor*. There are different types of psalms, each of which has a distinct form, distinct features, and distinct functions. Five of the major types are:

- Lament Psalms
- Declarative Praise Psalms
- Descriptive Praise Psalms
- Royal/Messianic Psalms
- Wisdom Psalm

Wisdom Literature (Proverbs)

The Hebrew noun *mashal*, translated proverb means a comparison. Whether it is used in wisdom literature, prophetic oracles, poetic sayings or popular speech, the term refers to a comparison that the author has created to teach truth through representational imagery. Most often, *mashal* refers to a short, pithy, memorable saying that expresses a general truth, as in Proverbs 10-29 (e.g., 10:1). However, at times it can refer to extended didactic discourse, as in Proverbs 1-9 (e.g., 1:8-19) and to an extended allegory as in Ezek. 17:2-24.

The Book of Proverbs is the largest collection of traditional proverbial sayings in Scripture, containing both the longer didactic discourses (Proverbs 1-9, 30-31) and the shorter sentence sayings (Proverbs 10-29). Traditional proverbial sayings also appear elsewhere in the Old Testament (1 Sam. 10:11-12; 24:14; Ezek. 16:44) and New Testament (Luke 4:23).

The three most common forms of proverbs found in the book of Proverbs are the *short sentence proverb*, the *wisdom saying*, and the *mashal ode or long didactic discourse*. Additional forms such as the numerical saying or the alphabetic acrostic can also be found in Proverbs but with much less frequency.

Prophetic Discourse

The prophetic books of the Old and New Testaments are composed of two very different types of material, prophetic speeches and apocalyptic visions. The apocalyptic material recounts and explains visions given by God to communicate a message. In Chapter 24 we will discuss apocalyptic literature. The prophetic speeches are sermon-like discourses spoken by God through the prophet to a group of people. They can be as short as one verse or as long as several chapters. In Chapter 23 we will discuss the interpretation of these speeches.

Most of the prophetic books consist of a collection of prophetic speeches, apocalyptic visions, and historical narratives edited and compiled by the prophet by whose name the book is known or by a compiler who did so in the name of the prophet. Some of the material is arranged chronologically and some more topically. Often several speeches are grouped together to form a larger address.

There are four basic types of speeches, each having unique form, features, and function. They are: *Legal Disputation, Judgment Speech, Call to Repentance,* and *Salvation Speech*. In Chapter 23, we will also consider two other types of writings found in the prophetic books, the *Call Narrative* and *Songs of Confidence*.

Apocalyptic Literature

The term apocalyptic comes from the Greek noun, ἀποκαλυψις (*apocalupsis*), meaning unveiling, uncovering, revealing; and the verb, ἀποκαλυπτω (*apocaluptō*), meaning to unveil or to uncover what is hidden, to reveal.

When used with reference to prophetic literature, the term apocalyptic designates a special kind of prophetic visionary literature that unveils or reveals God's future prophetic program leading up to the establishment of the future kingdom. Most of the apocalyptic material in the Bible is found in Isaiah, Ezekiel, Daniel, Zechariah, and Revelation.

New Testament Genres
- Gospel
- Parables of Jesus
- Epistles

New Testament Genres

Gospel

The word, gospel, derived from the Anglo-Saxon god-spell, was used to translate the Greek word, εὐαγγελλιον (*euangellion*) meaning good news. A Gospel is a writing that gives the message of Jesus Christ in the context of his life. The biblical Gospels are portraits of Jesus Christ that concentrate upon his teaching, life, and atoning work.

The Gospels are not autobiographies since Jesus did not write them. The Gospels are not biographies about Jesus. They say very little about his early life but concentrate upon three and one-half years of his life, placing great emphasis upon the last week of his life on earth. The Gospels are individual accounts of the life and teaching of Jesus to explain who he was, what he did and why he should be honored and praised.

Parables of Jesus

A **parable** is a true-to-life story that illustrates a spiritual truth by drawing a comparison between the characters and actions in the storyline with real characters, such as God, believers, and unbelievers, and their actions. It is a true-to-life short story that employs stereotypical characters and activities common to everyday life to illustrate a spiritual truth. Parables are sub-genres found mainly in the Gospels.

Epistles

The English term, **epistle** is derived from the Greek term, ἐπιστολη (*epistolē*) and means a letter. Paul and Peter use the noun *epistolē* with reference to many of the epistles that they wrote (e.g., Rom. 16:22; 1 Cor. 5:9; 2 Cor. 7:8; Col. 4:16; 1 Thess. 5:27; 2 Thess. 2:15; 3:14,17; 2 Pet. 3:1,16). The verb, ἐπιστελλω (*epistellō*) to write a letter, is used in the epistle to the Hebrews (Heb. 13:22).

This word is appropriate because the New Testament epistles consist of both personal letters written to specific individuals or churches and public treatises written as tracts to be circulated among all the churches.

The New Testament epistles consist of the 21 compositions found from Romans through Jude. They are classified as the Pauline Epistles (Romans through Philemon), General Epistles (Hebrews through Jude).

Pauline		Non-Pauline	
Romans	1 Thessalonians	Hebrews	1 John
1 Corinthians	2 Thessalonians	James	2 John
2 Corinthians	1 Timothy	1 Peter	2 John
Galatians	2 Timothy	2 Peter	Jude
Ephesian	Titus		
Philippians	Philemon		
Colossians			

Summary

One important principle of the HGRT Methodology is the Principle of the Literary Genre, which states that the most probable interpretation of a passage is the one that best harmonizes with the literary genre in which it was written.

A *literary genre* is a kind of literary composition that is distinguished by unique forms, features, and functions. A proper interpretation is *genre dependent*, that is, a passage must be interpreted in the light of its literary genre. *Genre analysis* is the process of identifying the specific literary genre of a biblical passage and then using its elements to help interpret. *Genre competence* is the ability to recognize the literary genre of a biblical book and to use that awareness to better interpret that book.

Three elements characterize a literary genre. Each genre has a *typical form*, a recurring pattern or plan. Each genre exhibits *typical features*, unique characteristics of language, style, structure, and tone. Each genre expresses *typical functions*.

We must not perform genre analysis in isolation, but rather as a refinement to the general principles of hermeneutics. We must understand that authors creatively and selectively apply typical elements of a genre. We should not attempt to force a book or passage into the typical pattern but rather understand the genre as an interpretive grid to help in interpretation. Genre analysis should be done early in the interpretive process before analysis of the plan of the book.

Key Terms

Literary Genre	Genre Dependence	Genre Analysis
Genre Competence	Interpretive Grid	

Review Questions

1. What is the principle of interpretation that relates to the literary genre?
2. What is meant by literary genre, genre dependence, genre analysis, and genre competence?
3. What are the three elements of a literary genre?
4. What is meant by typical form?
5. What is meant by typical features?
6. What is meant by typical functions?
7. What is the relationship between genre analysis and general hermeneutics?
8. In what way does a literary genre provide an interpretive grid for interpretation?
9. When should genre analysis be performed?
10. What are the eight aspects of the interpretive process?
11. What are the names of the genres of the Old and New Testaments

References

[1] Klein, William W., Craig L Blomberg, and Robert L Hubbard, Jr. *Introduction to Biblical Interpretation*. Dallas: Word Publishing, 1993. pp. 260.

This page intentionally left blank.

Chapter 13

Theological Analysis
Considering the Biblical Context

Outline

Principle of Interpretation 156

Theological Interpretation 156

    Definition 156

    Historical Development.. 156

        Rule of Faith.. 156

        Analogy of Faith.. 157

        Historical-Critical Methodology 157

    The Role of Theological Interpretation in Exegesis 158

Guidelines for Theological Interpretation.. 158

    Identify Parallel Passages 158

    Interpret Difficult Passages in light of the Clear 158

    Consider Theological Presuppositions of Author and Readers 158

    Test Exegetical Conclusions Using the Rule of Faith............................ 159

    Seek Affirmation from the Believing Community................................... 159

Summary 160

Review Questions... 160

Learning Objectives

After completing this chapter, you should be able to

- ❑ State the general principle of interpretation related to theological interpretation.
- ❑ Define theological interpretation.
- ❑ Describe the historical development of theological interpretation.
- ❑ List and evaluate the proposed roles of theological interpretation.
- ❑ List the guidelines for theological interpretation.

Principle of Interpretation

> **Principle**
> Correct interpretation of a passage will harmonize with and help to explain God's ultimate goal in providing the Scriptures.

In Chapter 2 we introduced the HGRT Method of interpretations. The fourth principle in this method is the *Theological Principle*. It is based on the assumption that the Scriptures are divinely inspired and therefore must be unified and consistent. Based on this, the following principle of interpretation can be derived.

> *Correct interpretation of a passage will harmonize with and help to explain God's ultimate goal in providing the Scriptures.*

A corollary to this is the **principle of non-contradiction** which states, no passage of Scripture when properly interpreted with contradict the clear teaching of Scripture on a given topic.

Theological Interpretation

Defined

> **Theological Interpretation**
> Attempts to see the theological connections between the individual statements found in the Bible, and makes or tests the interpretations of individual passages based on these connections

The historical-grammatical-rhetorical method of interpretation emphasizes the diversity of the individual books of the Bible and their human authorship. Each text has a unique cultural and situational context. Each has a unique purpose and genre. Each has a unique rhetorical context and message. Thus, the HGR method provides principles and guidelines for the study of the individual books of the Bible authored by individual human beings. However, this method says nothing about understanding the Bible as a whole, authored by God.

The theological principle assumes that the Bible as a whole is inspired, authored by God and intended to move its readers to devotion and service for God. Thus, **theological interpretation** *attempts to see the theological connections between the individual books and statements found in the Bible and makes or tests the interpretations of individual passages based on these connections.*

Historical Development

Rule of Faith

> **Rule of Faith**
> Trinitarian teaching handed down from the apostles, now equated with the Bible.

The concept of theological interpretation has existed in the Church since its inception. Early Church fathers such as Irenaeus, Clement of Alexandria, and Tertullian in their opposition to heresy argued that the true Church was identified by its Trinitarian teaching that was handed down from the apostles. They called this teaching **the rule of faith**. It represented the unbroken continuity of teaching from Jesus, to the disciples, and finally to the Church.

With the passing of the apostles and their immediate successors, the apostolic writings were recognized as the lasting repository of this teaching. This led to the collection of these writings during the 2nd and 3rd centuries. However, not all of the religious writings created during this period were accepted by the Church. The process of recognizing which writings were inspired is called **canonization**. By the end of the 4th century the Church universally recognized the 66 books that are included in the Protestant Bible as the inspired Word of God.

One of the major criteria in the selection process was the rule of faith. Only those books whose teachings reflected the rule of faith were recognized. Thus, the individual writings are themselves theologically a cohesive whole. As such Protestant theologians now use the term, **rule of faith** to refer to the Scriptures.

The Analogy of Scripture

The Protestant Reformers used the phrase, the **analogy of faith** or the **analogy of Scripture** to describe the unity and consistency of the biblical teaching on any particular subject. Based on the analogy of Scripture the theologian can expect that it is possible to harmonize all the individual scriptural statements on a particular subject. Thus, if all the passages that deal with sin are properly understood and harmonized, the result would be a coherent and consistent teaching about sin.

> **Analogy of Scripture**
> The unity and consistency of the biblical teaching on any particular subject

The analogy of Scripture should be distinguished from the rule of faith. It is more specific than the rule of faith. It suggests that the theological unity and consistency of the Bible is not only in its adherence to basic Trinitarian teaching but also in its uniformity of teaching about all theological subjects addressed in Scripture.

The rationale for the analogy of Scripture is based on the assumption that all of the individual writings in Scripture are inspired by God. God is the ultimate author of the individual books and therefore, these books will present coherent and consistent teachings.

Historical-Critical Methodology

In the 18th century liberal scholars began to deny the supernatural origins of the Bible and instead sought to explain its origins as a completely human process. They assumed that a proper understanding of the text could only be derived from an understanding of its development and the application of hermeneutical principles derived from the nature of human communication. They rejected the idea that the Bible exhibited theological unity. Instead they attempted to demonstrate the diverse and even conflicting theological teachings found within the Bible.

> **Historical-Critical Method**
> Understanding of the text based on its human development and the nature of human communication

Though most evangelical scholars reject the hermeneutic of unbelief that is typical of many who promote the historical-critical method, they do see benefits in the method. An overemphasis on theological interpretation has resulted in ignoring the literary diversity found in the Bible and in imposing unwarranted conclusions upon the text. The historical-grammatical-rhetorical method is akin to the historical-critical method to the degree that both provide principles for interpreting the text that are based on human authorship.

However, Evangelicals disagree with liberal scholars about the divine origins of the Bible and its theological unity. They remain convinced that theological interpretation is a valid element in the exegetical process.

The Role of Theological Interpretation in Exegesis

Evangelical scholars agree that theological interpretation should play a role in the exegesis of individual passages; but exactly what kind of role should it play? There are four options.

- It should be a substitute for exegesis.
- It should dictate the exegesis.
- It should be one element of exegesis.
- It should be a check after exegesis.

Proper Roles
- One element of exegesis
- A check after the exegesis

There is a great deal of debate among Evangelicals about which of these four roles theological interpretation should play in interpretation. The first two options should be rejected since they lead to dogmatic interpretation. Within conservative evangelical circles, the third and fourth options are preferred. The third option is based on the conclusion that it is impossible and even unwarranted to eliminate completely our theological presuppositions during exegesis. However, we must identify them and keep them in check. The fourth option should certainly be used. We should always test the viability of our interpretations, using the Analogy of Faith.

Guidelines for Theological Interpretation

Identify Parallel Passages

Identify Parallel Passages
- Other passages that deal with the same topic.

A **parallel passage** or **cross-reference** is a passage which deals with the same topic of discussion. MacArthur states, "Cross-referencing, implemented with competent sensitivity to clues in each context, avoids making invalid connections and adds insights for preaching. It is best not to strain a cross-reference if evidence for a relationship is not solid."[1]

We must be cautious in the use of cross-references. The two passages must exhibit real cohesion. This cohesion is not simply the occurrence of similar words. There must be a valid topical connection between the two passages. The most probable parallels are those written by the same author, those dealing with the same situation, and those contained in the same genre.

Use a good reference Bible or topical index to discover potential parallel passages. However, critically examine each cross-reference. Not every cross-reference suggested is a real parallel.

Interpret Difficult Passages in light of the Clear

Use Clear Passages
- Always interpret unclear passages in light of those that are clear

When real parallels are found, we must base our interpretation on those that are the clearest. Such passages normally employ less figurative language and are rarely found in genres that employ high levels of figurative or indirect language such as parables, poetry, apocalyptic writings, and narratives. *Always interpret difficult to understand, ambiguous, vague, and figurative passages based on those that are clear, concrete, and obvious.*

Consider Theological Presuppositions of Author and Readers

The theological presuppositions of the author and the original readers provide an appropriate theological backdrop for theological consideration of the text. Walter Kaiser states, "Only the doctrine and the theology prior to the time of the writer's composition of his revelation (which theology we propose to call here the 'Analogy of Scripture') may be legitimately used in the task of theological exegesis."[2] Though Kaiser may have understated the legitimacy of using the analogy of faith, he does appropriately underscore the need to consider the theological presuppositions of the author and his readers. We must attempt to discover the theological presuppositions of the author and the original readers.

Test Exegetical Conclusions Using the Rule of Faith

No interpretations that contradicts the rule of faith are valid. Therefore, it is imperative that we test our interpretations against the rule of faith. However, we must be cautious that we do not substitute a specific theological position for the rule of faith. The rule of faith is a general Trinitarian construct such as the Apostles' Creed. More specific theological constructs must be derived from the Scriptures and therefore must not be the basis for interpreting the Scriptures.

Test Exegetical Conclusions
- No interpretation that contracts the rule of faith is valid

Seek Affirmation from the Believing Community

The Church, the believing community, is the interpretive community in which God's Spirit dwells and to which the rule of faith was given. Valid interpretation should find affirmation within this community. We must submit our exegetical conclusions to this believing community. However, we must remember that the Church today is not a completely unified community. Doctrinal distinctions exist. We should not expect that our interpretations will receive universal affirmation from every location. Yet, we should expect general affirmation. *Novel interpretations that have never been suggested should be accepted with great caution.*

Affirmation of the Church
- Novel interpretations should be accepted with great caution

160

Summary

An important theological principle of interpretation is that *correct interpretation of a passage will harmonize with and help to explain God's ultimate goal in providing the Scriptures*. Theological interpretation attempts to see the theological connects between the individual statements found in the Bible and makes or tests the interpretations of individual passages based on these connections.

Early Church fathers argued that the true Church was identified by its Trinitarian teaching called **the rule of faith**. This rule of faith provides the theological cohesion that pervades the Bible. The Protestant Reformers used the phrase, **the analogy of faith** or the **analogy of Scripture** to describe the unity and consistency of the biblical teaching on any particular subject. Based on the analogy of Scripture the theologian can expect that it is possible to harmonize all the individual scriptural statements on a particular subject. Liberal biblical scholars deny the supernatural origins of the Bible and reject the idea that the Bible exhibits theological unity. Evangelicals reject this conclusion but disagree as to what role theological interpretations should play in exegesis. Some suggest it should be one element of exegesis. Others suggest it should be used only as a check after the exegesis.

To use theological interpretation properly, you should:

- Identify parallel passages dealing with the same topic
- Interpret difficult passages in light of clear passages
- Consider the theological presuppositions of the author and the original readers
- Test Exegetical conclusions using the rule of faith
- Seek affirmation from the believing community

Key Terms

Theological Interpretation	Rule of Faith	Analogy of Scripture
Canonization	Historical-Critical Method	Parallel Passage
Cross-reference		

Review Questions

1. What is the principle of Non-Contradiction?
2. What is meant by rule of faith and analogy of Scripture?
3. What role should theological interpretation play in exegesis?
4. What guidelines should you use in theological interpretation?

References

[1] John MacArthur, *Rediscovering Expository Preaching* Dallas: Word Pub., 1997, c1992. 133.
[2] Walter Kaiser, "The Single Intent of Scripture" *Rightly Divided: Readings in Biblical Hermeneutics*, Kregel Publications, 1996 pg. 169.

Chapter 14

The Application Process
Responding to God's Word

Outline

Introduction 162

    Definition of Application 162

    Importance of Application 162

    Applicational Relevance of All Scriptures 162

Principles for Applying Scripture 163

    Challenges to Correct Application 163

        Differences between Original Readers and Us 163

        Differences in Dispensation 163

        Differences in Audience 164

        Differences in Culture 164

    Two Basic Kinds of Application 165

    Direct Application 165

    Indirect Application 165

Guidelines for Applying Scripture 166

    Guidelines for Determine General Principles 166

    Guidelines for Evaluating General Principles 167

    Guidelines for Applying Scripture Summarized 168

Summary 168

Review Questions 169

Learning Objectives

After completing this chapter, you should be able to

- ❏ Define application.
- ❏ Explain the challenge to applying Scripture.
- ❏ Distinguish between direct and indirect application.
- ❏ List the guidelines for deriving general principles from biblical narratives.
- ❏ List the guidelines for defining general principles from specific commands.
- ❏ Explain how to evaluate the validity of general principles.
- ❏ Use a set of guidelines to properly apply a passage of Scripture.

Introduction

Definition of Application

Application
The process of determining the relevance of a passage to our lives, and putting the passage into practice

Application is the process of determining the relevance of a passage to our lives and putting the passage into practice in our lives. It follows observation, interpretation, and correlation as the fourth step in the inductive Bible study process. It is the goal of all Bible study.

The Importance of Application

Importance of Application
Application is the ultimate goal in Bible Study

Application is the ultimate goal of the entire Bible study process. Interpretation is a means to an end, not the end it itself (Col. 1:28; 1 Tim. 1:5). Jesus did not call us to make students, teaching them to know everything, but to "make disciples; teaching them to do everything I have commanded you" (Matt. 28:19-20). If we do not force ourselves to go beyond interpretation to the step of application, we will be in danger of becoming hearers only and not doers of the Word of God (Jas. 1:22-25).

The Applicational Relevance of All Scriptures

Relevance of Scripture
Both Old Testament and New Testament have applicational relevance for Christians

All Scripture is not only inspired, but also profitable for teaching, rebuke, correction and training in righteousness (2 Tim. 3:16-17). Both the Old Testament and the New Testament have applicational relevance for Christians. Everything in Scripture was written for our instruction (Rom. 15:4; 1 Cor. 10:11). Although Christians live in the church age and are under the law of Christ rather than the Law of Moses, the Old Testament is still relevant to us (Matt. 5:17-20; 2 Tim. 3:16-17).

Principles for Applying Scripture

The Challenges to Correct Application

Correct interpretation does not guarantee correct application. The reason is that the original message was written to a different audience, at a different time, in a different culture. Exegesis explains what the message meant to them. But, it does not necessarily follow that our response to the message should be the same as theirs. To demonstrate this, let's look at two commands Paul made in 2 Timothy 4.

> Preach the Word; be prepared in season and out of season; correct, rebuke and encourage – with great patience and careful instruction.
>
> 2 Tim. 4:2

> When you come, bring the cloak that I left with Carpus at Troas, and my scrolls, especially the parchments.
>
> 2 Tim. 4:13

Most Christians are quick to see the relevance and application of the first command. We understand that God wants us to evangelize. However, the second command seems to have little relevance. Certainly, God does not expect us to go to Troas in search of Paul's cloak and scrolls. This leads us to two questions. First, how do I determine which statements are directly applicable to me? Second, is there any relevance to statements that are not directly applicable to me?

Challenge of Application
Some passages seem to have little relevance while other passages seem to have much relevance

Differences between Original Reader and Us

To answer these questions, we first need to understand why our responses to Scripture might be different from those of the original readers. They involve three differences between them and us – a difference in *dispensation*, a difference in *audience*, and a difference in *culture*.

Differences between Original Reader and Us
- Dispensation
- Audience
- Culture

Differences in Dispensation

The term **dispensation** refers to the distinct periods in Biblical history in which God revealed new promises and responsibilities to his people in such a way that the historical period can be distinguished from what preceded and what followed. Each new period began when God inaugurated a new historical covenant in the history of salvation. Each historical covenant has distinctive promises and responsibilities. The following table summarizes the dispensational periods and historical covenants.

Adamic Covenant	Gen. 1:26-31	Adam to Noah
Noahic Covenant	Gen. 9:1-17	Noah to Abraham
Abrahamic Covenant	Gen. 12:1-3	Abraham to Moses
Mosaic Covenant	Exod. 19-24; Deut. 5-31	Moses to 1st Coming of Christ
New Covenant	Jer. 31:31-34	1st Coming to 2nd Coming

Believers today are under the New Covenant in contrast to the Mosaic Covenant (2 Cor. 3:6-16; Heb. 8:6-13). The Mosaic Covenant commanded Israel to observe certain ceremonial laws that are not obligatory under the New Covenant (Heb. 8:6-13). This is the reason that the Church does not observe the Day of Atonement and other Jewish ceremonial rituals.

This does not mean, however, that the Old Testament is irrelevant to us. For example, the prohibition against murder (Gen. 9:5-6) revealed under the Noahic Covenant carries forward throughout all the historical dispensations. Likewise, New Testament authors quote Old Testament commands about holiness and obedience, suggesting that the moral laws that underlay the ceremony and cultural laws of the Old Testament are still relevant for New Testament believers. For example, Peter quotes Leviticus 19:2, "You shall be holy for I the LORD your God am holy," as the basis for his exhortations to holy living (1 Pet. 1:16) for those living under the New Covenant.

Generally speaking, Old Testament statements about moral standards and statements in New Testament books are more directly applicable to us.

Differences in Audience

Each author wrote to a distinct historical audience. While all Scripture was written for us, not all Scripture was written directly to us (Rom. 15:4). In some cases, the audience was very specific (e.g., Paul's Epistle to Philemon). In other cases, the audience was more general and the author intended his material to have a more universal application (e.g., the Book of Proverbs).

Biblical books that were written to a wider and universal audience are more directly applicable to us. Biblical books that were written to a narrow and specific historical audience are less directly applicable to us. For example, the Pastoral Epistles, 1 and 2 Timothy and Titus, were addressed to two young pastors, instructing them how to lead their churches (1 Tim. 3:14-15; Tit. 1:5). Much of what the Pastoral Epistles say has primary reference to pastors and church leaders. Thus, a layperson in the church should not appoint elders as Paul instructed Titus (Tit. 1:5). Such a command to Titus would best apply to pastors and church leaders who are in positions similar to Titus.

Differences in Cultural

Some practices and commands in Scripture reflect an ancient practice or custom that was unique to the author's culture but foreign to our modern culture. We must wrestle with the issue of whether or not that ancient practice or custom is **cross-cultural**—that is, authoritative at all times in all cultures. In some cases, only the principle behind the ancient custom is authoritative. However, in other cases, the ancient practice may be appropriate in the Christian community even though it is foreign to modern secular culture.

For example, it was customary in ancient Near Eastern cultures for people to greet one another with a kiss. This practice is reflected throughout the Old Testament (Gen. 27:26-27; Exod. 4:7; 18:7; Prov. 27:6) and the New Testament (Matt. 26:48-49; Mark 14:44-45; Luke 7:25; Acts 20:37). Paul adopts this custom but admonishes believers that it must be practiced in a holy manner: "Greet one another with a holy kiss" (Rom. 16:16; 1 Cor. 16:20; 2 Cor. 13:12). In modern western culture, we do not greet one another this way. In fact, to do so might be quite misunderstood and have the opposite effect Paul intended. Thus, we should probably adopt the principle behind the custom without forcing the ancient Near Eastern custom upon our modern western culture. Instead of greeting one another with a holy kiss, we could greet one another with a holy hug or a hearty handshake.

The Two Basic Kinds of Application

Direct Application

Two Kinds of Application
• Direct Application
• Indirect Application

If the statement of a passage is not conditioned dispensationally, culturally or historically, we may say that the passage has **direct application** to us. In other words, we do not have to go through any process to determine how the passage should apply to us. An example of a passage that has direct application for us is, "Rejoice always" (1 Thess. 5:16). There are no differences in audience, culture, or dispensation that we need to overcome before we will know what we should do.

Direct Application
Applications taken directly from a passage that is not conditioned dispensationally, culturally or historically

Statements that have direct application have these characteristics. They are:

- Addressed to a General Audience
- General in Nature
- Repeated
- Repeatable
- Not Revoked
- Similar in Cultural Significance
- Moral and Theological in Natures

Indirect Application

If the statement of a passage is conditioned dispensationally, culturally or historically, we may say that the passage has **indirect application** to us. This does not mean that the command is any less relevant or authoritative; it simply means that we must first determine how the passage should apply to us. For example, Paul's command, "Greet one another with a holy kiss" (Rom. 16:16) would be a case of a passage having indirect application to us. We are obligated to apply the principle behind the custom–greet one another in a Christian manner–but we are not obligated to adopt the ancient custom itself.

Indirect Application
Applications based on principles from a passage that is conditioned dispensationally, culturally or historically

Statements that have only indirect application have these characteristics. They are:

- Addressed to Individuals
- Specific in Nature
- Not Repeated
- Not Repeatable
- Revoked
- Different in Cultural Significance
- Not Moral or Theological in Nature

Example

We should now be able to identify why 1 Timothy 4:2, "Preach the Word", is more directly applicable to us than is 1 Timothy 4:13, "Bring the cloak". The former passage includes a command that is general, repeated, repeatable, and is moral and theological in nature. On the other hand, the latter passage is specific, not repeated, not repeatable, and not moral or theological in nature.

Since 1 Timothy 4:13 has no direct application to us, we need to think generally about the command and seek a general principle that we can apply. One possibility is that we ought to help those saints who have physical needs.

Guidelines for Applying Scripture

Guidelines for Determining General Principles

General principles for application can be derived from both direct commands and implicit actions and statements found in biblical narratives. However, the approaches are not necessarily the same. We will first discuss how to derive principles from biblical narratives and then discuss how to derive principles from direct commands.

Guidelines for Deriving General Principles from Biblical Narrative

The Bible indicates that biblical narrative is intended for instructional and applicational use (1 Cor. 10:11). Biblical characters become both positive and negative models for us. However, we should not conclude that all activities and statements of individuals within that narrative are normative and should be used as the basis for developing applications. Consider, for instance, the request of Gideon for a sign from the Lord to confirm the Lord's promise to save Israel through him (Judges 6:36-40) – a sign he requested twice. The text makes no comment about the request, whether it was right or wrong. What should we conclude? Is Gideon's action an example for us to follow? Should we ask God for signs to confirm his will for our lives?

Generally, the actions and statements of individuals in narratives can be used to develop general principles for application when:

- The action or statement is commended or corrected in the narrative.
- The consequences of the action or statement imply that it was or was not commendable.
- The supposed principle is explicitly taught in the New Testament.

Guidelines for Deriving General Principles from Commands

When a command is not directly applicable to us, we must determine the general timeless principles that are implied in the command. In this process we tend to move from the specific to the general, from the temporal to the timeless, from the cultural to the universal. Below are some suggestions for discovering such principles.

- Examine the broader context for a general principle that underlies the specific commands. In 1 Corinthians 10:23-24, 31-32 Paul suggests the general principles that lie behind his command to not eat meat sacrificed to idols (1 Cor. 8-10).

- Examine the reasons given for obeying the specific commands. In Ephesians 6:5 slaves are commanded to obey their masters because the Lord will reward everyone for whatever good he does.

- Examine the context for a doctrinal issue that underlies the specific commands. In Galatians 5:2-3 Paul warns the Galatians about being circumcised. The issue is not so much the specific act of circumcision as it is the replacing of God's grace with Jewish legalism.

- Consider whether a specific command can be stated as a general principle. For instance, Paul's prohibition against drunkenness in Ephesians 5:18 can be generalized to deal with any drug dependency.

Guidelines for Evaluating General Principles

To ensure that we do not base our applications on invalid principles, we should evaluate any principle we develop. Ask the following questions.

- Is the principle timeless and universal in scope?
- Does the principle have clear correspondence with the passage from which it was taken?
- Is the principle explicitly stated elsewhere in Scripture?
- Is the principle cross-cultural?

Guidelines for Evaluating Principles
- Is it timeless, universal?
- Does it correspond with passage?
- Is it stated explicitly elsewhere?
- Is it cross-cultural?

Is the principle timeless and universal in scope?

A general principle must not include something that is limited to a given time or given situation. For instance, in Genesis 14:20 Abraham gave a tenth of the spoils of war to Melchizedek. To suggest that Christians should give a tithe of all that they receive is invalid. The problem is that tithing is not taught in the New Testament. Instead, proportion in giving is based on ability, not on an across-the-board ten percent (2 Cor. 8:12-15).

Does the principle have clear correspondence with the passage from which it was taken?

Paul pleads with Euodia and Synteche to "agree with each other in the Lord" (Phil. 4:2). A valid principle from the passage would be that Christian workers should be unified and cooperate with each other. There is a clear correspondence between Euodia and Synteche, and Christian workers since in 4:3 Paul states that they had worked with him in the cause of the gospel.

Is the principle explicitly stated elsewhere in Scripture?

Naaman, who at first refused to dip in the Jordan and was offended because the prophet would not come out to him, took the advice of a servant girl, humbled himself, and was cleansed of his leprosy (2 Kings 5). The story of Naaman suggests that to receive deliverance, we must replace arrogance and disobedience with humility and obedience. This is confirmed by direct statement elsewhere in Scripture (James 4:10).

Is the principle cross-cultural?

"Greet one another with a holy kiss" (Rom. 16:16) is clearly not cross-cultural. However, neither is the statement, "Christians should shake hands at church." The second statement is just as culture-bound as the first. A better statement might be, "Christians should warmly greet each other in a truly holy manner."

Guidelines for Applying Scripture Summarized

Guidelines for Applying Scripture
- Determine if passage has direct application

If not directly applicable
- Determine the timeless principle
- Determine appropriate modern response

To summarize our approach, we should follow these steps to apply Scripture:

- Determine if the passage has direct application to us.

If the passage is not directly applicable:

- Determine the timeless principle expressed in the passage.
- Determine the appropriate response to the principle in our culture.

Summary

Application is the process of determining the relevance of a passage to our lives and putting the passage into practice. Application is important since it is the ultimate goal of Bible study. All Scripture is relevant and can be applied to our lives.

The problem is that not all Scripture was written to us and therefore not all Scripture is directly applicable to us. This is due to differences between the original readers and us: differences in dispensation, in audience, and in culture. When these differences do not exist, the passage has direct application to us. When they do exist, the passage has only indirect application to us. Before it can be applied, we must discover the general principle that underlies the statements in the passage.

General principles can be derived from the actions and statements found in biblical narratives when:

- The action or statement is commended or corrected in the narrative.
- The consequences of the action or statement imply that it was or was not commendable.
- The supposed principle is explicitly taught in the New Testament.

General principles can be derived from specific commands by doing the following:

- Examine the context for a general principle underlying the specific commands.
- Examine the reasons given for obeying the specific commands.
- Examine the context for a doctrinal issue that underlies the specific commands.
- Consider whether a specific command can be stated as a general principle.

To summarize our approach, we should follow these steps to apply Scripture:

- Determine if the passage has direct application to us.

If the passage is not directly applicable:

- Determine the timeless principle expressed in the passage.
- Determine the appropriate response to the principle in our culture.

Key Terms

Application	Dispensation	Cross-cultural
Direct Application	Indirect Application	

Review Questions

1. Why is it that not all Scripture can be directly applied to our lives?
2. What three differences might exist between the original readers and us?
3. What is meant by dispensation and how does it relate to application?
4. What is meant by cross-cultural and how does it relate to application?
5. What are the characteristics of statements that can be directly applied to us?
6. What are the characteristics of statements that can only be indirectly applied to us?
7. What guidelines should you follow to derive general principles from the actions and statements of individuals in narratives?
8. What guidelines should you follow to derive general principles from specific commands?
9. What guidelines should we use to evaluate the validity of general principles?
10. What is the basic three-step process for applying Scripture?

This page intentionally left blank.

Chapter 15

Gospel Genre
Interpreting the Four Gospels

Outline

Defining Gospel 172

    Gospel Versus gospel 172

    The Four Gospels 172

Function of the Gospels 173

Form of the Gospels 174

Features of the Gospels 174

    Pericope Stories 174

    Saying of Jesus 176

    Synoptic Parallels 176

Guidelines for Interpreting the Gospels 176

Summary 177

Review Questions 178

References 178

Learning Objectives

After completing this chapter, you should be able to

❑ Explain the typical form of the Gospels.
❑ Explain the typical function of the Gospels.
❑ List the typical features of the Gospels.
❑ Compare and contrast the Four Gospels.
❑ List the guidelines for interpreting the Gospels.

Defining Gospel

Gospel Versus gospel

gospel (lowercase)
The message of salvation through the work of Jesus Christ

Gospel (uppercase)
A book that gives the message of Jesus Christ in the context of his life

The word, gospel, derived from the Anglo-Saxon god-spell, was used to translate the Greek word, εὐαγγελλιον (*euangellion*) meaning good news.

In the Bible, the lower-case word, gospel, refers to the message of salvation through the work of Jesus Christ, while the capitalized word, Gospel, has a literary application. A Gospel is a book that gives the message of Jesus Christ in the context of his life. The biblical Gospels are portraits of Jesus Christ that concentrate upon his teaching, life, and atoning work.

The Gospels are not autobiographies since Jesus did not write them. The Gospels are not biographies about Jesus. They say very little about his early life but concentrate upon three and one-half years of his life, placing great emphasis upon the last week of his life on earth. The Gospels are individual accounts of the life and teaching of Jesus to explain who he was, what he did and why he should be honored and praised.

The Four Gospels

There are four Gospels in the Bible: Matthew, Mark, Luke and John. The four different Gospels are by different authors, have different audiences in mind and reflect different purposes. We are greatly enriched in our understanding of who Jesus is by having four different Gospels.

The Gospels Compared

Figure 15.1
The Gospels Compared

	Audience	Theme
Matthew	Jews	Jesus is Messiah
Mark (Peter)	Gentiles	Jesus is suffering Savior
Luke (Paul)	Church	Jesus is historical fact
John	Gentiles	Jesus is Son of God

The Function of the Gospels

Though each Gospel has a unique specific function, all four have the same general theological function, to show that Jesus Christ, the Savior of the world, died to provide salvation and rose again as prove of this accomplishment. John explicitly mentions this purpose when he writes:

> Jesus did many other miraculous signs in the presence of his disciples, which are not recorded in this book. But these are written that you may believe that Jesus is the Christ, the Son of God, and that by believing you may have life in his name.
>
> John 20:30-31

Though the other gospel writers do not state this purpose explicitly, an analysis of the content of their Gospels reveals it. The following chart indicates how much emphasis the writers placed on the final week of Christ's life, which ended with his death and resurrection. This is the clear emphasis of all four Gospels. We can conclude that the overall purpose was not merely biographical but theological. The writers wanted to explain who Jesus is, what he did, and why he should be worshiped as Savior.

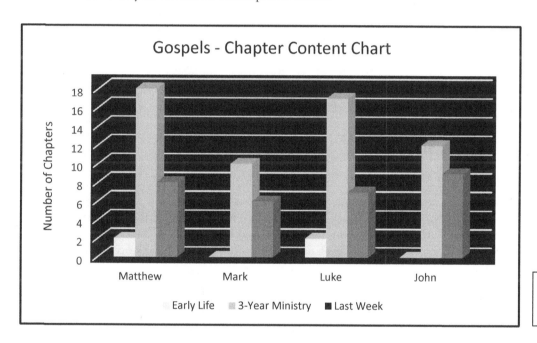

Figure 15.2
Gospels Chapter
Content Chart

Along with this general function, each gospel writer also had a unique special function that closely related to his original audience and their situation. See Figure 15.1 for a summary of these unique purposes. See Chapter 6 for the general guidelines for discovering the author's purpose.

The Form of the Gospels

As Figure 15.2 indicates, the Gospel writers emphasized the last three years of Jesus life with special emphasis on the last week of his life. In general, all four Gospels follow the same order and pattern. Below is the general plan found in all four Gospels.

Figure 15.3
Form of the Gospels
	I. Announcement of the Christ
	II. Ministry of the Christ
	    A. Public Ministry to Israel
	    B. Opposition and Rejection
	    C. Private Ministry to Disciples
	III. Atoning work of Christ
	    A. Final Week in Jerusalem
	    B. Trial
	    C. Crucifixion
	    D. Resurrection

The Features of the Gospels

Pericope Stories

Definition of Pericope

A **pericope** is a section of a book. We use the term to refer to the short stories from the life of Jesus found in the Gospels. After the ascension of Jesus, the disciples told these stories, passing them down to the next generation of Christians. Most likely a story was told with little concern about its relationship to other stories. The story took on its own identity.

Pericope
A short story from the life of Christ

When the Gospel writers recorded the stories, they placed them in a loosely ordered chronology. However, it was clearly not their purpose to establish an exact chronology. Instead the stories are woven together somewhat chronologically and somewhat topically. At times, the writers wove several stories together into a longer narrative.

Two Study Approaches

When studying these stories, we should take two approaches. Gordon Fee and Douglas Stuart call these the *horizontal* and the *vertical* approaches.[1]

Two Approaches to Study
- Vertical: study in light of the historical and literary context of a Gospel
- Horizontal: study in parallel with other Gospels

Vertical Study. Each pericope should be studied in light of the occasion and purpose of the author as well as in light of the literary context of the Gospel in which it is found.

For example, because Matthew writes to Jews, only Matthew records Jesus' citation of the Jewish law about rescuing animals on the Sabbath (Matt. 12:11-12) when he heals a man's withered hand. Compare Matt. 12:9-14 with Mark 3:1-6 and Luke 6:6-11.

Horizontal Study. Each pericope should be studied in parallel. We study it in light of all the descriptions and statements in the other Gospels. For example, only by reading in all four Gospels do we know what was written on the cross superscription.

Matt 27:37	Mark 15:26	Luke 23:38	John 19:19
Above his head they placed the written charge against him: THIS IS JESUS, THE KING OF THE JEWS.	The written notice of the charge against him read: THE KING OF THE JEWS.	There was a written notice above him, which read: THIS IS THE KING OF THE JEWS.	It read: JESUS OF NAZARETH, THE KING OF THE JEWS.

The process of reconciling any differences in content or location of an event found in one or more Gospels by weaving them together into a larger picture is called harmonization. A Harmony of the Gospels is a helpful tool for this type of study. Below is a sample.

The NIV Harmony of the Gospel
By Thomas & Gundry[2]

240   *The Death of Christ*   Sec. 236-237

CRUCIFIXION

Sec. 236   Mockery by the Roman soldiers
    – Jerusalem, in the Praetorium –

Matt. 27:27-30	Mark 15:16-19
27 Then the soldiers of the governor took Jesus into the Praetorium and gathered the whole Roman [1]cohort around Him. 28 And they stripped Him, and put a scarlet robe on Him. 29 And after weaving a crown of thorns, they put it on His head, and a [2]reed in His right hand; and they kneeled down before Him and mocked Him, saying, "[1]Hail, King of the Jews!" 30 And they spat on Him, and took the reed and began to beat Him on the head.	16 And the soldiers took Him away into the [3]palace (that is, the Praetorium), and they called together the whole Roman [1]cohort. 17 And they [*]dressed Him up in [4]purple, and after weaving a crown of thorns, they put it on Him; 18 and they began to acclaim Him, "Hail, King of the Jews!" 19 And they kept beating His head with a [2]reed, and spitting at Him, and kneeling and bowing before Him.

[1]Or, *battalion.* [2]Or, *staff (made of a reed).* [3]Or, *court.* [4]A term for shades varying from rose to purple.

Sec. 237   Journey to Golgotha

Matt. 27:31-34	Mark 15:20-23	Luke 23:26-33a	John 19:17
31 And after they had mocked Him, they took His robe off and put His garments on Him, and led Him away to crucify *Him.* 32 And as they were coming out, they found a man of Cyrene named Simon, [l]whom they [m]pressed into service to bear His cross.	20 And after they had mocked Him, they took the purple off Him, and put His garments on Him. And they [*]led Him out to crucify Him. 21 And they [*m]pressed into service a passer-by coming from the country, Simon of Cyrene (the father of Alexander and Rufus), to bear His cross.	26 And when they led Him away, they laid hold of one Simon of Cyrene, coming in from the country, and [m]placed on him the cross to carry behind Jesus. 27 And there were following Him a great mul-	17 They took Jesus therefore, and He went out, [l,m]bearing His own cross.

[l](Matt. 27:29; Mark 15:18) The mockery and crude treatment of Jesus came in two stages of which this is the second. Before His condemnation, Pilate seems to have allowed ill-treatment in hopes of provoking the crowd's sympathy toward Jesus and thereby persuading them to ask for His release (John 19:1-5, Sec. 235). In this section, however, following His condemnation the soldiers took the initiative and carried the brutal mockery to a much greater extreme.

[m](Matt. 27:32; Mark 15:21; Luke 23:26; John 19:17) At the outset of the journey to Golgotha, Jesus appears to have carried the cross (or the transverse beam of the cross) Himself, in accordance with John's description. Being so weakened from lack of sleep and the cruel scourging, however, He was unable to complete the journey. The soldiers therefore forced Simon of Cyrene to carry it for Him. It is possible that Simon's son Rufus, who appears to have been known to Mark's Roman readers (Mark 15:21), is the person whom Paul greets in Romans 16:13.

Sayings of Jesus

The Gospels also include much of what Jesus said. These sayings include short similes, parables, and longer discourses. The Gospels differ as to the timing, organization, and wording of these sayings. At times material found in longer discourses in one Gospel are given in shorter form in another Gospel. At times sayings are repeated. And at times the wording of the sayings differs.

These differences can be explained in several ways. First, the standard for quoting someone differs today than it did when the Gospels were written. Generally, the test for accuracy related to the overall message, not to the individual words. Second, Jesus spoke in Aramaic but the Gospels were written in Greek. Two translations can be accurate though they express the original ideas in different words. Third, the longer discourses seem to be summaries rather than complete statements of what Jesus said. The intent was to provide the gist of what Jesus said, not the exact words. Finally, it is very possible that Jesus said the same thing more than once. He was an itinerate preacher with a single theme. It only makes sense to assume that he would repeat many of his sayings to different audiences in slightly different ways and even with slightly different intent.

Synoptic Parallel

Because of the similarity of content and order in Matthew, Mark and Luke, these three Gospels are known as **The Synoptic Gospels**. Matthew reflects 90% of Mark, and Luke reflects 50% of Mark. All three generally follow the same plan and are strikingly similar in places. Compare Mark 2:10, Matt. 9:6, and Luke 5:24. Yet each also has unique material about the Lord Jesus. The study of the differences and similarities of these Gospels, their date and relationship, is called **The Synoptic Problem**.

Guidelines for Studying the Gospels

When studying the pericopes and sayings of Jesus found in the Gospels, you should consider the following.

- The overall theological purpose of the Gospel in which the pericope or saying is found.

- The occasion for writing and unique purpose of the Gospel in which the pericope or saying is found.

- The literary context of the Gospel in which the pericope or saying is found.

- The historical context of the life of Christ and overall emphasis that all four Gospels place on his ministry and atoning work.

- The parallel accounts in the other Gospels.

Summary

The Gospel is a unique literary genre. Gospel, capitalized, a written record of the life of Christ, must be distinguished from gospel, lower-case, the message of salvation. The Bible contains four Gospels, Matthew, Mark, Luke, and John. Each was written to a unique audience under unique circumstances and with unique purposes. However, the general function of all the Gospels is to show that Jesus, the Savior, died to provide salvation and rose as proof of it.

All four of the Gospels have the same general form.

- o Announcement of the Christ
- o Ministry of the Christ
  - Public Ministry to Israel
  - Opposition and Rejection
  - Private Ministry to Disciples
- o Atoning work of Christ
  - Trial
  - Crucifixion
  - Resurrection

The Gospels exhibit several interesting features. They include short stories from the life of Christ, called pericopes. These stories should be studied vertically, in the historical and literary context of the Gospel in which they are found, and horizontally by comparing them with the parallel accounts in the other Gospels. For this, you can use a Gospel harmony.

Another feature of the Gospels is the sayings of Jesus. These sayings include short similes, parables, and longer discourses. Differences in the parallel accounts of these sayings can be explained at follows.

- The standard for accuracy was measured differently than today.
- Jesus spoke in Aramaic while the gospels are written in Greek.
- Longer discourses are summaries, not complete statements of what Jesus said.
- Jesus repeated much of his statements in slightly different ways.

Matthew, Mark, and Luke are known as *The Synoptic Gospels* since they are very similar in content and plan. The *Synoptic Problem* deals with explaining both the similarities and differences of these gospels.

Key Terms

Gospel	gospel	Pericope
Parallel	Harmony	Synoptic Gospels
Synoptic Problem		

Review Questions

1. What is the difference between the capitalized Gospel and the lower-case gospel?
2. What are the names of the four Gospels?
3. What is the overall purpose of the Gospels?
4. What is the typical form of the Gospels?
5. What are the three unique features of the Gospels?
6. What is a pericope?
7. What are the two ways to study a pericope?
8. What is a harmony of the Gospels and how would you use it?
9. How can you explain the differences in the parallel accounts of the sayings of Jesus?
10. What is the synoptic problem?

References

[1]Fee, Gordon D., and Douglas Stuart. *How To Read The Bible For All Its Worth*. Grand Rapids: Zondervan Publishing House, 1993. pp. 121-126.

[2] Thomas, Robert L., and Stanley N. Gundry, ed. *The NIV Harmony of the Gospels*. San Francisco: Harper, 1988. pp. 240.

Chapter 16

Parables of Jesus
Interpreting the Parables

Outline

Defining Parable 180

    Definition 180

    Types of Parables 180

Form of the Parables 180

    Introduction to Parable 180

    Body of the Parable 181

    Explanations 181

Features of the Parables 182

    True-to-life Story 182

    Characterization 182

    Central Truth 182

Function of the Parables 183

    Encourage Reflection 183

    Conceal and Reveal Truth 183

Guidelines for Interpreting the Parables 183

Summary 184

Review Questions 184

References 184

Learning Objectives

After completing this chapter, you should be able to

- ❑ Explain the typical form of the parables.
- ❑ Explain the typical function of the parables.
- ❑ List the typical features of the parables.
- ❑ List the guidelines for interpreting the parables.

Defining Parable

Definition

> **Parable**
> A true-to-life story that illustrates a spiritual truth

A **parable** is a true-to-life story that illustrates a spiritual truth by drawing a comparison between the characters and actions in the storyline with real characters, such as God, believers, or unbelievers, and their actions. It is a true-to-life short story that employs stereotypical characters and activities common to everyday life to illustrate a spiritual truth.

Types of Parables

> **Types of Parables**
> - Similitude
> - True Parable

Though parables can be found in the Old Testament, we will be dealing only with the parables of Jesus. The majority of the parables are complete stories. We call these **true parables**. Others are only shorter illustrations called **similitudes**.

The Form of the Parables

> **Form of Parable**
> - Introduction
> - Body
> - Explanation

The parable consists of three basic parts, an introduction, the body or parable itself, and concluding explanations. Not all the parts are always present.

Introduction to the Parable

> **Types of Introductions**
> - General introduction identifying the parable
> - Formal Formula
> - No introduction

Most of Jesus' parables have a general introduction that identifies the parable. They are similar to the following.

Matt 13:3	Then he told them many things in parables, saying...
Matt 13:24	Jesus told them another parable...
Luke 5:36	He told them this parable...

Some of the parables begin with a more formal formula like the following.

Matt 13:24	The kingdom of heaven is like...
Mark 4:30	What shall we say the kingdom of God is like...

In a few instances, a story that seems to be a parable may not include any reference to it being a parable. The story of the rich man and Lazarus, though thought to be a true story by some, is best taken as a parable (Luke 16.19-31).

Body of the Parable

The body of the parable is the true-to-life story that is used to communicate the central truth. The story is not an allegory. In allegory every detail has meaning and correspondence. However, in a parable, many of the details are provided only to assist in making the story realistic.

All the details in a parable contribute to the story. However, only some are directly related to the central spiritual truth. The details that help teach, reveal, develop or enhance the basic spiritual truth in the parable may be called the **primary details**. The details that are included in the parable because they are necessary to make the storyline true-to-life may be called the **secondary details**.

> **Body of Parable**
> The true-to-life story that is used to communicate the central truth

> **Types of Details**
> • Primary
> • Secondary

The Explanation of the Parable

The explanation of the parable is not always present. When it is present, it becomes a very important component for interpretation. The explanations can take on many different forms.

> **Types of Explanation**
> • Jesus explains central point
> • Jesus explains details
> • Occasion helps to explain

Sometimes Jesus explains the central point of the parable.

- Sometimes Jesus states the central point before telling the parable (Mark 13:33-37; Luke 15:4-7; 14:15-24; Matt. 18:10-14; 24:44-51).

- Sometimes Jesus states the principle after telling the parable (Luke 11:5-10; 16:1-9; 17:7-10; 18:9-14; Matt. 20:1-16; 22:1-14; 25:1-13).

Sometimes Jesus or the writer explains the details or purpose.

- Sometimes Jesus will explain the point of each of the details in the parable (e.g., Matt. 13:18-23; 13:36-43; 15:15-20).

- Sometimes the writer will explain the purpose of why Jesus told the parable (e.g., Luke 18:1, 18:9; 19:11).

Sometimes the historical occasion helps to explain the parable.

- Sometimes Jesus tells a parable to answer a question (e.g., Luke 10:25; 10:29; Matt. 9:14; 18:21; 20:1; 21:28; 21:33).

- Sometimes Jesus tells a parable in response to a request (e.g., Luke 11:5-8 responds to 11:1 and Luke 12:16-21 responds to 12:13).

- Sometimes Jesus tells a parable in response to a complaint by others (e.g., the complaint in Luke 7:39-40 leads to 7:41-43; the complaint in 15:2 leads to the parables in 15:4-7, 8-10, 11-32).

- Sometime Jesus tells a parable to address or illustrate a situation that had just occurred (e.g., Luke 7:29-35; 13:1-8; Matt. 7:24-27).

The Features of the Parables

True-to-life Story

Features of Parables
- True-to-life Story
- Characters
- Central Spiritual Truth

The parables are cast in the form of a short true-to-life story, which serves as an illustrative vehicle to teach a basic spiritual truth. The storyline is taken from common life situations in Israel.

While not everyone grasped the profound spiritual truth in the parables, everyone—even common people—could follow the storylines of the parables because they were drawn from their everyday life experiences.

True-to-life Story
Storyline is taken from common life situations in Israel

Characterization

Each parable has 1-3 main characters featured in a short storyline that describes an activity of the character(s) or unfolds a narrative plot. The true-to-life storyline involves stereotypical characters that can be understood on their own, apart from an exegetical search for the underlying spiritual truth. Often the characters will have some parallel in the central truth of the parable. They may represent God, believers, unbelievers, or even those to whom the parable was given.

Characterization
- 1-3 main characters
- Stereotypical
- Often parallel people related to central truth

Central Spiritual Truth - The Heart of the Parable

Parables differ from allegories. In an allegory, every detail corresponds to something. In a parable there is only one central spiritual truth. There are many details in each parable but normally only one primary spiritual truth around which all the details revolve.

Central Spiritual Truth
- Parable is not allegory
- Only one central truth
- Several parables may work together to illustrate the central truth

Jesus' explanations of His parables focus on a single central all-embracing spiritual truth (e.g., Matt. 20:16; Luke 15:10; 19:7). Even when Jesus explained several details in a parable, all the details revolved around the one central truth, e.g. parable of the sower (Matt. 13:1-9, 18-23) and the wheat and the weeds (Matt. 13:24-30, 36-43).

Sometimes a set of parables occur together as multiple illustrations of the same basic central truth. This is true of the parables of the lost sheep (Luke 15:4-7), lost coin (Luke 15:8-10) and lost son (Luke 15:11-32).

Teachings Represented by Main Characters

Allegorical interpretation of the parables has historically been common in the church. However, most Protestant and Evangelical scholars reject this approach. Klein, Blomberg, and Hubbard point out that some recent Evangelical scholars are proposing a limited sense of allegorical interpretation. They suggest that each main character in the parable may represent a different truth or teaching. For instance, in the parable of the Prodigal Son, the son illustrates repentance, the father illustrates divine love, and the older brother illustrates the hard-heartedness of the Jewish leaders. These sub-ideas differ from the central truth that teaches that there is joy in heaven over a sinner who repents.[1]

The Functions of the Parables

Two types of parables can be identified based on their function. Some parables are designed to help the hearers apprehend very basic truth. These encourage reflection and personal evaluation. Others are designed to conceal truth from those who have rejected the truth that was clearly given. These parables are the mystery parables of the kingdom.

To Encourage Self-Reflection and Personal Evaluation

Jesus used parables to make people think. The primary purpose of these types of parables is to encourage self-evaluation and personal reflection. These parables call upon the hearer to render a personal judgment upon his/her own spiritual condition before God. For instance, in the Parable of the Ten Mina (Luke 11:11-27), one is forced to ask, "Am I like the faithful servants or the unfaithful one?"

To Conceal Truth from the Unresponsive

At times, Jesus spoke in parables to conceal truth from those who did not believe (Matt. 13:10; Mark 4:11). Rather than speaking clearly, Jesus used parables to obscure and hide the truth from the unresponsive. In private he interpreted these parables to his disciples, making plain the meaning. These parables deal with the mysteries of the Kingdom of God (Matt. 13:24).

Everyone could understand the storyline, but only His disciples could fully understand the theological point of the parable. This was because Jesus interpreted the parables privately to the disciples (Matt. 13:10,18). Those not given the interpretations were unable to grasp the spiritual truth that was hidden in these parables.

Guidelines for Interpreting the Parables

- Observe whether the point of the parable is explained in the introduction or conclusion of the parable.

- Observe whether the surrounding literary context or historical occasion explains the purpose of the parable.

- Analyze the storyline before you try to determine the underlying spiritual truth.

- Identify whom the main characters represent (God, believer, unbeliever, the kingdom of God, etc.).

- Distinguish between the primary details that directly relate to and reveal the central spiritual truth, and the secondary details, that are present merely to make the storyline true-to-life.

- Identify the single, central, all-embracing spiritual truth that unifies the entire parable and around which all the details revolve.

- Determine if the main characters suggest additional teachings or truths.

- Observe these cautions when interpreting the parables.

  o Do not seek a spiritual lesson behind every detail in the parable.
  o Do not use the interpretation of a parable as the sole basis for a doctrine.

Summary

A *parable* is a true-to-life story that illustrates a spiritual truth. True parables have a three-part form, *Introduction*, *Body*, and *Explanation*. The introduction may be general, a formal formula, or not present at all. The body is the story itself. It is not an allegory since not all of the details have correspondence in the central truth. The details that do have correspondence are called the *primary details*. The parable may or may not have an explanation. Some different types of explanation are:

- Jesus explains only the central point.
- Jesus explains only the details.
- The occasion helps to explain the central point.

Parables have three important features, *the true-to-life story*, *characters*, and *the central truth*. The story is taken from common life and is easy to grasp. The story normally includes 1-3 main stereotypical characters who often have some parallel in the central truth. Parables illustrate one central truth. The main goal in interpreting the parables is to discover this truth.

Parables differ based on their function. Some parables are intended to encourage self-reflection and personal evaluation. Others, called the Mystery Parables, are designed to conceal truth from the unresponsive.

Use the following guidelines when studying parables.

- Observe the introduction and conclusion
- Observe the surrounding literary context
- Analyze the storyline
- Identify who the main characters represent
- Distinguish between primary and secondary details
- Identify the central truth
- Determine if the main characters suggest additional teachings or truth.

Key Terms

Parable	Similitude	True Parable
Primary Details	Secondary Details	

Review Questions

1. What is a parable?
2. What are the basic parts of the typical form of the parables?
3. In what ways are the parables explained?
4. What are the key features of the parables?
5. What are the two functions of parables and why do they differ?
6. What guidelines should you follow when studying the parables?

References

[1] Klein, William W., Craig L. Blomberg, and Robert L. Hubbard, Jr. *Introduction To Biblical Interpretation*. Dallas: Word Publishing, 1993. pp. 336-340.

Chapter 17

New Testament Epistles
Interpreting the Epistles

Outline

Introduction 186

    Definition of Epistle.. 186

    Extent of Epistles 186

    Two Basic Categories 186

Form of the Epistles 187

    Greco-Roman Form.. 187

    Modified New Testament Form.. 188

    Example.. 189

Features of the Epistles 189

    Logical Features 189

    Rhetorical Features 190

    Practical Features 190

Function of the Epistles 190

    Doctrinal Instruction.. 190

    Ethical Instruction 190

Guidelines for Interpreting the Epistles 191

Summary 192

Review Questions.. 192

References... 192

Learning Objectives

After completing this chapter, you should be able to

- ❑ Define epistle.
- ❑ Explain the typical form of the epistles.
- ❑ Explain the typical functions of the epistles.
- ❑ List the typical features of the epistles.
- ❑ List the guidelines for interpreting the epistles.

Introduction

Definition of Epistle

Epistle
A letter, either personal or private

The English term, **epistle** is derived from the Greek term, ἐπιστολη (*epistolē*) and means a letter. Paul and Peter use the noun *epistolē* with reference to many of the epistles that they wrote (e.g., Rom. 16:22; 1 Cor. 5:9; 2 Cor. 7:8; Col. 4:16; 1 Thess. 5:27; 2 Thess. 2:15; 3:14,17; 2 Pet. 3:1,16). The verb, ἐπιστελλω (*epistellō*), to write a letter, is used in the epistle to the Hebrews (Heb. 13:22).

This word is appropriate because the New Testament epistles consist of both personal letters written to specific individuals or churches and public treatises written as tracts to be circulated among all the churches.

Extent of Epistles

Extent of NT Epistle
- Pauline 13
- General 8

The New Testament epistles consist of the 21 compositions found from Romans through Jude. They are classified as the Pauline Epistles (Romans through Philemon), Non-Pauline Epistles (Hebrews through Jude).

Pauline		Non-Pauline	
Romans	1 Thessalonians	Hebrews	1 John
1 Corinthians	2 Thessalonians	James	2 John
2 Corinthians	1 Timothy	1 Peter	2 John
Galatians	2 Timothy	2 Peter	Jude
Ephesian	Titus		
Philippians	Philemon		
Colossians			

Two Basic Categories

Two Basic Categories
- Private Letters
- Public Letters

Letters and Epistles

In light of the vast number of Greco-Roman papyrus discoveries, scholars often make a distinction between letters and epistles. The letters are non-literary and were intended only for the person to whom they were addressed. They were not written for the public or posterity. The epistles were literary (generally longer, more carefully structured, more artistic in composition, and more didactic) and written as a treatise intended for the public at large and posterity in the future.

Little Distinction in New Testament

This distinction between letter and epistle is helpful in some ways, but it should not be pressed too rigidly because God ultimately intended both the letters and epistles of the New Testament for all Christians.

Most of the New Testament epistles may be classified as public epistles written to a local church as a whole, intended to be read publicly and then circulated among the other churches (e.g., Col. 4:16; 1 Thess. 5:27). Three epistles are more personal letters written to a single individual: Philemon, 2 John and 3 John. But even these had the broader audience of the local church in view (e.g., Philemon 2:2; 2 John 1; 3 John 9). Three other epistles were written to individuals: 1 Timothy, 2 Timothy and Titus. But these also are actually public epistles intended for the local church as a whole (e.g., 1 Tim. 3:14-15; 2 Tim. 4:22).

While it is helpful to distinguish between the more personal letters and public epistles, remember that all Scripture was inspired to instruct all believers throughout the ages (e.g., Rom. 15:4; 2 Tim. 3:16-17).

Form of the Epistles

Just as the structure of modern letters, whether personal or business, is standardized, the structure of Greco-Roman epistles was standardized – so standardized that students were taught the pattern in the ancient schools. By comparing the New Testament epistles with the first-century Greco-Roman epistles, we will be able to recognize what is typical and atypical in the New Testament epistles, that is, the conventional and the creative.

Greco-Roman Form

The typical structure of Greco-Roman epistles consisted of five parts. A partial example of this form is found in Acts 23:26-30.

Salutation	Identification of writer, Identification of recipients Standard greeting ("Greetings and health!")
Personal Opening	Thankfulness for the physical well-being of the recipients
Body of the Epistle	The main content of the letter, which is the major reason for writing to his recipients
Personal Closing	Personal advice or more personal exhortations after the body of the letter
Farewell	The final words of closing

Greco-Roman Form
- Salutation
- Personal Opening
- Body
- Personal Closing
- Farewell

Modified New Testament Form

New Testament Form
- Salutation
- Opening Prayer & Thanks
- Body
- Personal Closing
- Farewell

The New Testament epistles follow the standard structure of the Greco-Romans epistles. However, they also include a few modifications, which were designed for theological or rhetorical impact. Thus, the New Testament epistles have both conventional and creative elements in their form.

Salutation

All of the New Testament epistles (except Hebrews and 1 John) open with an identification of the writer and recipients, and a greeting. The description of the writer and recipients is often expanded. These expansions offer hints about the author's attitudes, the occasion for writing, and the author's purpose for writing. The standard greeting of the secular epistles, "Greetings and health!" is modified for theological and rhetorical reasons to one like, "Grace and peace."

Opening Prayer and Thanksgiving

The personal opening includes prayers and thanksgivings to God that are more theological than an average secular letter. In the secular Greco-Roman epistles, the focus is on the physical well-being of the recipients; while in the New Testament epistles the primary focus is on their spiritual well-being (e.g., 3 John 2). While the opening well-wishes and thanksgivings in the secular letters were considered a common courtesy and more a matter of good form, they are real heartfelt prayers in the New Testament epistles.

Expansions and/or omissions in the opening prayer often hint at the occasion for writing or the author's purpose. For instance, Galatians, an epistle written to address a major theological problem at the church, has no thanksgiving and 1 Thessalonians, an epistle to commend new believers for their faithful endurance, has two (1 Thess. 1:2-10 and 2:13-16).

Main Body of the Epistle

As in typical first-century Greco-Roman epistles, the body of the New Testament epistles develops the author's purpose for the letter as a whole. The body of the epistles generally consists of a balance between doctrinal teaching (facts) and practical exhortations (commands). Often the more doctrinal or didactic material comes first and is followed by the more practical and hortatory material as in Ephesians where the opening chapters are mainly doctrinal (Ephesians 1-3) and final chapters are mainly practical (Ephesians 4-6).

Closing Personal Remarks

The epistles often conclude with personal remarks or instructions about personal issues to specific individuals within the church. These remarks often contain historical information that is helpful in determining the time and place of writing. Examples: Rom. 16:1-24; 1 Cor. 16:5-18; Eph. 6:21-22; Phil. 4:10-19; Col. 4:7-17; 2 Tim. 4:9-18; Titus 3:12-14)

Concluding Farewell

As in secular epistles, New Testament epistles conclude with a personal farewell and greetings from other people to the recipient. The New Testament epistles often also conclude with material unparalleled in the secular epistles, namely, a benediction of spiritual blessings from God and/or a doxology of praise to God.

Example: The Epistle to the Colossians

The structure of the Epistle to the Colossians may be outlined in the following manner, according to the typical form of the Epistles:

Introductory Salutation 1:1-2
Opening Thanksgiving and Prayer 1:3-14
Main Body of the Epistle 1:15-4:6
    Doctrinal Instruction 1:15-2:5
    Practical Instruction 2:6-4:6
Closing Personal Remarks 4:7-17
Concluding Farewell 4:18

Note: It would be permissible for the introductory salutation and the opening thanksgiving and prayer to be summarized into one major point with two sub-points. Likewise, the closing personal remarks and concluding farewell also could be summarized into one major point with two sub-points. However, the outline above is rigidly following the standard Greco-Roman epistle structure.

Features of the Epistles

Logical Features

The genre of epistle is in many ways similar to the modern letter-to-the-editor genre. Epistles tend to be longer than personal letters. They were written for public reading. And they exhibit logical argumentation, especially in the doctrinal sections.

> **Logical Features**
> - Argument
> - Classical Argument Form
> - Old Testament Quotes
> - Logical Connectives
> - Rhetorical Questions

Argument. An argument consists of claims and evidences designed to prove to an audience that some general claim is true. Much of the doctrinal material found in the epistles is in the form of an argument. Mapping the arguments is an important step in understanding the epistles. This mapping involves identifying claims and evidences, and then seeing how claims work together to support broader claims.

Classical Argument Form. Often these arguments include classical argument forms. For instance, in I Corinthians 15:12-20, Paul employs the *Argumentum Ad Absurdum* argument. In this argument, the debater begins by affirming his opponent's position (15:13). He then demonstrates that such a position leads to an absurd conclusion and therefore must be rejected (15:13-19). He ends by affirming an alternative position (15:20).

Old Testament Evidences. The Old Testament is often used to provide evidence or proof of a claim. A good example is the quotation from Genesis 15:6 found in Romans 4:3. Paul's claim is that Abraham gained righteousness by faith. Genesis 15:6 is the historic record that proves this to be so. We must pay special attention to quotations from the Old Testament.

Logical Connectives. The arguments in the epistles consist of groups of paragraphs linked by logical connectives. In this way, the author develops his argument over larger sections. You should carefully observe and consider connectives that link paragraph to paragraph. See Chapter 7 on discourse analysis.

Rhetorical Questions. Paul often uses questions to introduce a new topic or line of reasoning as in Romans 4:1. In such cases, the question provides the topic of discussion and the following paragraphs give the development.

Rhetorical Features

Rhetorical Features
- Parallelism
- Climax
- Paradox

Leland Ryken notes the eloquent rhetorical style of the New Testament epistles.[1] This style, though similar to classical rhetoric and oratory, is unique. Some examples of this style are listed below.

Parallelism. The writers of the epistles, especially Paul, used eloquent styles that at times imitated the parallelisms found in Hebrew poetry. For instance, Paul often parallels faith, hope, and love (1Thess. 1:3 and 1 Cor. 13:13). Understanding of these parallels can be helpful in interpretation.

Climax. Paul often employs a crescendo, increasingly lifting the emotional level of the thought as he completes a section. For example, in 1 Corinthians 3:21-23 Paul begins by discussing the value of leaders in the church and ends by mentioning life and death.

Paradox. Paradox involves two contradictory statements that after contemplation reveal a deeper truth. Paul often expressed himself my means of paradox (2 Cor. 6:8-10).

Practical Features

The practical sections of the epistles are identified by exhortations and commands. Though exhortations are sometimes interspersed within the doctrinal sections, they more often are grouped in a single section that follows the doctrinal section. You should look for a shift from logical discourse to commands and exhortations. A good example is at Romans 12:1. The earlier material is logical statement. The later material is exhortation.

Functions of the Epistles

Functions of Epistles
- To Teach Doctrine
- To Motivate to respond

The basic functions of the New Testament Epistles are two-fold, namely, to teach doctrine and to motivate the readers to respond practically. These two functions are so distinct that commonly the body of the epistle can be divided into two sections, the first doctrinal and the second practical.

Doctrinal Instruction

In general, the doctrinal content of the epistles focuses on the person and work of Jesus Christ. However, the epistles cover a broad range of doctrinal issues. In the early Pauline epistles, the doctrinal issues center on the doctrine of justification. In the Pastoral Epistles, 1-2 Timothy and Titus, the instruction primarily deals with church order.

Task Theology
Theology written to address a specific situation

The theology and teachings found in the epistles were written to address a specific situation and were not intended to be exhaustive treatments on any given doctrine. Therefore, the theology of the epistles is **task theology**; that is, theology written to address a specific situation. Since this is true, the only way to discover the overall teaching of the epistles on a given subject is to correlate all the material on that subject from various epistles. There is no single place in the epistles or in any other part of the Bible that gives an exhaustive treatment of a doctrine.

Ethical Instruction

The epistles are pastoral in nature. That is, the writers wrote in pastoral or shepherding roles. Their intent was not simply to share doctrine, but to change lives. They not only gave doctrinal facts but practical exhortations. The exhortations are both individual and corporate. However, both exhort believers to respond to Christ in heart, word, and action.

Guidelines for Interpreting the Epistles

- Consider the occasion for writing and the author's purpose.
- Look for hints about the occasion in the personal closing of the epistle.
- Study the salutation for hints about the content of the epistle.
- Consider how opening prayers and thanksgivings relate to the occasion and purpose of the epistle
- Consider the overall plan of the epistle.
- Distinguish between the doctrinal and practical sections in the body of the epistle.
- Consider the near context of all passages.
- Map the broader argument and understand all passages within the framework of the argument.
- Note the use of Old Testament materials.
- Correlate the doctrinal teachings of a passage with similar teachings in the other epistles.

Guidelines for Interpretation
- Consider occasion and purpose
- Look for occasion in closing of epistle
- Study salutation
- Consider opening prayer
- Consider the overall plan
- Distinguish between doctrinal and practical
- Consider the near context
- Map the argument
- Note use of Old Testament materials
- Correlate the doctrinal teachings

Summary

An *epistle* is a letter designed for public reading. New Testament epistles have a five-part form, *Salutation, Opening Prayer & Thanksgiving, Body, Personal Closing* and *Farewell*. This form is patterned after the Greco-Roman form but includes several modifications of a theological and rhetorical nature. The body is commonly divided into a doctrinal section and a practical section.

Epistles feature logical arguments with classical argument forms, Old Testament quotations, logical connectives, and rhetorical questions. They also contain many stylistic rhetorical features such as parallelism, climax, and paradox.

The body of the epistles tends to be divided based on two functions. The first section teaches doctrine with an emphasis on the person and work of Jesus Christ. The theology is called, *task theology* since the theology is given to address a specific situation. The second section is designed to motivate the readers to live for Jesus.

Use the following guidelines when studying the epistles.

- Consider the occasion for writing and the author's purpose.
- Look for hints about the occasion in the personal closing of the epistle.
- Study the salutation for hints about the content of the epistle.
- Consider how opening prayers and thanksgivings relate to the occasion and purpose of the epistle
- Consider the overall plan of the epistle.
- Distinguish between the doctrinal and practical sections in the body of the epistle.
- Consider the near context of all passages.
- Map the broader argument and understand all passages within the framework of the argument.
- Note the use of Old Testament materials.
- Correlate the doctrinal teachings of a passage with similar teachings in the other epistles.

Key Terms

Epistle   Task Theology

Review Questions

1. What is an epistle?
2. What is the typical form of New Testament epistles?
3. How is the body of most New Testament epistles divided?
4. What are the key features of the epistles?
5. What are the two functions of the epistles?
6. What guidelines should you follow when studying the epistles?

References

[1]Ryken, LeLand. *The Literature Of The Bible*. Grand Rapids: Zondervan Publishing House, 1976. pp. 317-332.

Chapter 18

Biblical Narrative

Interpreting Old Testament Narratives

Outline

Introduction 194

    What Narrative Is Not 194

    What Narrative Is... 194

Form – The Narrative Plot 194

    Definition of Plot.. 194

    Five-Part Plot Structure 195

    Visual Representation of the Narrative Plot.. 195

    Contextual Levels of Plot Narratives.. 196

Features of the Narrative 196

    General Features 196

        Selectivity 196

        Arrangement.. 197

        Literary Devices 197

    Character Development.. 197

        Characterization.. 197

        Character Roles... 198

        Character Types 198

Function of the Narrative 199

    Theological Function... 199

    Ethical Function.. 199

Guidelines for Interpreting Narratives 199

Summary.. 200

Review Questions... 200

Learning Objectives

After completing this chapter, you should be able to

- ❑ Describe biblical narrative.
- ❑ Explain the five-part plot structure of biblical narrative.
- ❑ List the three contextual levels of narrative plot.
- ❑ Describe the general features of biblical narrative.
- ❑ Discuss character development in biblical narrative.
- ❑ List the two basic functions of biblical narrative.
- ❑ Analyze biblical narratives using the guidelines for interpreting biblical narrative.

Introduction

What Narrative Is Not

Narratives Are Not
• Boring History
• Allegory

Biblical narratives are not boring history lessons nor merely historical accounts of irrelevant past events. Narratives are not allegories with hidden spiritual meanings nor are they merely prophetic typologies foreshadowing the person and work of Christ.

What Narrative Is

Narratives Are
• History of redemption
• Both history and theology
• Ethical stories

Biblical narratives are *prose accounts that dramatically chronicle the unfolding of God's mighty deeds in the history of redemption.* They are historical-rhetorical-theological accounts that have theological and practical significance for the people of God throughout all ages. Biblical narratives contain both history and theology and are designed to teach us about God and his ways. As such they are ethical stories that we are to understand and apply.

Form – The Plot Narrative

Definition of Plot

Plot
The storyline that develops around a central character or important event in a dramatic way

The **plot** is the storyline that develops around a central character or important event in a dramatic way. The plot encompasses a unified sequence of events in the storyline that unfold in a cause-effect sequence, building to a climactic conclusion. The best way for the reader to determine the basic message of a narrative is to carefully study the plot, especially the interplay of opponents and the interaction between major and minor characters.

Five-Part Plot Structure

The plot includes five basic elements, *Prologue, Presentation of the Conflict, Development of the Plot, Resolution of the Problem,* and *Epilogue.*

Prologue

The typical narrative opens with an introduction of the main character (protagonist) and identification of the setting. It prepares the reader for the rest of the narrative by introducing important information.

Presentation of Conflict

The plot formally begins when the main character is presented with a conflict or problem. It may be a temptation, attack from an antagonist, or a trial or challenge from God to trust or obey Him in an extraordinary manner.

Development of the Plot

In the development of the plot, the main character takes actions to resolve the problem. The plot thickens and tension mounts. Complications may arise or a sub-plot may develop. The actions of some of the characters may pave the way toward resolving the problem or they may make it more difficult.

Resolution of the Problem

The resolution of the problem is the dramatic turning point in the narrative. Sometimes the main character solves the problem through his wisdom, faith or obedience to God. Sometimes, God is the hero who intervenes either directly or indirectly through His word (revelation) or work (deliverance). At times, the main character fails and sins. He then suffers the natural consequences of sin or is directly disciplined or judged by God.

Epilogue

The typical narrative will conclude with a brief epilogue that brings closure to the episode and prepares the way for the next episode. The epilogue is sometimes quite short and does not always appear.

Visual Representation of the Narrative Plot

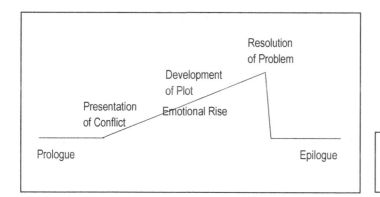

Figure 18.1
Visual Representation of the Narrative Plot

Elements of the Plot
- Prologue
- Presentation of Conflict
- Development of Plot
- Resolution of Problem
- Epilogue

Prologue
Introduction of main character and identification of the setting

Presentation of Conflict
Main character presented with a temptation, trial, or challenge

Development of the Plot
Attempts to resolve problem with complications added

Resolution of the Problem
Dramatic turning point as the problem is resolved

Epilogue
Brings closure to the episode and prepares the way for the next episode

Contextual Levels of the Narrative Plot

Contextual Levels of Plot
- Individual Episode
- Complete Narrative Story
- Overall Redemptive Program

Plot can function at three levels: the *individual narrative episode*, the *complete narrative story* or the *overall redemptive program*.

Individual Narrative Episode

Individual Episode
Smallest literary unit in which the narrative plot and storyline operates

The smallest literary unit in which the narrative plot and storyline operates is the individual narrative episode. The account of Abraham's journey to Egypt (Gen. 12:10-20) is an example of an individual narrative episode.

Complete Narrative Story

Complete Narrative Story
Larger literary unit composed of many episodes

In most cases, an individual episode is part of a larger literary unit composed of many episodes called the complete narrative story. For example, the complete Abraham Narrative (Gen. 12:1-25:11) is composed of about 20 individual episodes (e.g., 12:1-9, 10-20, 13:1-18; etc.). Just as an individual episode has a basic plot or storyline, the complete story also has a basic five-part plot, only on a much larger scale.

Ultimately, each individual episode must be viewed in the light of its place in the complete overall story and analyzed in the light of its contribution to the dramatic unfolding of this bigger picture. For example, Abraham's risk in permitting Sarah to be given to Pharaoh and the importance of God's deliverance of Sarah (Gen. 12:10-20) can only be fully appreciated in the light of God's promise to Abraham of offspring (Gen. 12:1-9).

Overall Redemptive Program

Overall Redemptive Program
Overall history of redemption that unfolds throughout the Scriptures

Ultimately, each complete narrative story must be viewed in the light of its place in and contribution to the overall history of redemption that unfolds throughout the Scriptures. For example, the complete Abraham Narrative (Gen. 12-25) cannot be fully understood apart from its role in God's plan to raise up Israel as the channel of universal redemptive blessings to the apostate nations.

Features of Narrative

General Features

Selectivity

Selectivity
Limiting content to what is significant to the plot.

Biblical narrative is short and compact most likely because the stories were originally communicated orally. They purposefully exclude what is not necessary and include only what develops the narrative plot. We call this **selectivity**. Biblical authors selectively limited their narrative accounts to those events that were theologically significant. Because everything in the narrative is either theologically significant or relates to the development of the plot, we should always be asking, "Why did the narrator include this particular detail in the narrative?"

For example, we are told very little about what David wore when he encountered Goliath but the author describes the armor of Goliath in great detail to express the prowess of the enemy (1 Sam. 17:4-7) and ultimately to impress the reader with the grandeur of God's deliverance.

Arrangement

While most narratives are arranged in chronological order, some are arranged in a more topical order to emphasize a central theological theme rather than merely retracing the mere order of events. Without compromising the historicity of their accounts, narrators often artistically arrange material into chiastic structures to highlight the turning point of an episode, parallel actions or reversals of fortune.

For example, the narrative about David and Goliath is told in basic chronological order except for a little information about David's family that is introduced at the point where David enters the story (1 Sam 17:12-15).

> **Arrangement**
> - Generally chronological
> - Sometimes
> - Topical
> - Chiastic

Literary Devices

Word Plays. Biblical narrators often emphasize the main point or major theme of a narrative by repeating key words or creating word plays in the Hebrew. This is especially true with the names of places. For example, in Judges 15:14-17 Samson killed a thousand Philistines with a jawbone at Lehi, which means jawbone. Many places in the Bible get their names from the events that took place there.

Sarcasm and Ridicule. Narrators often employ irony, sarcasm and ridicule to cast a shadow on certain characters or actions in an episode. Note how Goliath ridicules David in 1 Samuel 17:43-44.

Dialogue. Dialogue is limited in biblical narratives. When it is used, it is significant. Narrators often make strategic use of dialogue to emphasize important theological content or reveal the motivation of a character's actions. For instance, in the story of David and Goliath (1 Samuel 17), the dialogue reveals David's trust in God (17:45-47) and Goliath's unbelief and pride (17:43-44).

Poetry. Hebrew poetry was more spontaneous than Western poetry and therefore is sometimes found within narrative. It is used to highlight an especially important theological statement (e.g., Gen. 12:2-3; Lev. 10:3). At times, complete poems are included as songs of praise (e.g., Exodus 15:1-18).

Dramatic Reversal. Narrators often emphasize striking and dramatic reversals in the actions or fate of the characters, from the beginning to the end of the episode. Often these reversals are the results of divine actions as in the destruction of Pharaoh's army in Exodus 14:23-28.

> **Literary Devices**
> - Word Plays
> - Sarcasm & Ridicule
> - Dialogue
> - Poetry
> - Dramatic Reversal

Character Development

Characterization

Biblical narrators usually do not describe the physical appearance or identify the nationality, lineage or background of the characters. However, when the narrator does provide this, it is usually important.

Biblical narrators rarely articulate the motives or thoughts of the characters. These are left to the reader to infer through the characters' actions. However, when they are provided, they are crucial to the narrative.

Narrators do not usually evaluate the moral character of the actors. Their character is revealed by their actions and words. However, when a narrator does evaluate this, it is very important.

Character Roles

Character Roles
• Protagonist
• Antagonist
• Agent

The major characters in the narrative play one of three roles: *protagonist*, *antagonist*, or *agents*. It is important to identify these roles to properly understand the narrative. Each is described below.

The Protagonist

Protagonist
Main character or hero of the narrative

This is the main character or hero of the narrative. It may be a single individual (e.g., Abraham) or an entire group (e.g., Israel). The antagonist usually confronts the protagonist with a problem. The plot develops around the protagonist's success or failure in solving the problem.

The Antagonist

Antagonist
Enemy of the protagonist and the character who often causes the problem

This is the enemy of the protagonist and the character who often causes the problem in the narrative plot. The antagonist may be an individual, an entire group, or an inanimate problem. The antagonist serves as the foil against which the protagonist responds.

The Agents

Agents
Help to thwart the protagonist or antagonist

These characters function in the background of the narrative. The agent is involved in the action of the narrative, but in a secondary role, helping to thwart or advance the cause of the protagonist or antagonist.

Character Types

Character Types
• Round Character
• Flat Character
• Non-Character

Character types relate to the personality of the characters. Some characters are complex and it is difficult to predict their actions. Others characters are stereotypes and act in very predictable ways. We will identify three types of characters: *round*, *flat*, and *non-characters*.

The Round Character

Round Character
Multidimensional, complex, unpredictable

A round character is multidimensional and has many traits, in contrast to a flat character that is one-dimensional. The narrator not only recounts the round character's actions and dialogue, but also relates to us his secret inner thoughts and motives. A round character seems real because he or she is complex. The protagonist is usually a round character. Normally, the theological and application points of the narrative revolve around round characters.

The Flat Character

Flat Character
One-dimensional, predictable

A flat character is one-dimensional because the narrator focuses on only one trait crucial to the plot. Such characters are predictable and consistent in their actions. You can almost guess what they will do next. While the narrator describes the flat characters actions and words, the narrator almost never reveals his inner thoughts, emotions or motives. Frequently, flat characters in the narrative function as foils to or against whom the round characters (main character or protagonist) respond and react.

The Non-Character

Non-Character
No personality, appears to move the story along

The non-character is presented with no personality to speak of and appears merely to perform an action that moves the story along. The descriptions of such characters are minimal. They may appear in the narrative momentarily and then fade into the background or they may be present in the narrative the whole time but far in the background.

Functions of the Narrative

Narrative serves two functions, to teach us about God, the *theological function*, and to teach us about right and wrong, *the ethical function*. The most important principle to remember about narrative is that its functions are *fulfilled implicitly*. We rarely find either theological discourse or ethical instruction given directly. Instead we are given stories. From these stories we are expected to learn about God as we see him work and to learn about our obligations to him as we see individuals' choices and the consequences.

Functions of Narrative
- Theological
- Ethical
- Fulfilled Implicitly

The Theological Function

Biblical narratives are not merely historical in nature. They have a theological purpose to teach us about the nature and dealings of God. In this role, we learn about God through his past workings in history.

Unlike many other genres that give explicit teachings about God and his ways, narrative normally reveals doctrine implicitly. We learn about God from observing what he does and how he is described.

Theological
Implicitly teaches about the nature and dealings of God through history.

The Ethical Function

While Biblical narratives have a theological function, they also have an ethical function, that is, they are didactic discourses that offer us lessons in faith and obedience to God (Rom. 15:4).

While they do not contain commands or promises addressed directly to us, they teach by means of positive and negative examples (1 Cor. 10:6, 11). Biblical narratives are relevant to the people of God of all ages because they relate timeless, eternal, unchanging truth about God, man and our basic relationship with God.

Ethical
Implicitly offers lessons in faith and obedience by example

Guidelines for Interpreting Narratives

- Chart the plot of the individual episode.
- Identify the protagonist, antagonist, and agents in the narrative.
- Identify the character type of each major character.
- Consider the selectivity in the descriptions of characters, use of dialogue, etc.
- Identify the arrangement of the story and look for topical and chiastic features.
- Identify special literary devices such as word play, dialogue, etc.
- Identify the place of the episode in the complete narrative story.
- Consider what the story teaches about God.
- Consider what the story teaches about a proper response to God.

Guidelines for Interpretation
- Chart the plot
- Identify the protagonist, antagonist, and agents
- Identify the character type of each character.
- Consider selectivity
- Identify the arrangement
- Identify special literary devices
- Identify place of episode in the complete narrative
- Consider what the story teaches about God
- Consider what the story teaches about a proper response to God

Summary

Biblical narrative gives us a history of redemption and is both theological and ethical. The best way to study a narrative is to analyze its five-part plot structure consisting of *Prologue, Presentation of Conflict, Development of Plot, Resolution of Problem,* and *Epilogue.* The plot exists on three contextual levels, *the Individual Episode, the Complete Narrative Story,* and *the Overall Redemptive Program.*

Narratives include several general features, including *selectivity, arrangement,* and the following *literary devices: word plays, sarcasm and ridicule, dialogue, poetry, and dramatic reversal.* The most important feature of narrative is character development. We must determine who is the *protagonist, antagonist,* and who are the *agents.*

Biblical narrative has two main functions. The *doctrinal* function is designed to teach us about God and his ways. The *ethical* function is designed to teach us about moral values. Both functions are developed implicitly in the stories. The stories are examples from which we can draw universal principles.

Use the following guidelines when studying the narratives.

- Chart the plot of the individual episode.
- Identify the protagonist, antagonist, and agents in the narrative.
- Identify the character type of each major character.
- Consider the selectivity in the descriptions of characters, use of dialogue, etc.
- Identify the arrangement of the story and look for topical and chiastic features.
- Identify special literary devices such as word play, dialogue, etc.
- Identify the place of the episode in the complete narrative story.
- Consider what the story teaches about God.
- Consider what the story teaches about a proper response to God.

Key Terms

Biblical Narrative	Plot	Prologue
Epilogue	Episode	Complete Narrative Story
Selectivity	Protagonist	Antagonist
Round Character	Flat Character	Non-character

Review Questions

1. What is the basic nature of biblical narrative?
2. What is meant by plot?
3. What is the five-part plot structure of narrative and what does each part do?
4. What are the three contextual levels of the narrative plot?
5. Why is selectivity important when analyzing a narrative?
6. In what ways might a narrative be arranged?
7. What are the key literary devices used in biblical narrative?
8. What are the three roles of major characters in a narrative?
9. What are the three types of characters in a narrative?
10. What are the two functions of narrative and how are they developed?
11. What are the guidelines for interpreting narratives?

Chapter 19

Biblical Law
Interpreting Law Codes

Outline

Introduction 202

Two Basic Forms 202

    Apodictic Law Form 202

    Casuistic Law Form 203

Features of Mosaic Law Codes 203

    Correspondence Explained 203

    Correspondence in Exodus 20-23 204

    Correspondence in Deuteronomy 5-26 204

Functions of Law 204

    Function of Apodictic Laws 205

    Functions of Casuistic Laws 205

Guidelines for Interpreting Law Codes 207

Summary 208

Review Questions 208

Learning Objectives

After completing this chapter, you should be able to

- ❑ Describe the two forms of biblical law.
- ❑ Show how the Old Testament case laws correspond to the Ten Commandments.
- ❑ Explain the function of apodictic laws in the Bible.
- ❑ Explain the function of case laws in the Bible.
- ❑ Discuss the degree to which case laws in the Bible can be applied to the Christian.
- ❑ Analyze biblical laws using the guidelines for interpreting biblical law.

Introduction

The literary genre known as Biblical law encompasses the many commandments, prohibitions and case laws found in Scriptures. The genre of Biblical law not only includes the Old Testament commands and prohibitions, but also the New Testament commands and prohibitions. In the Old Testament, this genre is composed of the material that constitutes the Law of Moses while in the New Testament it is composed of the material that constitutes the Law of Christ (e.g., 1 Cor. 9:21; Gal. 6:2).

Two Basic Forms

Two Basic Forms
- Apodictic
- Casuistic

There are two basic forms of Biblical law, namely, the *apodictic* and the *casuistic* law forms. It is both important and helpful to distinguish these and to understand the differences between these two forms of biblical law.

Apodictic Law Form

Apodictic Law Form
Law form that is characterized by direct commandments and prohibitions

The term, **apodictic** means direct commandment and it refers to the law form that is characterized by direct commandments and prohibitions. The apodictic form is generally introduced with the words, "You shall..." when it is a direct command or with the words "You shall not..." when it is a direct prohibition.

The best-known examples of apodictic law in the Old Testament are the Ten Commandments (Exod. 20:1-17; Deut. 5:6-21). There are also other apodictic laws in the Old Testament outside of the Ten Commandments (e.g., Gen. 2:16-17; 9:4-5; Lev. 18:7-24; 19:11-19). Apodictic forms appear in the New Testament also (e.g., Eph. 4:2-3; 4:25-5:2; Col. 3:5-10; 1 Thess. 5:16-22).

Casuistic Law Form

The term, **casuistic** refers to legal case laws, legislation that deals with specific legal cases. The Biblical case laws are similar to the legal case laws that our courts and lawyers appeal to for legal counsel and precedents. The case laws are usually introduced by the conditional term, "If..." or the circumstantial term, "When...". The standard form of the case laws is, "If such-and-such happens, then do such-and-such" or "When someone does this, then do this." Casuistic commands provide practical instructions about how to deal with specific situations as they arise in everyday life.

The most important case laws in the Old Testament appear in Exodus 21-23 and Deuteronomy 12-26. Case law forms also occur elsewhere in the Old Testament (e.g., Lev. 12:1-15:33; 19:20-25). Casuistic forms also appear in the New Testament in commands that provide instructions about how to deal with specific situations (e.g., Matt. 18:15-20; 1 Cor. 7:12-16; 7:36-40; 1 John 5:16).

> **Casuistic Law Form**
> Legislation that deals with specific legal cases

The Features of the Mosaic Law Codes

Correspondence between Apodictic and Casuistic Laws

Correspondence Explained

There are two basic law codes in the Old Testament, each of which is composed of apodictic and casuistic laws: the original Mosaic Law (Exod. 20-23) and the Law given to the second generation (Deut. 5-26). In each case, the apodictic commandments of the Decalogue are given first (Exod. 20:1-17; Deut. 5:6-21) and the casuistic instructions are given afterwards (Exod. 21-23; Deut. 6-26).

As several scholars have shown (e.g. Stephen Kaufmann, Walter Kaiser), each case law is a specific application of one of the commandments in the Decalogue and can be classified under one of the Ten Commandments. As Moses explained, the case laws were detailed explanations of how the apodictic laws of the Ten Commandments should be applied in everyday real-life situations in ancient Israel (Exod. 20:18-21; 24:3-4; Deut. 5:22-33).

This striking correspondence between apodictic commandments and casuistic application instructions is presented in the material below.

> **Correspondence between Types of Law**
> In Mosaic Law case laws are related to and paralleled with the Ten Commandments

204

Correspondence in Exodus 20-23

The law code originally delivered to Moses on Sinai was composed of two sections, namely, the apodictic Ten Commandments (Exod. 20:1-17) and the casuistic applications in the Book of the Covenant (Exod. 21:1-23:19). The case laws explained how the Decalogue applied to everyday life situations in ancient Israel (Exod. 20:18-21; 24:3-4). The chart that follows displays the correlation between the Decalogue and the case laws that follow.

Apodictic	Command	Central Theme	Case-Laws
20:2	(Prologue)	Deliverance from Slavery	21:2-11; 22:21
20:3	1	Exclusive Worship of YHWH	23:13
20:4-6	2	Prohibition of Idolatry	22:20
20:7	3	Name of YHWH	23:14-19
20:8-11	4	Sabbath-Keeping	23:10-12
20:12	5	Honoring Parents	21:15,17
20:13	6	Murder	21:12-15
20:14	7	Adultery	22:16-19
20:15	8	Theft	22:1-15
20:16	9	False Charges	23:1-9
20:17	10	Covetousness	22:22-27

Correspondence in Deuteronomy 5-26

When the second generation was about to enter Canaan, Moses wrote Deuteronomy (second law) in which he reiterated the law code, providing new case laws to govern their new life in Canaan. Like the original Law, it was composed of two sections, namely the apodictic Ten Commandments (Deut. 5:6-21) and the casuistic applications (Deut. 6:1-26:15). Moses explained that the case laws were explanations of how the Decalogue applied to the life of ancient Israel (Deut. 5:22-33). The chart below displays the precise correlation between the general principles in the Decalogue and the specific stipulations.

Apodictic	Command	Central Theme	Case-Laws
5:6	Prologue	YHWH is Savior and Lord	6:1-11:32
5:7	1	Exclusive Worship of YHWH	12:1-32
5:8-10	2	Prohibition of Idolatry	13:1-18
5:11	3	Name of YHWH	14:1-21
5:12-15	4	Sabbath-Keeping	14:22-16:17
5:16	5	Honoring Authority	16:18-18:22
5:17	6	Murder	19:1-22:12
5:18	7	Adultery	22:13-23:14
5:19	8	Theft	23:15-24:7
5:20	9	False Charges	24:8-16
5:21	10	Covetousness	24:17-26:15

The order of the case laws follows the exact order of the apodictic laws in the Decalogue. This supports the fact that the case laws in Deuteronomy 6-26 are application instructions of each of the Ten Commandments in Deuteronomy 5.

Functions of Law

Apodictic laws and casuistic laws differ in their functions. Apodictic laws provide the broad general principles and timeless truths upon which the case laws reside. The case laws are related to specific situations and provide examples of applying the general apodictic laws. The case laws are not exhaustive and are temporary in nature.

The Function of Apodictic Law

Provide General Principles

Function of Apodictic Laws
- Provide general principles
- Provide timeless, eternal standards

The purpose of apodictic commands is to provide general principles that should govern all basic areas in the life of the people of God. In contrast to casuistic laws that are culturally and situationally conditioned, apodictic commands and prohibitions are not culturally conditioned nor situationally limited. In other words, the apodictic commands and prohibitions are relevant in all cultures, not just in the culture of ancient Israel. For example, the prohibition "Do not murder" is not culturally conditioned: it is relevant in any culture and society.

Provide Timeless, Eternal Standards

In contrast to casuistic laws that deal with specific situations at a specific time, apodictic commands provide timeless, eternal, general standards of conduct that are relevant at all times for the people of God. The Hebrew verb forms used in the Ten Commandments emphasize their universal nature. They may be translated, "You shall always..." and the prohibitions may be translated, "You shall never...". For example, the prohibition, "Do not murder" is not limited to one historical period; it is a timeless eternal principle. The timelessness of the Ten Commandments is demonstrated by the fact that they are all restated in the New Testament. (Note: The Sabbath command is modified to commemorate the resurrection of Christ).

The Function of Casuistic Law

Apply Apodictic Law to Specific Situations

Function of Case Laws
- Apply apodictic laws to specific situations
- Provide specific instruction and concrete examples
- Not exhaustive
- Provide precedents for future judgment
- Temporary in nature

While the apodictic laws legislated the general principles governing the life of the people of God, casuistic laws were designed to apply the general apodictic laws to specific situations in everyday life.

For example, the apodictic laws of Exodus 20 (Ten Commandments) are explained and applied to everyday life situations in the casuistic commands in Exodus 21-23 (Book of the Covenant). Likewise, the apodictic laws of Deuteronomy 5 (Ten Commandments) are explained and applied to everyday life situations in the casuistic commands in Deuteronomy 6-26 (Laws of Deuteronomy).

Provide Specific Instructions and Concrete Examples

The Old Testament case laws provided specific instructions and concrete examples of how the more general apodictic laws of the Ten Commandments should be applied to everyday situations in the life of ancient Israel.

For example, Moses applied the apodictic command, "Do not murder" (Deut. 5:17) to a variety of everyday situations in ancient Israel, explaining what did and did not constitute murder (Deut. 19:1-22:12). For instance, in the case laws, Moses explained that neither capital punishment nor holy war was murder (Deut. 20:1-20; 21:18-23).

Not Exhaustive

Biblical case laws were not intended to be exhaustive, nor were they designed to cover every situation which might hypothetically occur; rather, they deal with the common everyday real-life situations which were occurring or would be certain to occur in the near future. The case laws in Deuteronomy were designed to deal with the specific historical situations that Israel would face when it entered the land of Canaan in the Late Bronze Age (e.g., Deut. 6:1; 18:9; 19:1).

Provide Precedents for Future Judgments

While the Biblical case laws are not designed to be exhaustive, they were designed to provide precedents that illustrate the way in which the general principle could and should be applied to other situations. In this sense, the Biblical case laws are similar to modern legal case laws which provide legal rulings on specific situations that have arisen: these judgments provide precedents for future cases.

For example, when Ezra was faced with a new situation that was not directly addressed in Scripture, he studied the case laws to find precedence and principles to govern his actions (Ezra 9:1-10:44). Likewise, when modern Christians face new situations that are not directly addressed in Scripture, we should study Biblical case laws to discern the Biblical principles that can guide our actions.

Temporary in Nature

Since the Old Testament case laws were historical, cultural applications for the life of ancient Israel, they were culturally conditioned and temporary in authority. In contrast to the verb forms for apodictic law, the Hebrew verb forms for casuistic law indicates that they were temporally and culturally limited to a specific situation at a specific time.

This limitation of the Old Testament case laws is seen in the fact that their authority was limited to ancient Israel under the Mosaic Covenant. They do not directly carry over into the New Covenant. New Testament believers are not under the authority of Old Testament case law. However, they still provide relevant principles for the life of the people of God (e.g., Deut. 25:4; 1 Cor. 9:9-10).

Guidelines for Interpreting Laws

- Determine if the law is apodictic or casuistic in form.
- For apodictic laws:
  - Identify the general principle taught in the law.
  - Identify the timeless, eternal standards of conduct taught in the law.
  - Determine if the law is restated in the New Testament.
  - Apply the law within the framework of the New Testament covenant.
- For casuistic laws:
  - Identify the apodictic law that underlies the case law.
  - Identify the relationships between the apodictic and case laws.
  - Identify the parallels between the situation the case law addresses and your modern situation.
  - Identify the timeless, eternal standards of conduct inherent in the law.
  - Determine how the underlying standards can be used to create relevant modern case laws.

Guidelines for Interpretation
- Determine if the law is apodictic or casuistic in form.

For apodictic laws:
- Identify the general principle
- Identify the timeless, eternal standards
- Determine if restated in the New Testament.
- Apply within framework of the New Testament

For casuistic laws:
- Identify underlying apodictic law
- Identify the relationships to apodictic
- Identify the parallels between modern and original situation
- Identify the timeless, eternal standards
- Determine how the underlying standards can be used to create relevant modern case laws

Summary

Biblical law exists in two forms, *apodictic* and *casuistic* laws. The apodictic laws are direct commands and prohibitions that normally are introduced with words such as, "You shall..." or "You shall not...". The casuistic laws are case laws that apply the general apodictic laws to specific situations. They normally are in the form, "If... then" or "When... then...".

The Ten Commandments are the major apodictic laws of the Old Testament. In Exodus 21-22 and Deuteronomy 5-26 the related case laws are organized to reveal their relationship to the underlying Ten Commandments.

The apodictic laws provide general principles to govern all the basic areas in life of the people of God. They include direct timeless, eternal principles that generally can be applied directly to us. On the other hand, the case laws addressed specific situations in Israel's history and therefore are normally not directly applicable to us. They do provide examples and precedents on how to apply the apodictic laws. Though they are temporary and not exhaustive, they are helpful as models and examples.

Use the following guidelines when studying biblical laws.

- Determine if the law is apodictic or casuistic in form.
- For apodictic laws:
  - Identify the general principle taught in the law.
  - Identify the timeless, eternal standards of conduct taught in the law.
  - Determine if the law is restated in the New Testament.
  - Apply the law within the framework of the New Testament covenant.
- For casuistic laws:
  - Identify the apodictic law that underlies the case law.
  - Identify the relationships between the apodictic and case laws.
  - Identify the parallels between the situation the case law addresses and your modern situation.
  - Identify the timeless, eternal standards of conduct inherent in the law.
  - Determine how the underlying standards can be used to create relevant modern case laws.

Key Terms

Apodictic Law   Casuistic Law

Review Questions

1. What are the two forms of biblical law?
2. How do the two forms of law relate to each other?
3. How are the case laws found in Exodus and Deuteronomy related to the Ten Commandments?
4. What are the functions of the two types of biblical laws?
5. To what degree are case laws applicable to the Christian?
6. What guidelines should you follow when studying biblical laws?

Chapter 20

Hebrew Poetry

Outline

Introduction 210

    What is Hebrew Poetry? 210

    Where is Hebrew Poetry Used? 210

Basic Forms of Hebrew Poetry 210

    Poetic Parallelism 210

        Synonymous Parallelism 211

        Antithetical Parallelism 211

        Emblematic Parallelism 211

        Synthetic Parallelism 212

        Incomplete Parallelism 212

        External Parallelism 212

    Colon – Line Groupings 213

        Bicolon 213

        Tricolon 213

        Quatracolon 213

        Monocolon 214

    Stanzas 214

Special Features of Hebrew Poetry 215

Basic Function of Hebrew Poetry 217

    Lyric Poetry 217

    Didactic Poetry 217

Guidelines for Interpreting Hebrew Poetry 218

Summary 219

Review Questions 220

References 220

Learning Objectives

After completing this chapter, you should be able to

- ❑ Explain parallelism in Hebrew poetry.
- ❑ List the four major types of parallelisms.
- ❑ Explain the use of colon in Hebrew poetry.
- ❑ List the four major types of cola.
- ❑ Explain the meaning of stanza.
- ❑ Identify the seven important features of Hebrew poetry.
- ❑ Explain the two basic functions of Hebrew poetry.

Introduction

What is Biblical Hebrew Poetry?

Poetic Parallelisms
Parallels of thought and structure where one line of poetry has ideas that parallel another line

Biblical Hebrew poetry is a poetic form that is characterized by parallel structures, concise language, and figures of speech. Like most western poetry, Hebrew poetry employs a wealth of figures of speech and is highly structured. Unlike most western poetry, Hebrew poetry rarely employs parallels of sound, but rather employs parallels of thought and structure, called **poetic parallelisms**.

Colon
A set of poetic lines working together to form a parallelism

Notice the parallels of thought in the following lines of poetry. Line two parallels line one and line four parallels line three. Each set of parallel lines is called a **colon** or **stiche**. Thus, in the example there are two cola, each having two lines.

> My son, pay attention to what I say;
> Listen closely to my words,
> Do not let them out of your sight,
> Keep them within your heart.
>
> Proverbs 4:20-21

Where is Biblical Hebrew Poetry Used?

Found in:
- The Poetic Books
- The Prophetic Books
- Some in OT Narratives
- Some in New Testament

Biblical Hebrew poetry occurs throughout Psalms, Proverbs, Job, Song of Songs, Lamentations and parts of Ecclesiastes. These are known as the poetic books. The Hebrew prophets also employed poetic forms throughout their prophetic speeches. The prophetic books are composed largely of poetic material. Poetry also occurs within some Old Testament narratives (e.g., Gen. 2:23; Exod. 15:1-18). Poetry even occurs in the New Testament (e.g., Luke 1:46-55; 68-79).

Basic Forms of Hebrew Poetry

Poetic Parallelism

Types of Parallelism
- Synonymous
- Antithetical
- Emblematic
- Synthetic

As mentioned above, the most predominant structures in Hebrew poetry are structured parallelisms. In any parallelism, all the lines are paralleled. However, that does not mean that all the lines express the same thought. The parallel thoughts can also be contrasts, illustrations, or expansions of the first thought. Thus, there are four basic types of parallelism, *synonymous, antithetical, emblematic,* and *synthetic.*

At times the parallelisms are not perfect. Some ideas found in the first line of the colon are not found in the remaining lines or they are not paralleled perfectly. This is called *incomplete parallelism.*

Synonymous Parallelism

When the thought in the first line of a colon is paralleled in the other lines of the colon using different but synonymous words, the parallelism is said to be **synonymous**. Most synonymous cola are two lines long. The following cola are examples of synonymous parallelism.

> Israel came to Egypt;
> Jacob sojourned in the land of Ham
>
> Psalm 105:23
>
> Wisdom shouts in the street,
> She lifts her voice in the square.
>
> Proverbs 1:20

Synonymous Parallelism
The lines in the colon say the same thing in different words

For additional examples see Job 11:7; Psalm 35:1; 35:14; Proverbs 5:1.

Antithetical Parallelism

When the thought in the first line of a colon is contrasted by an opposite idea in a second line, the parallelism is said to be **antithetical**. The second line is often, but not always, introduced by the conjunction, "But . . .". Most antithetical cola are two lines long. The following are examples of antithetical parallelism.

> In the morning it flourishes and is renewed;
> In the evening it fades and withers.
>
> Psalm 90:6
>
> A wise son makes glad his father;
> But a foolish son causes grief for his mother.
>
> Proverbs 10:1

Antithetical Parallelism
The second line of a colon is a paralleled but contrasting thought

For additional examples see Psalm 37:17; 145:20; Proverbs 10:7; 16:9.

Emblematic Parallelism

When the thought in one line of a colon is illustrated by a simile or metaphor in the other line, the parallelism is said to be **emblematic**. The illustration line is usually introduced by the comparative, "As.." and the other line is introduced with "So..". Most emblematic cola are two lines long. The following are examples of emblematic parallelism.

> *As* a father cares for his children,
> *So* the Lord cares for those who fear Him.
>
> Psalm 103:13
>
> *As* a dog returns to its vomit,
> *So* a fool repeats his folly.
>
> Proverbs 26:11

Emblematic Parallelism
One line of a colon is a figurative illustration of the thought of the other line

For additional examples see Psalm. 42:1; 103:11; Proverbs 26:21; 28:15.

Synthetic Parallelism

When the thought in one line of a colon is expanded, or explained in the additional lines of the colon, the parallelism is said to be **synthetic**. Synthetic cola are often more than two lines long. The following is an example of synthetic parallelism. While the first few words of the sentence are not paralleled, the remaining words are paralleled with each line adding something to the thought.

> Blessed is the man who
> does not walk in the counsel of the wicked,
> nor stand in the path of sinners,
> nor sit in the seat of scoffers.
>
> Psalm 1:1

For additional examples see Psalm. 14:2; 23:5; 143:10

Parallelism Often Incomplete

When part of the thought found in the first line of the colon is not paralleled in the additional lines, the parallelism is said to be **incomplete**. Often the subject of the first line is not repeated in the remaining lines as in Psalm 132:2. At times both the subject and the verb are missing as in Psalm 132:4. At times the poet, possibly for rhythmic reasons, will fill in this incomplete part with some non-paralleled thought. This is called **compensation**. So, you will find both incomplete cola with no compensation and incomplete cola with compensation. The following are examples of incomplete cola. The first has an intentional gap while the second example compensates for dropping the first clause by expanding the second clause.

> I will allow no sleep to my eyes,
> no slumber to my eyelids.
>
> Psalm 132:4

> Blessed is the man who fears the Lord
> Who finds great delight in his commands.
>
> Psalm 112:1

For additional examples see Psalm 24:1; 22:20; 49:5

External Parallelism

External parallelism occurs when multiple cola are paralleled. In Isaiah 1.3 two synthetic parallelism form an external antithetical parallelism.

> An ox knows its owner,
> And a donkey its master's manger,
> But Israel does not know,
> My people do not understand."

Often every other line is paralleled as in Habakkuk 1.2.

> How long, O LORD, will I call for help,
> And You will not hear?
> I cry out to You, "Violence!"
> Yet You do not save.

Colon – Line Groupings

As mentioned above, a set of parallel poetic lines is called a colon. Most commonly a colon contains two lines. However, a colon can contain any number of lines of parallel thought. The more lines in the colon, the more uncommon it is. Most cola are between two and four lines. To these we give the names, *bicolon, tricolon,* and *quatracolon*. Sometimes the poet employs an isolated line to introduce or conclude a section. This is called a *monocolon*.

Types of Colon
- Bicolon
- Tricolon
- Quatracolon
- Monocolon

Bicolon

A bicolon consists of two lines of poetry that express parallel ideas. The bicolon is most frequent. The following six lines of poetry consist of three bicola. A blank line has been added between each bicolon to make them easier to see.

Bicolon
Two parallel lines of poetry that express parallel ideas

> Praise the LORD, O my soul,
> All my innermost being, praise His holy name.
>
> Praise the LORD, O my soul,
> And forget not any of His benefits.
>
> He forgives all your sins.
> And heals all your diseases.

Psalm 103:1-3

For additional examples see Psalm. 14:2; 23:5; 143:10

Tricolon

The tricolon consists of three lines of poetry that express parallel ideas. The following are examples of tricola.

Tricolon
Three parallel lines of poetry that express parallel ideas

> He made the earth by His power,
> He set up the world by His wisdom
> He extended the heavens by His skill.

Jeremiah 10:12

> All her images shall be beaten to pieces,
> All her earnings shall be burned with fire,
> All her idols I will lay waste.

Micah 1:7

For additional examples see Psalm 2:2; 22:23

Quatracolon

The quatracolon includes four parallel lines. This is unusual and is only used to express grand degrees of emotion.

Quatracolon
Four parallel lines of poetry that express parallel ideas

> I have come into my garden, my sister, my bride,
> I have gathered my myrrh with my spice,
> I have eaten my honeycomb and my honey,
> I have drunk my wine and my milk.

Song Sol. 5:1

For additional examples see Psalm 59:1,2; Isaiah 42:15

Monocolon

The monocolon is rare. It consists of an isolated poetic line that usually appears before or after a set of bicola, functioning as an emphatic introduction or conclusion. The first example below illustrates a monocolon used as a dramatic conclusion. The second example illustrates a monocolon used to introduce a tricolon.

> The days of punishment are coming,
> The days of reckoning are at hand;
> Let Israel know this!

Hosea. 9:7

> Who is this looking out like the dawn?
> Fair as the moon,
> Bright as the sun,
> Awesome as the stars?

Song Sol. 6:10

Stanza

Cola are grouped together to form **stanzas**. The stanza is to poetry what the paragraph is to prose. Several related cola working together within a poem form a stanza. The typical poem is composed of several stanzas, each of which functions as a major section within the poem. Similar to the paragraph in prose literature, the stanza is unified around a central topic that is developed throughout each colon. Klein[1] calls the stanza a sense unit and suggests several key indicators for identifying it. They include:

- Changes in content, grammar, speaker or literary form
- Repetition of key words
- Presence of refrains and iteration

Modern translations attempt to identify stanzas by placing a blank line between them. As is true with paragraphs, translators will differ as to where they divide a poem into stanzas.

The sample section contains two stanzas. The topic of the first stanza is the psalmist's cry to God. In the second stanza, the topic is God's hatred of evil men.

> Give ear to my words, O LORD,
> consider my sighing.
> Listen to my cry for help, my King and my God,
> for to you I pray.
> In the morning, O LORD, you hear my voice;
> in the morning I lay my requests before you,
> and wait in expectation.
>
> You are not a God who takes pleasure in evil;
> with you the wicked cannot dwell.
> The arrogant cannot stand in your presence;
> you hate all who do wrong.
> You destroy those who tell lies;
> bloodthirsty and deceitful men the LORD abhors.

Psalm 5:1-6

Special Features of Hebrew Poetry

Word-Pairs

Hebrew Poetry features **word-pairs**; that is, paralleled terms regularly used together in parallel lines. Biblical scholars have identified over one thousand word-pairs that are commonly used in Biblical Hebrew poetry.

Recognizing the presence of a word-pair is helpful because the A word can help you understand the meaning of the parallel B word.

In the example below, the difficult, literal phrase "her earnings" is clarified by the parallel phrases, "her images" and "her idols". The "earnings" must also refer to idols, which are the source of her income.

> All her <u>images</u> shall be beaten to pieces,
> All her <u>earnings</u> shall be burned with fire,
> All her <u>idols</u> I will lay waste.

Micah 1:7

> **Word-Pairs**
> Sets of words that are regularly paralleled in cola

Grammatical Differentiation

The key to Hebrew parallelisms is the parallel of thought between the lines, not parallel grammatical structure. At times, the poet may change the grammatical structure purposefully for emphasis. This is called **grammatical differentiation**.

In the following example in the first two lines of the tricolon the passive verb is used but in the third line an active verb is used. However, the lines remain perfectly paralleled. The third line is more emphatic.

> All her images <u>shall be beaten</u> to pieces,
> All her earnings <u>shall be burned</u> with fire,
> All her idols <u>I will lay waste</u>.

Micah 1:7

> **Grammatical Differentiation**
> Two parallel lines with different grammatical structure, often for emphasis

Chiastic Structures

A **chiastic structure** is an inverted structure often with a central turning point that highlights the correspondence between parallel elements. Depending upon its length, a chiasm may be represented by the following letters, ABA, ABCBA, ABBA, ABCCBA, etc. Chiastic structures in the original Hebrew are lost in some English translations, which rearrange the word order to make a smoother English translation. As a result, two translations may differ as to whether a structure is chiastic.

In a simple chiasm, the two lines of a bicolon are inverted. Notice how the terms, Judah and Ephraim, are inverted.

> Ephraim shall not be jealous of Judah;
> Judah   shall not harass   Ephraim.

Isaiah 11:13

> **Chiastic Structures**
> A structure that inverts a thought, often with a central turning point

In this more extensive chiasm the whole psalm is organized chiastically.

> God be gracious to us and bless us
> And cause His face to shine upon us-   Shelah
>> That Your way may be known on the earth
>> Your salvation among all nations
>>> Let the peoples praise You, O God;
>>> Let all the peoples praise You
>>>> Let the nations be glad and sing for joy
>>>> For You will judge the peoples with uprightness Selah
>>>> And guide the nations on the earth
>>> Let all peoples praise You, O God;
>>> Let all the people praise You.
>> The earth has yielded its produce;
>> God, our God, blesses us.
> God blesses us,
> That all the ends of the earth may fear Him.

Psalm 67

Acrostic Structures

> **Acrostic Structures**
> A set of lines or stanzas, each of which begins with the next letter of the Hebrew alphabet

An **acrostic** structure consists of a set of lines or stanzas, each of which begins with the next letter of the Hebrew alphabet. Unfortunately, this artistic structure is lost when translated into English. The most famous acrostic is Psalm 119, where the lines of each stanza begin with a different Hebrew letter.

Refrains

> **Refrain**
> A repeated colon used to complete the stanzas of a poem

A refrain is a repeated colon used to complete the stanzas of a poem. The refrain marks out the stanzas and ties the poem together. Kaiser indicates that some eighteen psalms employ refrains.[2] Psalm 46 in verses 7 and 11 uses the refrain:

> The Lord Almighty is with us;
> the God of Jacob is our fortress.   *Selah*

For additional examples see Psalm 56:4,11; Psalm 57:5,11

Iteration

> **Iteration**
> A repetition of words and phrases within several lines of a colon or stanza

Iteration is the repetition of words and phrases within several lines of a colon or stanza. Iterative parallelism occurs when every word of the lines of a colon are repeated. Most often, only a few of the words in a line are repeated. The non-repeated words tend to build upon each other, creating an emotional crescendo, thus, forming a type of synthetic parallelism. Notice the use of iteration in Psalm 150.

> Praise the Lord.
> Praise God in his sanctuary;
> Praise him in his mighty heavens.
> Praise him for his acts of power;
> Praise him for his surpassing greatness.
> Praise him with the sounding of the trumpet;
> Praise him with the harp and lyre,

Psalm 150:1-3

For additional examples see Psalm 136; Psalm148;

Biblical Hermeneutics: A Guide for Studying the Bible

Figures of Speech

Hebrew poetry also features extensive use of figures of speech, e.g., simile, metaphor, personification, anthropomorphism, etc. For the various categories of the major figures of speech, see Chapter 11.

Basic Function of Hebrew Poetry

Lyric Poetry

Much of Hebrew poetry is **lyric**, that is, it attempts to communicate feelings. It is often characterized by great shifts in emotion. The poem may begin with despair and end with a sudden confidence. The psalms are extensively lyric.

Lyric Poetry Attempts to communicate feelings

Notice the strong feeling expressed in the following section.

> Help, Lord, for the godly are no more;
> the faithful have vanished from among men.
> Everyone lies to his neighbor;
> their flattering lips speak with deception.

Psalm 12:1-2

For examples outside of Psalms, see Song of Songs

Didactic Poetry

Hebrew poetry can also be **didactic**, that is, it attempts to teach moral lessons or doctrinal truths. Didactic poetry is mostly found in the wisdom literature though it also is seen in the prophetic literature and Psalms.

Didactic Poetry Attempts to teach moral lessons or doctrinal truths

Notice the teaching expressed in the following section.

> Get wisdom, get understanding;
> do not forget my words or swerve from them.
> Do not forsake wisdom, and she will protect you;
> love her, and she will watch over you.

Proverbs 4:5-6

For examples in Psalms, see Psalm 1.

Guidelines for Interpreting Hebrew Poetry

- Group the lines of the poem into cola (monocolon, bicolon, tricolon, or quatracolon).

- Identify the kind of parallelism for each colon (synonymous, antithetical, synthetic, or emblematic parallelism).

- Use your understanding of word-pairs to help you define vague or unclear words.

- Identify the figures of speech in each poetic line, being sensitive to the parallel words or ideas that might help you understand the figure.

- Look for chiastic structures, refrains, iterations, and other highly stylistic structures that may help you to understand the overall plan of the poem.

- Divide the poem into stanzas and summarize the thought of each.

- Determine if the poem is primarily lyric or didactic and summarize the overall message of the poem.

- Remember you are studying poetry, not discourse. Do not over analyze. Take time to appreciate the emotion and beauty of the poem.

Summary

This chapter described the general nature of Hebrew poetry that employs parallels of thought called **parallelisms**. Each parallelism consists of two or more lines of poetry, called a **colon**. There are four basic types of parallelism:

- Synonymous   the idea of the first line is repeated in the additional lines
- Antithetical   the idea of the first line is contrasted in the additional lines
- Emblematic   the idea of one line is illustrated in the additional lines
- Synthetic   the idea of the first line is expanded in the additional lines

Often some of the words found in the first line are not paralleled in the additional lines in which case the parallelism is said to be **incomplete**.

The number of lines that form a colon differs. The most common cola are named:

- Monocolon   one line of poetry often used to introduce or conclude
- Bicolon   two parallel lines of poetry
- Tricolon   three parallel lines of poetry
- Quatracolon   four parallel lines of poetry

Several cola are grouped together to form a **stanza**.

Hebrew poetry includes many stylistic features including:

- Word Pairs
- Grammatical Differentiation
- Chiastic Structures
- Acrostic Structures
- Refrains
- Iteration
- Figures of Speech

In function, Hebrew poetry is either **lyric** or **didactic**. Lyric poetry communicates feeling and is highly emotional. Didactic poetry teaches moral and theological truth.

When attempting to interpret a poem, follow these steps:

- Group the lines of the poem into cola.
- Identify the kind of parallelism for each.
- Use your understanding of word-pairs to help define vague or unclear words
- Identify the figures of speech in the poem.
- Look for highly stylistic structures that reveal the poem's plan.
- Divide the poem into stanzas and summarize the thought of each.
- Determine if the poem is lyric or didactic.
- Remember you are studying poetry, not discourse,

Key Terms

Parallelism	Synonymous Parallelism	Antithetical Parallelism
Emblematic Parallelism	Synthetic Parallelism	Colon
Monocolon	Bicolon	Tricolon
Quatracolon	Stanza	Chiastic
Acrostic	Lyric	Didactic

220

Review Questions

1. What is the most basic structural component of Hebrew poetry?
2. In what ways is Hebrew poetry different from most western poetry?
3. What is the name of a group of parallel lines of Hebrew poetry?
4. In what parts of the Bible are you most likely to find Hebrew poetry?
5. What are the four basic types of Hebrew parallelisms?
6. What is meant by an incomplete parallelism?
7. What is meant by incomplete parallelism with compensation?
8. What are the four most common types of cola?
9. What are the two common usages of a monocolon?
10. In what way is a stanza of a poem similar to a paragraph of prose?
11. What are seven special features of Hebrew poetry?
12. What does word-pair mean and how can it be helpful in interpretation?
13. What does grammatical differentiation mean and why is it used?
14. What is a chiastic structure?
15. What is an acrostic structure?
16. What is a refrain and why is it used?
17. What does iteration mean and why is it used?
18. What are the two basic functions of Hebrew poetry?
19. What is lyric poetry?
20. What is didactic poetry?
21. What steps should you take when interpreting Hebrew poetry?

References

[1]Klein, William W., Craig L. Blomberg, and Robert W. Hubbard, Jr. *Introduction to Biblical Interpretation*. Dallas: Word Publishing, 1993. pp. 252.

[1]Kaiser, Jr., Walter C. and Moises Silva. *An Introduction to Biblical Hermeneutics*. Grand Rapids: Zondervan Publishing House, 1994. pp. 90.

Chapter 21

PSALMS
Interpreting the Psalms

Outline

Introduction 222

    Psalm Defined 222

    Psalm Headings 222

Basic Types of Psalms 222

    Lament Psalms 223

    Declarative Praise Psalms 224

    Descriptive Praise Psalms 225

    Royal/Messianic Psalms 226

    Wisdom Psalms 227

Guidelines for Interpreting Psalms 228

Summary 229

Review Questions 229

References 230

222

Learning Objectives

After completing this chapter, you should be able to

- ❑ Explain the basic nature of the psalms.
- ❑ Identify five basic types of psalms.
- ❑ For each type of psalm, identify its form, features, and functions.
- ❑ Interpret a psalm using an appropriate set of interpretive guidelines.

Introduction

Psalm Defined

> **Psalm**
> Poem that was sung to the accompaniment of music played on strings

The book of Psalms is a collection of psalms. The term, psalm, comes from the Greek word, ψαλμος (*psalmos*), meaning a poem that was sung to the accompaniment of music played on strings. The Old Testament equivalent word is *mizmor*.[1]

Psalm Headings

Many of the psalms include headings that are not part of the original psalm but were added by editors most likely when the psalms were placed into collections. These headings, though not inspired, are ancient and represent the research of reputable Jewish scholars from the past. Therefore, they can be generally accepted.

The headings are most useful when establishing the occasion for writing. This is important since most of the Psalms are occasional documents. Knowledge of the occasion is very helpful in understanding the message of the psalm. The following is the heading to Psalm 51.

> For the director of music. A psalm of David. When the prophet Nathan came to him after David had committed adultery with Bathsheba.

Basic Types of Psalms

> **Basic Types**
> - Lament Psalms
> - Declarative Praise Psalms
> - Descriptive Praise Psalms
> - Royal/Messianic Psalms
> - Wisdom Psalm

There are different types of psalms, each of which has a distinct form, distinct features, and distinct functions. Five of the major types are:

- Lament Psalms
- Declarative Praise Psalms
- Descriptive Praise Psalms
- Royal/Messianic Psalms
- Wisdom Psalm

Being able to recognize the form, features, and function of each kind of psalm will enhance your ability to properly read and interpret the psalms.

The Lament Psalms

Lament Psalms are prayers of strong petition in which the psalmist cries out to God for help. The emotional atmosphere swings from despair to confidence.

Form of Lament Psalms

The typical Lament has a three-fold structure that is summarized below. While most Laments fit this pattern, some have a few creative variations.

Introduction: Cry to God for Help

Main body: Description of Problem and Request for Deliverance

Conclusion: Confession of Trust or Vow to Praise God (optional)

Features of the Lament Psalms

Petition. The Lament Psalms feature a petition to God for help during a time of trial.

Sudden Shift in Emotion. The most striking feature is a sudden change in emotion from despair to confident trust.

Praise. Some Lament Psalms also include a public declaration of praise, a declaration that God has heard the psalmist's prayer and delivered him. Lament Psalms that end with praise are called **closed Laments**. Those that do not end with praise but conclude with the psalmist still waiting on God are called **open Laments**.

Function of the Lament Psalms

Appeal to God. The historical occasion of the Lament Psalm is a difficult trial or life-threatening situation that afflicts the psalmist. The psalmist's immediate purpose in the Lament Psalm was to appeal to God to deliver him from the calamity that was threatening him before it was too late.

Lament Psalms can be either individual or national. In the **Individual Lament** Psalms, the psalmist cries out for deliverance from sickness, affliction, slander, persecution, or the threat of death. In the **Communal Lament** Psalms, Israel cries out corporately for deliverance from a national catastrophe, such as war, drought or plague.

Encourage Readers to Trust. However, the psalmist also has a second purpose in writing, one more related to the reader. His purpose is to encourage those who are going through similar calamity to trust God to deliver them.

Relevance of the Lament Psalms

Model Prayer for Trials. The Lament Psalms are instructive models of the way that we should seek God in times of trial or calamity, pouring out our hearts in prayer and appealing to God to intervene.

Encourage Confidence in Trials. The closed Laments show that prayer can turn our concern into confidence, fear into faith, petition into praise, and worry into worship. Sometimes the greatest thing that changes when we pray is our own heart.

Truthful Tension in Trials. The open Laments reveal the tension in prayer. We know God can intervene, but sometimes we are not sure that he will intervene in the way we ask. We must submit our will to his will and wait on him to do his will.

Examples

Examples of Lament Psalms include Psalm 3, 4, 10, 13, 16, 17, 22, 25.

The Declarative Praise Psalm

The Declarative Praise Psalm is a testimony of praise. The testimony tends to be personal and specific and leads the psalmist to praise God for deliverance. The atmosphere is joyous.

Form of the Declarative Praise Psalms

The typical Declarative Praise Psalm has a standard three-fold structure that is summarized below. While most Declarative Praise Psalms fit this conventional pattern, there are some creative variations in a few individual psalms.

Introduction: Proclamation to Praise God

Main body: Report of God's Deliverance

Conclusion: Praise of God and/or Exhortation to People

Features of the Declarative Praise Psalms

Public Praise. The Declarative Praise Psalm features a public praise to God in which the psalmist declares to other people how God answered his prayers and delivered him from calamity.

Description of Problem. Descriptions of the past problem and God's deliverance are general, so that the psalm is relevant to all who hear/read it.

Joyous Atmosphere. The emotional atmosphere is joyous, thankful, and confident.

Function of the Declarative Praise Psalms

Glorify God for Deliverance. One purpose of the Declarative Praise Psalm is that the psalmist wants to glorify God for His deliverance.

Encourage Believers to Trust. In addition, the psalmist wants to encourage other believers to trust the Lord in the midst of similar trials.

Relevance of Declarative Praise Psalms

Model of Pubic Testimony. The Declarative Praise Psalms are instructive models of the way that we can give our public testimony of God saving us and answering our prayers.

Reminders to Praise. These psalms remind us that God wants us to praise him publicly after he has answered our prayers. They also remind us that testimony is a vital way to encourage others.

Examples

Examples of Declarative Praise Psalms include Psalm 9, 18, 34, 63, 116.

The Descriptive Praise Psalms

The Descriptive Praise Psalm is a call to corporate worship. It is distinguished from the declarative praise psalm by this call. It is more collective, calling upon the whole assembly to praise the Lord. While the declarative praise psalm emphasizes specific acts of God in deliverance of the psalmist or the nation, the descriptive praise psalms emphasize the grand works of God in creation, nation building and salvation.

Form of Descriptive Praise Psalms

The typical Descriptive Praise Psalm has a standard three-fold structure that is summarized below. While most Descriptive Praise Psalms fit this conventional pattern, there are some creative variations in a few individual cases.

> **Introduction:** Call to praise ("Hallelujah!")
>
> **Main body:** Cause for praise–person and work of God
>
> **Conclusion:** Call to praise ("Hallelujah!")

Features of the Descriptive Praise Psalms

Exhortation to Praise. These psalms feature a major exhortation to praise that usually includes the words, "Praise the LORD!" (hallelujah) occurring in the introduction and conclusion.

Descriptions of God. They also feature an extensive description of the person and work of God, describing God as creator and worker of mighty deeds.

Function of Descriptive Praise Psalms

Glorify God through Corporate Praise. One purpose of the Descriptive Praise Psalm is that the psalmist wants to glorify God through the corporate praise of the congregation.

Remind People of God's Person and Work. Another purpose is to remind the people of God about who God is and what He has done.

Relevance of the Descriptive Praise Psalms

Models on Motivating People to Praise. The Descriptive Praise Psalms are instructive models of how to motivate others to praise God.

- These psalms suggest that praise is based upon Biblical content.
- The main body of the Descriptive Praise Psalms suggests that we need to focus on both the person and work of God.

Examples

Examples of Description Praise Psalms include Psalm 29, 33, 95, 96, 106, 113, 135.

The Royal/Messianic Psalms

Royal/Messianic Psalm
Psalms that describe the ruling and reigning of God in the world

The Royal/Messianic Psalms are psalms that describe the ruling and reigning of God in the world. This rule is at times related to God's earthly king who rules on his behalf. As such, Israel, God's chosen nation, is viewed as the ruling nation among the nations. Ultimately, this rule will be fulfilled in the reign of the Messiah and the establishment of his eternal kingdom.

Form of the Royal/Messianic Psalms

Form Royal/Messianic Psalm
• No Typical Form

Unlike the Praise and Lament Psalms, the Royal/Messianic Psalms do not have a standard literary form. The structure of each Royal/Messianic Psalm must be determined on an individual basis, depending upon the major stanza divisions.

Features of the Royal/Messianic Psalms

Features of Royal/Messianic
• Focus on Davidic Covenant
• Historic Material
• Prophetic Material

Focus on Davidic Covenant, Davidic Dynasty, and Messiah. These psalms focus on three related themes: the Davidic Covenant, the Davidic Dynasty, and the ultimate Davidic King, the Messiah.

Historic Material. They often include historical materials that focus on the historical Davidic King (e.g., Solomon).

Prophetic Material. They also often contain prophetic materials because they describe the reign of the ultimate Davidic King.

The challenge in interpreting these psalms is to distinguish between the historical features that focus on the historical Davidic kings and the prophetic features that focus on the ultimate Davidic King (Messiah).

Function of the Royal/Messianic Psalms

Function of Royal/Messianic
• Focus on God's promises in Davidic Covenant
• Describe Kingdom of Messiah

Focus on God's Promises in Davidic Covenant. The historical purpose of these psalms was to focus on God's promises in the Davidic Covenant to bless and protect the Davidic Dynasty. The psalmist may petition God to be faithful to these promises or praise God for doing so.

Describe Kingdom of Messiah. The prophetic purpose of these psalms is to describe the future kingdom reign of the Messiah who will reign over the entire world in righteousness and justice.

Relevance of the Royal/Messianic Psalms

Teach About God's Faithfulness. The Royal/Messianic Psalms teach us that God is always faithful to his promises to his people, especially his promises about the Messiah.

Describe Messianic Kingdom. Because the ultimate fulfillment of the Royal/Messianic Psalms is still to come, they provide us with a picture of the future kingdom when Jesus Christ will reign over the world in righteousness and justice.

Examples

Examples of Royal Messianic Psalms include Psalm 2, 21, 45, 72, 110.

The Wisdom Psalms

Wisdom psalms consist of a small number of psalms that are similar to the biblical wisdom books (Job, Proverbs, and Ecclesiastes) in their themes and context. These psalms are designed to instruct the reader on ethical issues and cause the reader to think about life in relationship to God. Many deal with topics of human suffering and injustice in the world. Unlike the strongly emotional lament and praise psalms, these psalms express little emotion and are more contemplative in nature.

Wisdom Psalm
Psalms designed to instruct the reader on ethical issues and cause the reader to think about life in relationship to God

Form of the Wisdom Psalms

Unlike the Praise and Lament Psalms, the Wisdom Psalms do not have a standard literary form. These psalms tend to be addressed to people rather than the Lord. The structure of each Wisdom Psalm must be determined on an individual basis, depending upon the major stanza divisions.

Form of Wisdom Psalm
- No Typical Form

Features of the Wisdom Psalms

Wisdom Themes. Themes common to the Old Testament wisdom literature are developed in these psalms. Topics such as the study of the law (Ps. 119), the contrast of the godly and the ungodly (Ps. 1), and concern about reward and retribution (Ps. 73) are the emphasis of the wisdom psalms.

Wisdom Vocabulary. These psalms employ a high degree of wisdom vocabulary (heart, path, way, wise, fool, stupid).

Features of Wisdom Psalm
- Wisdom Themes
- Elements of lament and praise
- Contemplative Mood

Elements of Laments and Praise. At times the psalmist includes laments or praises similar to those found in lament and praise psalms. The difference is that these elements are secondary to the overall purpose and plan of the psalm.

Contemplative Mood. Wisdom Psalms are less emotional than the lament and praise psalms. They have a contemplative atmosphere similar to Proverbs and Ecclesiastes.

Function of Wisdom Psalms

Teach Godly Living. Some Wisdom Psalms are designed to teach godly living. They are similar to Proverbs and may contrast the righteous and the ungodly (Psalm 1).

Discuss Ethical Questions. Some Wisdom Psalms are designed to answer difficult moral questions, such as, why righteous people suffer (Psalm 49).

Function of Wisdom Psalm
- Teach Godly Living
- Discuss Ethical Question
- Teach About God
- Cause People to Ponder Existence Before God

Teach About God. Some Wisdom Psalms are designed to instruct on the nature of God or His Word (Psalm 33).

Cause People to Think About Life with God. Wisdom Psalms often deal with the difficult issues of life to cause an individual to ponder the meaning of their existence before God.

Relevance of the Wisdom Psalms

Contribute to Theology. The Wisdom Psalms provide teachings about God and as such contribute to our theology. They are especially helpful in their teachings about God as Creator and in their teachings about man.

Contribute to Ethics. The Wisdom Psalms provide teachings about man's relationship with God. They are especially helpful in providing instruction about God's word and our reactions to it.

228

Examples

Examples of Wisdom Psalms include Psalm 1, 14, 15, 19, 23, 24, 119.

Other Types of Psalms

In addition to the types of psalms described above, there are also songs of confidence, such as Psalm 27. Also, some psalms are mixed types often combing lament, praise, and wisdom elements.

Guidelines for Interpreting the Psalms

Guidelines for Interpretation
- Determine the historical occasion
- Determine the purpose and plan
- Analyze the poetry
- Determine if the psalm is quoted in the New Testament

- Determine the historical occasion of the psalm.

  Many psalms include headings describing the occasion. These are not original and scholars debate their accuracy. The psalm normally reveals the historical occasion sufficiently for interpretation.

- Identify the type of psalm based on its typical form, features, and function, keeping in mind that the writer may alter or enhance the typical form to fit his purpose.

- Determine the psalmist's purpose and plan.

  Use your understanding of the occasion to help determine the purpose.
  Use your observation of the category of the psalm (lament, description praise, etc.) to help determine the purpose and plan.

- Analyze the psalm's poetry.

- Determine if the psalm is quoted in the New Testament.

  This may reveal prophetic aspects of the psalm.
  This may reveal other doctrinal issues or key applications.

Summary

A psalm is a poem that was sung to the accompaniment of music. The psalms, when collected into the Book of Psalms, were given headings that can be helpful in identifying the occasion for writing. There are five basic types of psalms, each having unique form, features, and functions. When analyzing the psalm, these should be used to help identify the author's purpose and plan.

- Lament Psalms
- Declarative Praise Psalms
- Descriptive Praise Psalms
- Royal/Messianic Psalms
- Wisdom Psalm

Use the following guidelines when interpreting the psalms.

- Determine the historical occasion of the psalm.

  Many psalms include headings describing the occasion. Though these are not original and scholars debate their accuracy, they can be helpful.
  The psalm normally reveals the historical occasion sufficiently for interpretation.

- Identify the type of psalm based on its typical form, features, and function, keeping in mind that the writer may alter or enhance the typical form to fit his purpose.

- Determine the psalmist's purpose and plan.

  Use your understanding of the occasion to help determine the purpose.
  Use your observation of the category of the psalm (lament, description praise, etc.) to help determine the purpose and plan.

- Analyze the psalm's poetry.

- Determine if the psalm is quoted in the New Testament.

  This may reveal prophetic aspects of the psalm.
  This may reveal other doctrinal issues or key applications.

Key Terms

Lament Psalm	Open Lament	Closed Lament
Individual Lament	Communal Lament	Declarative Praise Psalm
Descriptive Praise Psalm	Royal/Messianic Psalm	Wisdom Psalm

230

Review Questions

1. What does the word psalm mean?
2. What are the five basic types of psalms?
3. For each type of psalm, what are its form, features, and functions?
4. Why might the emotional atmosphere of a lament psalm shift?
5. How does a declarative praise psalm differ from a descriptive praise psalm?
6. In what sense is a Royal/Messianic Psalm both historic and prophetic?
7. What are some of the major topics dealt with in Wisdom Psalms?
8. What is the value of the headings of the psalms?
9. What guidelines should be followed when interpreting the psalms?

References

[1]Leupold, H. C. *Exposition Of The Psalms*. Grand Rapids: Baker Book House, 1961. pp. 1.

Chapter 22

PROVERBS
Interpreting Proverbial Sayings

Outline

Introduction 232

    Meaning of Proverb 232

    Nature of Proverbial Sayings 232

    Traditional Proverbial Sayings in Scripture 232

Forms of Proverbs 232

    Short Sentence Proverbs 233

    Wisdom Sayings 234

    Long Didactic Discourses 234

    Other Forms of Proverbial Wisdom 234

Features of Proverbs 235

    Standard Poetic Features 235

    Unique Literary Features 235

Functions of Proverbs 236

    General Purposes 236

    Nature of Proverbial Sayings 236

Guidelines for Interpreting Proverbs 237

Summary 238

Review Questions 238

Learning Objectives

After completing this chapter, you should be able to

❏ Define proverb.
❏ Identify the three basic forms of proverbs.
❏ Identify the poetic and literary features of proverbs.
❏ Explain the function of proverbs and nature of proverbial sayings.
❏ Interpret a proverb following appropriate guidelines.

Introduction

Meaning of the Term, Proverb

> **Proverb**
> A short, pithy, memorable saying that expresses general truth

The Hebrew noun *mashal*, translated proverb means a comparison. Whether it is used in wisdom literature, prophetic oracles, poetic sayings or popular speech, the term refers to a comparison that the author has created to teach truth through representational imagery.

Nature of Proverbial Sayings

Most often, *mashal* refers to a short, pithy, memorable saying that expresses a general truth, as in Proverbs 10-29 (e.g., 10:1). However, at times it can refer to extended didactic discourse, as in Proverbs 1-9 (e.g., 1:8-19) and to an extended allegory as in Ezek. 17:2-24.

Traditional Proverbial Sayings in Scripture

The Book of Proverbs is the largest collection of traditional proverbial sayings in Scripture, containing both the longer didactic discourses (Proverbs 1-9, 30-31) and the shorter sentence sayings (Proverbs 10-29). Traditional proverbial sayings also appear elsewhere in the Old Testament (1 Sam. 10:11-12; 24:14; Ezek. 16:44) and New Testament (Luke 4:23).

Forms of Proverbs

> **Forms of Proverbs**
> • Sentence Proverb
> • Wisdom Saying
> • Long Didactic Discourse

The three most common forms of proverbs found in the book of Proverbs are the *short sentence proverb*, the *wisdom saying*, and the *mashal ode or long didactic discourse*. Additional forms such as the numerical saying or the alphabetic acrostic can also be found in Proverbs but with much less frequency.

Short Sentence Proverbs

Description

The short sentence proverb normally consists of one set of parallel lines, usually a bicolon but sometimes longer that expresses a general truth. Many of these proverbs are found in Proverbs 10:1-22:16 and Proverbs 25-27. These sentence proverbs classify persons, discuss positive and negative actions and provide advice about life, frequently by using pictures from everyday situations. Consider these examples.

> **Short Sentence Proverb**
> Set of parallel lines, usually a bicolon but sometimes longer, that expresses a general truth

> A simple man believes anything,
> but a prudent man gives thought to His steps.
>
> Proverbs 14:15

> A man who remains stiff-necked after many rebukes
> will suddenly be destroyed without remedy.
>
> Proverb 29:1

Standard Forms

Sentence proverbs have several standard forms. Below are some common forms.

> **Standard Forms of Sentence Proverbs**
> - Emblematic Parallelism
> - Antithetical Parallelism
> - Better...than Proverbs
> - If...how much more Proverbs

Emblematic parallelism

> Like a gold ring in a pig's snout
> is a beautiful woman who shows no discretion.
>
> Proverbs 11:22

> Like a bad tooth or a lame foot
> is reliance on the unfaithful in times of trouble.
>
> Proverbs 25:19

Antithetical parallelism

> The rod of correction imparts wisdom,
> but a child left to himself disgraces his mother.
>
> Proverbs 28:15

> The horse is made ready for the day of battle,
> but victory rests with the Lord.
>
> Proverbs 21:31

Better ... than proverbs

> Better a meal of vegetables where there is love
> than a fattened calf with hatred.
>
> Proverbs 15:17

> Better a poor man whose walk is blameless
> than a rich man whose ways are perverse.
>
> Proverbs 28:6

Argument from the lesser to the greater

> If the righteous receive their due on earth
> how much more the ungodly and the sinner!
>
> Proverbs 11:31

> Death and Destruction lie open before the LORD
> how much more the hearts of men!
>
> Proverbs 15:11

Wisdom Sayings

Wisdom Sayings
Several lines developing a central topic

The wisdom saying consists of several lines developing a central topic. Many of these sayings are found in Proverbs 22:17-24:34. The wisdom saying provides instruction or advice by briefly pointing out the merits or problems of a certain topic. The key to understanding these sayings is to identify the central issue being discussed.

Some examples of wisdom sayings are:

On Credit

> Do not be a man who strikes hands in pledge
> or puts up security for debts;
> if you lack the means to pay,
> your very bed will be snatched from under you.

Proverbs 22:26-27

On Justice

> Do not move an ancient boundary stone
> or encroach on the fields of the fatherless,
> for their Defender is strong;
> he will take up their case against you.
> Apply your heart to instruction
> and your ears to words of knowledge.

Proverbs 23:10-12

On Discipline

> Do not withhold discipline from a child;
> if you punish him with the rod, he will not die.
> Punish him with the rod and save his soul from death.

Proverbs 23:13-14

The Long Didactic Discourse

Long Didactic Discourse
One or more stanzas and are composed of many sets of parallel lines that develop a central theme

Long didactic discourses consist of one or more stanzas and are composed of many sets of parallel lines that develop a central theme. Such didactic discourses can be found in Proverbs 1-9 and 30-31. The long didactic discourse is a poem of several stanzas that develops one topic at length. Such poems provide an extended discussion of a key subject of wisdom.

Examples of the long didactic discourse include Proverbs 7:1-27 which is about the prostitute, or foolishness personified, and Proverbs 8:1-21 where wisdom is personified as a wise woman who offers understanding to any who will listen.

Other Forms of Proverbial Wisdom

Other Forms
• Acrostic Poem
• Numeric Sayings

Acrostic Poem

A special poetic form is the acrostic or alphabetic poem. In the Hebrew text each line begins with the successive letter of the Hebrew alphabet and follows the Hebrew alphabet from beginning (aleph) to end (taw). While our English translations are unable to reproduce this ordering, each Hebrew letter is frequently noted above every eight verses of Psalm 119 where every eight verses begin with another letter of the Hebrew alphabet. Proverbs 31:10-31 is an acrostic poem that describes the character of the noble wife. Other acrostic poems are found in the Psalms and Lamentations.

Numerical Sayings

Numerical sayings initiate their discussion with the use of a number. Frequently one is added to the initial number to raise it to the next higher number. For example, a saying may be introduced thus: "There are <u>six</u> things which ... <u>seven</u> which..." Such sayings are called graded numerical sayings. Several numerical sayings are found in Proverbs 30 as well as other parts of Scripture (cf. Amos 1 & 2).

> Under three things the earth trembles,
> under four it cannot bear up:
> a servant who becomes king,
> a fool who is full of food,
> an unloved woman who is married,
> and a maidservant who displaces her mistress.

Proverbs 30:21-23

Features of Proverbial Sayings

Standard Poetic Features

Bicolon. In terms of structure, proverbs are composed of parallel lines, usually bicolons, but occasionally tricolons.

Stanzas. Some proverbial sayings are composed of several sets of parallel lines forming a stanza; some stanzas are short, others are longer.

Parallelisms. Proverbial sayings use all kinds of parallelism, especially antithetical parallelism and emblematic parallelism, as well as synthetic and synonymous.

Other Poetic Features. Proverbs utilize all the standard poetic features, e.g., figures of speech, A-B word-pairs, grammatical differentiation and chiastic structures.

Poetic Features
• Bicolon, some tricolon
• Stanzas
• Parallelisms
• Other Poetic Features

Unique Literary Features

Timeless Truth. Proverbial sayings are unique literarily because they express timeless, gnomic truth that is cleverly worded in a memorable way.

Striking Imagery. Proverbial statements seek to drive home truth by using striking imagery and expressing truth in vivid, dramatic and sometimes humorous ways.

Short, Compact Sayings. Most proverbs are short, compact statements that express truth about human behavior that is applicable in a variety of situations.

Theme of Moral Living. Proverbs generally focus on the themes of moral wisdom, righteousness and the fear of the Lord versus folly, wickedness and lack of conscience.

Literary Features
• Cleverly Worded Timeless Truth
• Striking Imagery
• Short and Compact
• Theme of moral living

Function of Proverbial Sayings

General Purposes

General Purposes
- Teach art of living wisely
- Commend moral living and fear of God
- Warn of consequences of moral actions

Teach the Art of Living Wisely and Successfully

One of the major themes in proverbs is "wisdom" (*ḥokmâ*) which is more than mere intellectual acumen. It is moral discernment and ethical understanding which enables a person to live with moral skill and success in the world.

A basic purpose of proverbs is to develop moral values and discernment, so that a person may succeed in life, both on a spiritual level before God and on a practical level in the everyday world (family, business, community).

Commend Wise Moral Living and the Fear of God

Wisdom and the fear of the LORD are intimately related. The relationship between the two is cyclical: the fear of the LORD is foundation to true wisdom, and once gained, wisdom leads to a deeper fear of the LORD.

The fear of the LORD refers to an attitude that leads a person to turn away from sinful folly and pursue ethically righteous behavior, knowing that God judges and sovereignly controls the consequences of all moral actions.

Warn about the Consequences of Moral Actions

A major purpose of proverbs is to motivate people to turn away from sin and folly and to pursue righteous behavior, in the light of the benefits of righteousness versus the dangers of wicked behavior.

They emphasize **retribution theology** that focuses on the consequences of actions. Those who live wisely and righteously will be blessed and succeed, while those who live foolishly and wickedly will experience calamity.

The Nature of Proverbial Sayings

Proverbs State General Principles that Are Normally True

Nature of Proverbs
- States principles that are generally true
- Are not unconditional promises

By their very nature, proverbs are generic statements and gnomic truths that state general principles about the way that life normally works. They do not address every situation or exceptional circumstance. Sometimes, there are exceptions to the rule.

Proverbs 26:4 and 26:5 illustrate this point. "Do not answer a fool according to his folly" (26:4); and "Answer a fool according to his folly" (26:5). Sometimes we should do one thing, other times another.

Because they are generic principles, proverbs cannot be applied to every random situation without exception. It requires discernment to know when a proverb applies to a particular situation (e.g., Proverbs 26:7).

Proverbs Are Not Unconditional Promises or Guarantees

Many proverbs are simply generalized observations of the way life usually works (Proverbs 6:6-11; 24:30-33). Sometimes there are exceptions to the rule.

For example, Proverbs states that the righteous will be rewarded, while the wicked will be disciplined. However, Ecclesiastes notes that sometimes the righteous experience calamity and the wicked prosper (Eccles. 8:14). And Job claims that he is an example of the exception to the rule!

Proverbs are not promises. They should not be viewed as guarantees nor a formula for success. They should not be claimed as unconditional promises, as in the unbalanced "name-it-and-claim-it" approach of many.

For example, many assume that Proverbs 22:6 promises that, if parents raise their child correctly; he/she will never depart from righteousness. While this may be true in general, there will always be exceptional cases in which parents do everything right, but the child still rebels.

Guidelines for Interpreting Proverbs

- Determine if the statement is part of a longer discourse or is a sentence proverb.
- If part of a longer discourse, understand the statement in light of the context of the discourse.
- If part of a wisdom saying, understand the statement in light of the central topic.
- Use your knowledge of Hebrew poetry to help understand the statement.
- Use your knowledge of figurative expressions to help understand the imagery.
- Study the proverb together with other proverbs dealing with the same topic.
- Seek to generalize the proverb and remove cultural limitations.
- Compare the proverb to other passages of Scripture to determine if exceptions to the truth exist.
- State the truth in the proverb as a truth that is generally true, though not necessarily always true.

238

Summary

A *proverb* is normally a short, pithy, memorable saying that expresses a general truth. At times proverbs can be longer *wisdom sayings* and even much *longer didactic discourses*. The *short sentence proverb* is usually a bicolon in the forms:

Emblematic parallelism   Antithetical parallelism
Better...than proverb   If...how much more proverb

The wisdom sayings consist of several cola working together to develop a central topic. The longer didactic discourses consist of several stanzas. Other forms of proverbs include acrostic poems and numeric sayings.

Proverbs are poetic and include all the features of Hebrew poetry. Most often they employ bicola with antithetical or emblematic parallelism though all types of parallelism can be found. They also include cleverly worded timeless truths and striking imagery.

Proverbs deals primary with wise moral living by providing general, gnomic statements that are generally true. However, they can have exceptions. Proverbs are not unconditional promises.

Use the following *guidelines when interpreting proverbs*.

- Determine if the statement is part of a longer discourse or is a sentence proverb.
- If part of a longer discourse, understand the statement in light of the context of the discourse.
- If part of a wisdom saying, understand the statement in light of the central topic.
- Use your knowledge of Hebrew poetry to help understand the statement.
- Use your knowledge of figurative expressions to help understand the imagery.
- Study the proverb together with other proverbs dealing with the same topic.
- Seek to generalize the proverb and remove cultural limitations.
- Compare the proverb to other passages of Scripture to determine if exceptions to the truth exist.
- State the truth in the proverb as a truth that is generally true, though not necessarily always true.

Key Terms

Proverb   Sentence Proverb   Wisdom Saying
Long Didactic Discourse   Retribution Theology

Review Questions

1. What is a proverb?
2. What are the three basic forms of proverbs?
3. What are the standard forms of a sentence proverb?
4. How does a wisdom saying differ from a longer didactic discourse?
5. What are the poetic and literary features of proverbs?
6. What are the general purposes of proverbs?
7. Why should proverbs not be understood as promises or absolute truths?
8. What are the guidelines for interpreting proverbs?

Chapter 23

Prophetic Discourse
Interpreting Prophetic Speeches

Outline

Introduction 240

    Two Types of Prophetic Material 240

    Nature of Prophetic Books 240

Features of All Prophetic Speeches 241

    Poetic Features 241

    Figures of Speech 241

    Covenant Imagery 241

Types of Prophetic Speeches 241

    Legal Disputation 242

    Judgment Speech 243

    Call to Repentance 244

    Salvation/Deliverance Speech 245

    Call Narrative 246

    Prophet's Responses 247

Guidelines for Interpreting Prophetic Speeches 247

Summary 248

Review Questions 248

Learning Objectives

After completing this chapter, you should be able to

- ❏ Define prophetic speech.
- ❏ Identify the features common to all prophetic speeches.
- ❏ Identify the forms, features, and functions of the four basic types of prophetic speeches.
- ❏ Identify the prophetic speeches found within a prophetic address.
- ❏ Interpret a prophetic speech following appropriate guidelines.

Introduction

Two Types of Prophetic Material

Prophetic Speech
Sermon-like discourses spoken by God through the prophet

The prophetic books of the Old and New Testaments are composed of two very different types of material, prophetic speeches and apocalyptic visions. The apocalyptic material recounts and explains visions given by God to communicate a message. In Chapter 24 we will discuss apocalyptic literature. The prophetic speeches are sermon-like discourses spoken by God through the prophet to a group of people. They can be as short as one verse or as long as several chapters. In this chapter we will discuss the interpretation of these speeches.

Nature of Prophet Books

Anthologies

Nature of Prophet Books
- Anthologies of speeches, visions, narratives
- Occasional Documents, closely related to history of Israel

Most of the prophetic books consist of a collection of prophetic speeches, apocalyptic visions, and historical narratives edited and compiled by the prophet by whose name the book is known or later by another individual. Some of the material is arranged chronologically and some more topically. Often several speeches are grouped together to form a larger address.

The prophetic books confuse many readers because they do not understand the basic features and forms of the prophetic speeches. Once the reader becomes aware of the typical features and forms of the prophetic speeches, the prophetic books are much easier to understand.

Occasional Documents

The Old Testament prophetic books are closely related to the history of Israel and Judah. They address situations within and related to these nations. Thus, an awareness of the historical situation is crucial to proper understanding of the speeches found within these books.

Basic Features of All Prophetic Speeches

Each type of prophetic speech has unique form, features, and function. We will discuss these later. First, we will discuss the features that are common to all the speeches. They include their *poetic features*, use of *figurative language*, and *covenant imagery*.

Basic Features
- Poetic Features
- Figures of Speech
- Covenant Imagery

Poetic Features

The prophetic speeches were written using Hebrew poetry. In this sense they are similar to the poetry found in the Psalms, Proverbs and Job. The poetic lines are usually arranged in bicola having synonymous parallelism.

Figures of Speech

Like all forms of Hebrew poetry, the prophetic books exhibit widespread use of figures of speech. Prophetic books are fond of figures of comparison (simile, metaphor, and hypocatastasis), figures of representation (anthropomorphism and personification) and figures of substitution (metonymy and synecdoche).

Covenant Imagery

The basic content of the prophetic books corresponds to the contents of the Mosaic Covenant, as articulated in Exodus 19-24 and Deuteronomy 4-30. The prophets were the enforcers of the covenant, announcing judgment for violations as well as salvation based on the promises.

The prophetic judgment speeches are based upon the warnings in the Mosaic Covenant that the Lord would discipline Israel when it sinned and violated the covenant (e.g., Deut. 28-29; Lev. 26).

The prophetic exhortations to Israel and Judah to repent are based upon the promise in the Mosaic Covenant that The Lord would relent of discipline if the nation would repent of its sins (e.g., Deut. 30).

The prophetic announcements of salvation are based upon the promise in the Mosaic Covenant that the Lord would deliver the nation from discipline and restore its covenant blessings if it repented (e.g., Deut. 28-30).

The ultimate hope announced by the prophets also looked at the covenant promises to Abraham and David, seeing God's ultimate faithfulness to them even though it would take a major work of grace accomplished by the Messiah.

Types of Prophetic Speeches

Types of Prophetic Speeches
- Legal Disputation
- Judgment Speech
- Call to Repentance
- Salvation Speech
- Call Narrative
- Songs of Confidence

There are four basic types of speeches, each having unique form, features, and function. They are: *Legal Disputation, Judgment Speech, Call to Repentance,* and *Salvation Speech.* We will also consider two other types of writings found in the prophetic books, the *Call Narrative* and *Songs of Confidence.*

Legal Disputation

Legal Disputation
Legal charges against Israel
for unfaithfulness, using a
courtroom setting

The Legal Disputation has the covenant as its background and often reads like legal proceedings in a courtroom (legal motif). Israel has broken the covenant and God, as Judge, makes a case against his people. Witnesses (usually the heavens and the earth) are called and the charges (sins) are listed to show Israel's unfaithfulness before God.

Form

Legal Disputation Form
• Summons to Jury
• Review of Evidence
• Verdict Issued

Summons to Jury	a call to hear the complaint (optional)
Review of Evidence	the reasons for the charges are given
Verdict Issued	the judgment is given (optional)

Features

Legal Disputation Features
• Introduction
• Legal Pleadings
• Rhetorical Questions

Introduction. Often short exhortations calling the court together introduce these speeches. This introduction is optional and not found in all legal disputations. Some examples are:

"Hear, O Heavens! Listen, O Earth!"	Isaiah 1:2
"Hear, O Mountains, the Lord's accusation"	Micah 6:2
"Hear, You deaf; look, you blind.	Isaiah 42:18

Legal Pleading. These speeches consist mainly of logical arguments that include charges, presentation of evidence, and reasoning of Israel's guilt.

"The ox knows...but Israel does not know"	Isaiah 1:3
"How have I burdened you? Answer me."	Micah 6:3
"It pleased the Lord to make his law great but..."	Isaiah 42:21ff

Rhetorical Questions. Within the legal pleadings, the Lord asks rhetorical questions as a way to charge Israel.

" How have I burdened you?"	Micah 6:3
"Who is blind but my servant?"	Isaiah 42:19

Function

Legal Disputation Function
To demonstrate God's justice
in pronouncing judgment
against Israel

The purpose is to demonstrate God's justice in pronouncing judgment against Israel. The evidence, which clearly reveals Israel's rebellion and sin, vindicates God's judgment of the nation. God has been offended and God's covenant violated in spite of all God's efforts to remedy the situation.

Examples

Examples of this type of speech occur in all of the prophetic books. See Isa. 3:13-26; 43:26-28; Hos. 3:1-12; Micah 6:1-5.

Judgment Speech

The judgment speech contains an unconditional announcement of judgment by God. It may be as short as one verse or as long as several chapters. The prophet announces that the Lord is about to judge the people as a punishment for their sin. By far, the judgment speech is the most common type of prophetic speech in Scripture.

Judgment Speech
An unconditional announcement of judgment by God

Form

Accusation of sin	reason for judgment
Announcement of judgment	punishment/discipline for the sin

Judgment Speech Form
- Accusation of Sin
- Announcement of Judgment

Features

Introduction. Often short statements indicating that the Lord is about to speak introduce these speeches. Some examples are:

"Hear the word of the Lord"	Isaiah 1:10
"The Lord spoke to me"	Isaiah 8:5
"This is what the Lord says"	Jeremiah 5:14

Announcement Formula. Often a simple formula is given between the accusation of sin and the announcement of judgment. They normally include the word, "therefore" followed by mention of the Lord bringing judgment. Some examples are:

"Therefore the Lord will..."	Isaiah 3:17
"Therefore once more I will..."	Isaiah 29:14
"Therefore, hear O nations..."	Jeremiah 6:18

Judgment Speech Features
- Introduction
- Announcement Formula
- Woe
- Funeral Dirge
- Varying Addressee

Woe. At times these speeches include the word, woe, to introduce a judgment of doom (Habakkuk 2:6, 9, 12, 15).

"Woe to you who add house to house"	Isaiah 5:8
"Woe to those who rise early in the morning."	Isaiah 5:11
"Woe to those who draw sin along with cords"	Isaiah 5:18

Funeral Dirge. Some judgment speeches include a lamentation for the nation as though it were dead.

"Babylon has fallen, has fallen"	Isaiah 21:9
"Fallen is virgin Israel, never to rise again"	Amos 5:2

Varying Addressee. A prophetic judgment speech may be addressed to individuals, the nation of Israel or Judah as a whole, or even to pagan Gentile nations.

Function

The purpose is to pronounce judgment upon the people for their sins. Though these speeches are not identified as conditional, at times God removed the judgment in response to repentance as in the case of Jonah 3:4. See also Jeremiah 18:8.

Judgment Speech Function
To pronounce judgment upon the people for their sins

Examples

Examples of this type of speech occur in all of the prophetic books (e.g., Hos. 4:1-3) and in some historical books (e.g., 1 Sam. 15:17-29). The bulk of them, however, occur in the prophetic books that were written just prior to the Assyrian Captivity of Israel in 722 BC and the Babylonian Exile of Judah in 586 BC.

Call to Repentance

Call to Repentance
Appeal to Israel to repent to avert the judgment or receive blessing

In the Call to Repentance, the prophet appeals to Israel to repent to avert a threatened judgment or to be restored after discipline. The judgments or blessings contained within the speech are conditional.

Form

Call to Repentance Form
- Appeal to Repent
- Reasons to Repent

Appeal to repent   exhortations to turn from sin

Reasons to repent   positive and negative motivation

Features

Call to Repentance Features
- Exhortations
- If... then logic
- Short length

Exhortations. The major feature is the presence of exhortations and appeals to turn from sin and obey God. Some examples are:

"If you call the Sabbath a delight"	Isaiah 58:13
"If you will return, O Israel, return to me"	Jeremiah 4:1
"Repent! Turn away from all your offenses"	Ezekiel 18:30

If...Then logic. Conditional sentences are often used where the 'if' clause states the necessary responses, and the 'then' clause gives the consequences.

"If you call the Sabbath a delight...then you will"	Isaiah 58:13-14
"If you will return...then the nation will be blessed"	Jeremiah 4:1-2

Length Short. These speeches are most often short appeals placed between other speeches, normally judgment speeches.

Function

Call to Repentance Function
To motivate Israel to repent to avoid judgment or gain blessing

The purpose is to motivate Israel to repent. The reasons appeal to the intellect, emotions, and will of the audience. They may be positive promises of forgiveness or negative reinforcements of discipline or judgment.

Most of the prophetic calls to repentance occur in the prophetic books that deal with the Assyrian Captivity of Israel in 722 BC and the Babylonian Exile of Judah in 586-516 BC.

Examples

Examples include Isaiah 58:13-14; Jeremiah 4:1-2; 4:3-4; Ezekiel 18:30-32; Hosea 6:1-3; Joel 2:12-17.

Salvation/Deliverance Speech

The salvation speech is an unconditional announcement of deliverance for Israel from punishment whether that punishment came directly from God or indirectly through an enemy. Salvation speeches are the second most common type of speech found in the Scriptures. They often follow judgment speeches.

Form

Allusion to the problem
Announcement of God's promise to deliver
Description of the results of deliverance

Features

Unconditional Promises. The ultimate hope announced by the prophets was based on the covenant promises to Abraham (Genesis 12) and David (2 Samuel 7:16). Thus, these speeches never include any conditions. The announced salvation will take place. However, this salvation normally is viewed as something in the far future that will occur after the discipline has refined Israel (Isaiah 44:1-5).

Divine Mercy. The promises of salvation are based on God's unfailing love and grace, and therefore, though Israel will be disciplined for sin, they will ultimately be redeemed and delivered. (Isaiah 43:1-7).

Joyous Atmosphere. The salvation speech is often addressed to grieving Israel after the announcement of judgment or during the time of judgment. It is designed to encourage and turn sorrow to joy and despair to hope. It is uplifting and positive (Isaiah 49:13)

Function

The purpose of the speech is to encourage and comfort by announcing deliverance for Israel from a threat or future blessing as a source of hope.

The name of this form of prophetic speech may be a bit misleading to the beginner because prophetic salvation speeches do not deal with salvation from hell or eternal condemnation, but rather a temporal deliverance from a threat to them. It may refer to protection or deliverance for Israel from national enemies. It may promise removal of God's own discipline from the nation due to their repentance. At times, the language is so hyperbolic and idyllic that it suggests an escalation to a fulfillment that will culminate in a future Messianic Kingdom.

Examples

Examples of prophetic salvation speeches include Isaiah 2-4; 11-12; 25-27; 35; 40-55; 59-63; Jeremiah 30-33; Ezekiel 33-48; Hosea 2-3; 14; Joel 2:18-32; Amos 9:11-15; Micah 4-5; 7; Zephaniah 3:9-20; Zechariah 1-8.

Call Narrative

The Old Testament prophetic books contain narrative sections along with their prophetic speeches. These narratives are used for several purposes. The call narrative is a recounting of the prophet's call to service by God as a way to demonstrate the authority of the prophet as the spokesman of God.

Form

The divine confrontation
The introductory word
The commission proper
The prophet's objection
God's reassurance
The sign

Function

The purpose of the call narrative was to demonstrate the authority of the prophet as the spokesman of God. To do so, the prophet gives his divine commission to become a prophet.

In the same way that a king would commission a messenger to deliver a message to the nation, the Lord commissioned his messengers, the prophets to deliver his message, the prophetic word of God, to Israel. When an ancient Near Eastern messenger would deliver his message, he would quote the words of his king word-for-word. Likewise, the Old Testament prophets were commissioned to deliver God's word verbatim.

The royal commission enabled the ancient Near Eastern messenger to speak in the authority of his king. Likewise, the Hebrew prophets spoke in the authority of the Lord, the King of Kings.

As in the ancient Near East, when a king commissioned a messenger, he proclaimed his unworthiness for the task, so the prophets proclaimed their unworthiness to be used by the King of Kings as a prophet. The ancient Near Eastern king would typically reassure his messenger that he would favor him in his task and give him a sign to substantiate this. Likewise, the Lord reassured his messengers of success or divine enablement.

Examples

Examples of this would include Moses (Exodus 3-4), Isaiah (Isaiah 6) and Jeremiah (Jeremiah 1).

Prophet's Responses: Songs of Confidence, Laments and Complaints

Like the call narratives, these are not prophetic speeches in which the prophet speaks for God. Instead, they are mainly the prophet's responses to what God declares.

Form

Many of these responses are similar in form to the praise psalms found in the book of Psalms. At times the prophet questions God's revelations with poems similar to lament psalms.

Function

The purpose of the songs of praise is to praise the Lord for his mercy and deliverance. The prophet calls upon Israel to praise the Lord for delivering them from their temporal turmoil, foreign affliction or divine discipline. While the deliverance appears to have taken place already, the song or confession is actually prophetic in nature. The prophet is emphasizing that future deliverance is so certain that Israel should begin to praise The Lord in the present. For examples see Nahum 1:2-10 and Habakkuk 3:1-19.

At times the prophet reacts to announcements of judgment with mourning and questions. These poems express the prophet's sorrow and remind God of His unconditional choice of His people. For examples see Jeremiah 8:18-22 and 12:1-4.

| **Prophet's Responses** |
| Similar to praise and lament psalms |

| **Form** |
| • Praise Psalm |
| • Lament Psalm |

| **Function** |
| • To praise the Lord for mercy and deliverance |
| • To question God's judgment and mourn |

Guidelines for Interpreting Prophetic Speech

- Determine the historical background and specific occasion for the speech.
- Study the context to determine if the speech is part of a larger address or topical context.
- Determine the type of speech.
- Analyze the speech based on its form, features, and function.
- Determine what aspects of the speech should be understood literally and what aspects should be understood symbolically.
- Determine what aspects of the speech are conditional and what aspects are unconditional.
- Determine what aspects of the speech are fulfilled and what aspects are still future. Use the New Testament for help.
- Determine what aspects of the speech are Messianic by looking for use of the passage in the New Testament.

Summary

The prophetic books are mainly collections of speeches, visions, and some narratives. The speeches are sermon-like discourses of the following types: *Legal Disputation, Judgment Speech, Call to Repentance,* and *Salvation Speech.* All of the various types of speeches are poetic, containing much figurative language, and covenant imagery. Each type of speech also has unique form, features, and function.

Use the following *guidelines when interpreting prophetic speeches.*

- Determine the historical background and specific occasion for the speech.
- Study the context to determine if the speech is part of a larger address or topical context.
- Determine the type of speech.
- Analyze the speech based on its form, features, and function.
- Determine what aspects of the speech should be understood literally and which aspects should be understood symbolically.
- Determine what aspects of the speech are conditional and what aspects are unconditional.
- Determine what aspects of the speech are fulfilled and what aspects are still future. Use the New Testament for help.
- Determine what aspects of the speech are Messianic by looking for use of the passage in the New Testament.

Key Terms

Prophetic Speech	Legal Disputation	Judgment Speech
Call to Repentance	Salvation Speech	Call Narrative

Review Questions

1. What are the two types of prophetic materials found within the prophetic books?
2. What are some of the major characteristics of a prophetic book?
3. Why is the fact that the prophetic books are occasional documents important?
4. What are the common features of all prophetic speeches?
5. What are the four basic types of prophet speeches?
6. What are the forms, features, and functions of each type of prophetic speech?
7. In what ways is a judgment speech different from a call to repentance?
8. In what ways is a salvation speech different from a call to repentance?
9. What is the purpose of a call narrative?
10. What other types of prophetic materials did the prophets write?
11. What guidelines should be followed when interpreting a prophetic speech?

Chapter 24

Apocalyptic Literature
Interpreting Prophetic Visions

Outline

Introduction 250

    Definition 250

    Nature of Apocalyptic Prophecy 250

    Major Examples 250

Basic Form 251

    Introduction of the Vision 251

    Description of the Vision 251

    Interpretation of the Vision 251

Basic Function 251

Basic Features 252

    Futuristic 252

    Dualistic 252

    Nationalistic 252

    Symbolic 252

    Visionary 252

Principles for Interpreting Symbols 253

Guidelines for Interpreting Apocalyptic Literature 254

Summary 254

Review Questions 254

Learning Objectives

After completing this chapter, you should be able to

- ☐ Describe apocalyptic prophecy.
- ☐ Identify the three major parts of an apocalyptic story.
- ☐ List the two functions of apocalyptic prophecy.
- ☐ List the major features of apocalyptic prophecy.
- ☐ List the principles for interpreting symbols.
- ☐ Interpret an apocalyptic vision following appropriate guidelines.

Introduction

Definition

Apocalyptic Literature
Prophetic visionary literature that reveals God's future program leading to the future kingdom

The term apocalyptic comes from the Greek noun, ἀποκαλυψις (*apocalupsis*), meaning unveiling, uncovering, revealing; and the verb, ἀποκαλυπτω (*apocalupto*), meaning to unveil or to uncover what is hidden, to reveal.

When used with reference to prophetic literature, the term apocalyptic designates a special kind of prophetic visionary literature that unveils or reveals God's future prophetic program leading up to the establishment of the future kingdom.

Nature of Apocalyptic Prophecy

Visions. Apocalyptic prophecy is symbolic visionary prophetic literature, consisting of visions recorded exactly as they were seen by the author and explained by a divine interpreter.

Eschatological. The content of apocalyptic prophecy is primarily eschatological, focusing on end-time events, tracing the major periods in human history leading up to the inauguration of the future age.

Occasioned by Oppression. God usually revealed apocalyptic prophecies when His people were undergoing periods of oppressive conditions, when they were under hostile Gentile nations or persecution.

Major Examples

Most of the apocalyptic material in the Bible is found in Isaiah, Ezekiel, Daniel, Zechariah, and Revelation.

Pre-Exilic Period:	Isaiah 24-27
Exilic Period:	Ezekiel 34-38
	Daniel 2; 7; 8; 10-12
Post-Exilic Period:	Zechariah 1-7
New Testament Period:	Book of Revelation

Basic Form

The key element in apocalyptic literature is the interpretation of a vision. Generally, the vision is first introduced, then described, and finally interpreted. We can call this the vision story. An apocalyptic segment can be outlined as follows:

> Introduction of the Vision
> Description of the Vision
> Interpretation of the Vision

Basic Form
- Introduction of Vision
- Description of Vision
- Interpretation of Vision

Introduction of the Vision

The vision is normally introduced with the prophet receiving a vision by being translated to another place (Ezekiel 37:1), by dreaming (Daniel 7:1), or by falling into a trance (Revelation 1:10). At times the vision is given to someone other than the prophet (Daniel 2:1-2).

Description of the Vision

Normally, the vision is described before any attempt is made to interpret it. Often God or an angel asks the prophet what he saw (Zechariah 4:2). Generally, the vision is described in detail (Daniel 7:4-14). The visions include a significant number of symbols. At times, it is difficult to picture the visions because the descriptions are so unusual (Zechariah 4:2-3).

Interpretation of the Vision

The final and most important part of the vision story is the interpretation. Often, the interpretation begins with God or an angel asking the prophet if he understands the meaning of the vision (Ezekiel 37:3) or with the prophet asking for the meaning of the vision (Daniel 7:15-16; Zechariah 4:4-5).

The actual interpretation is then given. The interpretations normally involve revelations about the end of time as in the book of Revelation. However, some focus on the time in which they were given (Zechariah 4:1-8). The interpretations can be vague and difficult to understand.

Basic Function

Basic Functions
- To Encourage oppressed people of God
- To Instruct about future kingdom

The original historical purpose of most apocalyptic visions was to encourage the faith of the oppressed people of God suffering under a hostile Gentile power by demonstrating that God would eventually overthrow the hostile Gentile nations and establish his eternal kingdom on earth which his people would inherit and wherein they would receive their rewards for perseverance.

The canonical purpose of apocalyptic literature is to instruct all the people of God throughout the ages about the future prophetic program of God, culminating in the inauguration of the Messianic Kingdom, to ultimately motivate them to live by faith and persevere in a wicked world.

Basic Features

Basic Features
- Futuristic
- Dualistic
- Nationalistic
- Symbolic
- Visionary

Futuristic

The content is primarily futuristic, focusing on the major historical periods leading up to the inauguration of the eternal earthly kingdom of God.

Apocalyptic prophecies often climax with the eschatological appearance of God on earth at the end of the present age, coming to vanquish his enemies and deliver his people from their enemies who threaten them.

Dualistic

Apocalyptic prophecies present a strong dualism between good and evil embodied in the kingdom of God versus the kingdom of the hostile Gentile powers under the control of Satan. The visions often reveal that the spiritual battle in the heavens is behind the historical situation on earth, with a major cosmic battle waiting in the future. The presence of angels is typical.

Nationalistic

Apocalyptic prophecies are often nationalistic rather than individualistic in tone. They focus on the deliverance of the nation Israel from the hostile Gentile nations of earth, or the deliverance of the church from the Antichrist's kingdom.

Symbolic

Apocalyptic prophecies contain highly symbolic materials that often are difficult to envision. For instance, in Daniel 8, Daniel received a vision of a ram and a goat. These animals represented the Medo-Persian and Greek empires. The details may represent certain ruler and battles that took place between the empires.

Visionary

Apocalyptic prophecies feature unusual visions and images that often cannot be understood apart from a divine interpreter, who is quite frequently an angel. Frequently, the author sees a vision of heaven or a vision of a distant land or events in a distant period. When the prophet sees God, it is usually in a majestic vision in which he is enthroned in glory, surrounded by the angels and overwhelming in his majesty. The divine interpretation tends to expand on an item or event in the vision, focusing on the basic concepts, not details.

Principles for Interpreting Symbols

What constitutes a symbol?

A symbol is some real or imagined object or action that is assigned a meaning for the purpose of depicting rather than stating the qualities of something else. Symbols and types are both representative of something else. While a type represents something to come, a symbol has no necessary time reference.

Guidelines for Interpreting Symbols

- Note the three elements in symbolic interpretation:

    Object   (symbol)
    Referent   (what the symbol refers to)
    Meaning   (resemblance between symbol and referent)

- Remember that symbols have their base in reality.

- Observe the meaning that the text explicitly assigns to the referent.

- If the verse does not give the meaning or resemblance of the symbol, then check which major characteristic the referent and the object have in common.

- Look for the one major point of resemblance.

- Realize several objects may depict one referent.

- Do not assume that everything is a symbol because some symbols are present.

- Do not symbolize descriptions of the future that are plausible to take literally.

Examples of Symbols

Symbolic objects	Oil	Holy Spirit	Zech. 4:1-6
Symbolic actions	Water	Cleansing by the Word	Eph. 5:26
Symbolic materials	Bread & wine	Body & blood of Christ	Luke 22:19-20
Symbolic gestures	Tearing garment	Great grief	Job 1:20
Symbolic numbers	40	Testing	Num. 32:13 Luke 4:2
Symbolic names	Lo-ruhamah	No Pity	Hos. 1:6

Guidelines for Interpreting Apocalyptic Visions

- Use the normal, literal method of interpretation in order to understand the most natural meaning of the vision.

- Avoid speculation about the meaning of the vision if it is not interpreted.

- Rely upon previous use of the same symbol in earlier apocalyptic literature (e.g., the ten-horned beast in Rev. 13:1-2, foreshadowed by Dan. 7).

- Be consistent in your method and approach in interpretation.

- Have modest goals.

Summary

Apocalyptic literature is prophetic visionary literature that reveals God's future prophetic program leading up to the establishment of the future kingdom. This literature contains vision stories consisting of three parts, the *introduction of the vision*, the *description of the vision*, and the *interpretation of the vision*. The basic historic function of the visions was to encourage the faith of the oppressed people of God. For us the visions provide instruction on God's future kingdom and motivate us to live by faith. Apocalyptic literature is futuristic, dualistic, nationalistic, symbolic, and visionary.

Symbols are a major feature of apocalyptic prophecy and thus interpreting them is very important. A symbol is some object or action that is assigned a meaning for the purpose of depicting rather than stating the qualities of something.

Key Terms

Apocalyptic Prophecy   Symbol

Review Questions

1. How does apocalyptic prophecy differ from prophetic speeches?
2. What is the basic form of a vision story?
3. What are the basic functions of apocalyptic prophecy?
4. What are the basic features of apocalyptic prophecy?
5. What is a symbol?
6. What are the guidelines for interpreting symbols?
7. What are the guidelines for interpreting apocalyptic prophecy?

Chapter 25

Typology

Outline

Introduction 256

    Definition of Typology 256

    Prophetic Nature of Typology.. 256

    New Testament Terms.. 257

    New Testament Terms for Typological Fulfillment 257

    Examples of OT Types and NT Antitypes 258

    Types Verses Illustrations, Parallels, Symbols, or Allegories 259

Identifying and Interpreting Types.. 259

    Characteristics of A Type 259

    Questions to Ask to Identify Types... 259

    Guidelines for Interpreting Types 260

    Examples of Illegitimate Typology 260

Summary 262

Review Questions... 262

Learning Objectives

After completing this chapter, you should be able to

❑ Define typology, type, and antitype.
❑ Identify New Testament terms used to describe types and antitypes.
❑ Distinguish between types, illustrations, parallels, symbols, and allegories.
❑ List questions to ask when working with types.
❑ List the guidelines for interpreting types

Introduction

Definition of Typology

Typology
Form of prophecy based on correspondence between persons, events and things in the Old Testament that foreshadow greater New Testament counterparts

The New Testament looks back on Old Testament persons, things and events that foreshadow then future New Testament persons, things and events and calls these things types. Typology is a form of prophecy based on correspondence between persons, events and things in the Old Testament that foreshadow greater New Testament counterparts.

Prophetic Nature of Typology

Prophetic Nature of Typology
• Forward-looking from God's perspective
• Backward-looking from man's perspective

Typology was forward-looking from God's perspective in his sovereign design of redemption history; however, it is backward-looking from man's perspective because man in retrospect only sees it when we look back on the Old Testament from the perspective of the New Testament.

Old Testament writers did not realize that certain persons, events and things in Old Testament history had a typological-prophetic significance foreshadowing New Testament realities. Old Testament writers simply viewed these things as non-prophetic and historical persons, events and objects in the history of Israel.

While the human authors of Scripture were probably unaware of the prophetic significance of these persons, events and objects, it is clear that the Divine author had sovereignly designed these into the fabric of Old Testament history as his sovereign but hidden foreshadowing of the New Testament. God planned the Old Testament patterns to anticipate the ultimate fulfillment of these patterns in the New Testament. Thus, types were prophetic from God's standpoint, but not from the human author's standpoint.

When the New Testament antitypes were revealed in salvation-history, it was evident that the typological prophetic element had been present all along. As New Testament authors looked back at Old Testament history from the perspective of the New Testament, they saw the divinely designed patterns by comparing the Old Testament type with the greater New Testament antitype.

New Testament Terms

The New Testament often uses special terms to describe Old Testament persons, events and things that have a divinely designed resemblance or correspondence to something in the New Testament. Below is a listing of the most important of these terms.

New Testament Terms for Types

Old Testament Pattern		New Testament Fulfillment	
tupos	example, model, type	*antitupos*	copy
tupikos	typical		
hypotuposis	example, pattern		
deigma	example, pattern	*hypodeigma*	copy
skia	shadow	*eikon*	substance, reality
		soma	reality, body

Figure 32.1
NT Terms for Types

The Old Testament person, event or thing is called the **type** (*tupos*) and the New Testament person, event or thing is the **antitype** (*antitupos*). Something is clearly typological when the New Testament identifies it with this terminology. However, sometimes the New Testament views something as typological without such terms (e.g. 1 Cor. 5:6-8). The Old Testament does not designate these persons, things or events as prophetic. They are only identified and designated as such in the New Testament in retrospect looking back on the Old Testament.

Type
The Old Testament person, event or thing

Antitype
The New Testament person, event or thing

The type is called a shadow in contrast to the antitype that is called the reality. From this we understand that the type is a vague prefiguring and general correspondence. We should not make the mistake of trying to see everything in the type that is found in the antitype.

New Testament Terms for Typological Fulfillment

The divinely designed typological patterns have a prophetic significance because they point forward (from God's perspective) to Christ. Therefore, in the New Testament, the antitype is often pictured as the fulfillment of the prophetic pattern in the type.

When the New Testament authors quote the Old Testament to draw out the prophetic significance of a typological pattern, they often use the formula, "in order that the words of the prophet might be fulfilled" or "that the Scripture might be fulfilled" (e.g., Matt. 2-4).

Examples of OT Types and NT Antitypes

Adam and Christ

Adam is designated as a type of Christ because, like Christ, his one single act brought eternal consequences to all mankind (Rom. 5:14-19).

First Adam	Second Adam: Christ
Adam's one act of sin	Christ's one act of righteousness
Condemnation to all men	Salvation to all who believe
The many died in Adam	Many receive eternal life through Christ
Death reigned through Adam	Righteousness reigns through Christ
The many became sinners	Many are made righteous

The Levitical System

The Levitical system is called a "shadow of the good things that were to come" because it anticipated the need for the great High Priest (Heb. 10:1-14).

Levitical Sacrifices	Sacrifice of Jesus Christ
Repeated sacrifices	One sacrifice for all time
High priest sacrificed endlessly	Christ sacrificed himself once
High priest always stood	Christ sat down afterwards
Animal blood never removed sin	Blood of Christ totally removed sin

The OT Festivals

The Old Testament religious calendar was a "shadow of things to come"–the festivals foreshadowed various aspects of the work of Christ (Col. 2:16-17). The correspondence between the timing and significance of the Jewish festivals and God's program of redemption is startling.

Spring Festivals	*First Coming of Christ*
Passover	Death of Christ (1 Cor. 5:7)
Unleavened Bread	Purification from Sin (1 Cor. 5:6-8)
First fruits	Resurrection of Christ (1 Cor. 15:20-23)
Weeks/Pentecost	Coming of Holy Spirit (Acts. 2:1-4)
Summer Gap	*Church Age*
No Festivals: Period of Harvest	Age of Worldwide Evangelism
Fall Festivals	*Second Coming of Christ*
Trumpets	Second Coming (Matt. 24:31; 1 Thess. 4:16)
Day of Atonement	Atonement Applied to Israel (Dan. 9:24)
Tabernacles	Earthly Kingdom (Zech. 14:16)

Types vs. Illustrations, Parallels, Symbols or Allegories

Prophetic types are distinct from illustrations or parallels. Parallels and illustrations do not have a heightening or escalation and are not called types (e.g., 1 Cor. 10:1-11). A prophetic type prefigures the antitype. An illustration or parallel is only an analogous situation in the Old Testament that has some parallel with a situation in the New Testament. A prophetic type looks forward because it has a prophetic foreshadowing while an illustration or parallel merely looks back and lacks prophetic foreshadowing.

Types are distinct from allegories. Allegories are symbolic images of a non-historical nature in which every detail parallels a spiritual truth, while types are real historical persons, events or objects which bear a basic or general correspondence with the greater New Testament reality.

Identifying and Interpreting Types

Characteristics of a Type

The key to the study of types is proper identification. The following characteristics must be present for something to be a legitimate type

> **Characteristics of a Type**
> - Pre-figuring
> - Genuine Resemblance
> - Heightening or Escalation
> - Divine Design
> - NT Designation

- *Pre-Figuring:* A type has a predictive and foreshadowing element from God's perspective. It looks ahead and anticipates or points to the antitype.

- *Genuine Resemblance:* A resemblance, similarity or correspondence exists between the type and the antitype. The resemblance must be a genuine and substantial correspondence. It must be natural and not forced.

- *Heightening or Escalation:* In typology, the antitype is greater than and superior to the type. There is an increase, a heightening and an escalation that fulfills (heightens) the type by bringing it to the climax.

- *Divine Design:* God planned the resemblance as an outworking of God's prophetic design on history, and as evidence of the inspiration of Scripture. The correspondence cannot be a product of an overly imaginative interpreter.

- *New Testament Designation:* A type is an Old Testament historical person, event or thing intended by God to foreshadow a New Testament person, event or thing. The only sure test is whether or not it is designated as a type in the New Testament (e.g., Rom. 5:14; 1 Cor. 5:6-8; Col. 2:17; Heb. 10:1).

Questions to Ask to Identify Types

- Is there a definite correspondence or resemblance between the Old Testament prophetic type and the New Testament fulfillment/antitype?

- Does the Old Testament prophetic type exhibit the same truths, principles and relationships as the corresponding New Testament fulfillment/antitype?

- Is the historical setting of the Old Testament type in harmony with the historical setting of the New Testament fulfillment/antitype?

- Is the Old Testament type a prefiguring or foreshadowing of the New Testament antitype, or is it merely a non-prophetic example, parallel, analogy or illustration?

- Is there a forward focus in the Old Testament type which looks ahead to something in the future, as fulfilled in the New Testament antitype?

- Does the New Testament antitype heighten or fulfill the type with the New Testament antitype being superior and an escalation of the pattern seen in the Old Testament type?

- Can divine design be observed in the typological relationship between the Old Testament prophetic type and the New Testament fulfillment/antitype?

- Does the New Testament in some way designate or suggest the prophetic relationship between the Old Testament type and the New Testament antitype?

Guidelines for Interpreting Types

Guidelines for Interpretation
- Observe If NT suggest a correspondence
- Determine historical sense of type
- Identify points of correspondence
- Identify points of contrast
- Identify how antitype heightens type
- Do not hunt for too many details

- Observe whether the New Testament directly asserts or suggests that there is a typological correspondence between an Old Testament person, event or object (type) and a New Testament person, event or object (antitype).

- Determine the literal, historical sense of the Old Testament type and understand it in its original historical context from the human author's perspective.

- Identify the specific point(s) of correspondence or resemblance between the Old Testament type and its New Testament antitype.

- Identify the specific areas of contrast or dissimilarity in order to avoid making the non-prophetic elements of the Old Testament type into an illegitimate allegory.

- Identify the manner in which the New Testament antitype heightens or escalates the prophetic pattern foreshadowed by the Old Testament type.

- Do not hunt for more details than are legitimate to draw out the typological correspondence.

Examples of Illegitimate Typology

Exodus 25:10-16

The ark typified the person of our Lord Jesus Christ. This is so obvious that it is hardly necessary to pause and furnish proof . . . The fact that the ark of the covenant was composed of two materials and of two only—the wood and the gold—clearly points to the two natures of our Lord: the human and the Divine . . . The ark was made of "shittim wood," a species of the acacia which is said by many to be imperishable. It is a tree, which is found in the arid desert. The "shittim wood" grown here on earth typified the humanity of our Savior. Isaiah 53:2 speaks in the language of the type: "For He shall grow up before Him as a tender plant, and as a root out of dry ground." There are three things about this shittim-tree, which makes it peculiarly fitting as a type of this. It is the tree now called the acacia *seyal*—the only tree that grows to any size in the deserts through which Israel passed. First, it is a tree that can thrive in a very dry soil. Second, it has very long, sharp thorns. Third, it is a tree from which is obtained the gum Arabic so largely used in medicinal preparations, which is procured simply by piercing the tree at nightfall, and that which oozes out is, without any preparation, the gum-Arabic of commerce. To the spiritual mind, these facts are sweetly suggestive of Him who, in a dry and thirsty land, where surely there was naught to sustain His spirit, was in the constant freshness of communion with God, for other than an earthly stream sustained Him. Though indeed crowned now with glory, a crown of thorns was all this world had for Him. And we remember too that it was He who was pierced for us in that blackest night of guilt, when the blood flowed forth from His side, to be the only balm for the troubled soul and sin-burdened conscience.

As the shittim-wood was one that never rotted, it was a most appropriate emblem of the sinless humanity of the Lord Jesus. It is indeed striking to find that in the Septuagint (the first translation ever made of the Old Testament–into Greek) it is always translated "incorruptible wood." The wood of the ark was overlaid with gold, within and without. This prefigured His divine nature.

–Arthur W. Pink. Gleanings in Exodus. Chicago: Moody, 1977, pp. 191-193.

Genesis 14:17-24

Melchizedek bringing forth the bread and wine is suggestive. It is the first presentation to us of the royalty and priesthood of Christ, and therefore is of the deepest interest. The bread and wine suggest the Lord's Supper. The bread speaks of the loaf in the Lord's Supper, and the wine speaks of the cup of the Lord. There is nothing more wonderful than the Lord's Supper, and nothing the devil has more deadly hostility to. If you get a taste of that, the king of Sodom has not much to attract you; you do not want even a shoe latchet from him.

–C.A. Coates. An Outline of the Book of Genesis. Kingston: Stow Hill Bible and Tract Depot, 1959, p. 119.

Joshua 2:21

Rahab depended for her preservation upon the promise of the spies, whom she looked upon as the representatives of the God of Israel. Her faith was simple and firm, but it was very obedient. To tie the scarlet line in the window was a very trivial act in itself, but she dared not run the risk of omitting it. Come, my soul, is there not here a lesson for thee? Hast thou been attentive to all the Lord's will, even though some of His commands should seem non-essential? Hast thou observed in his own way the two ordinances of believer's baptism and the Lord's Supper? These neglected, argue much unloving disobedience in thy heart. Be henceforth in all things blameless, even to the tying of a thread, if that commanded of God.

–Charles Haddon Spurgeon. Morning and Evening. Grand Rapids: Zondervan, 1976, p. 218.

Joshua 5

Does not the Jordan represent death? Most surely it does. And must not the believer cross it? Yes; but he finds it dry, because the Prince of Life has gone down into its deepest depths, and opened a pathway for His people, by which they pass over into their heavenly inheritance . . . Moses was prevented from going over Jordan. We know that the Law could not possibly bring the people into Canaan; so, Moses' course must end here, for he represents the law. But Christ, the true Joshua, has crossed the Jordan, and not only crossed it, but turned it into a pathway by which the ransomed host can pass over dry-shod into the heavenly Canaan . . . It is most desirable that the reader should with all simplicity and clearness, seize the true spiritual import of the river Jordan. It typifies the death of Christ . . . The more deeply we ponder the typical instruction presented in the river Jordan, the more clearly, we must see that the whole Christian position is involved in the standpoint from which we view it. Jordan means death, but for the believer, a death that is past–the death we have gone through as identified with Christ, and which through the resurrection, has brought us on the other side–the Canaan side–where He is now . . . Joshua stands before us as a type of the risen Christ, leading His people, in the power of the Holy Spirit, into their heavenly inheritance. The priests bearing the ark into the midst of the Jordan typify Christ going down into death for us, and destroying completely its power . . . Here then we have a type of the full Christian position.

–C.H. Mackintosh. The Mackintosh Treasury. Neptune, N.J.: Loizeaux Brothers, 1978, pp. 183-198.

Summary

Typology is a form of prophecy based on correspondence between persons, events, and things in the Old Testament that foreshadow greater New Testament counterparts. Typology is forward-looking from God's perspective in that he controlled history so that certain persons, events, and things would point forward to New Testament realities. Typology is backward-looking from man's perspective in that he only sees these correspondences when looking back from the New Testament.

The Old Testament person, event, or thing is called the *type* and the New Testament person, event, or thing is called the *antitype*. Legitimate types have the following characteristics:

Pre-figuring	Divine Design
Genuine Resemblance	New Testament Designation
Heightening or Escalation	

The following questions should be asked when identifying types:

- Is there a definite correspondence between the supposed type and the antitype?
- Does the supposed type exhibit the same truths as the antitype?
- Is the historical setting of the supposed type in harmony with the setting of the antitype?
- Is the supposed type a true prefiguring or foreshadowing of the antitype?
- Does the supposed type look ahead to something fulfilled by the antitype?
- Does the antitype heighten or fulfill the pattern seen in the supposed type?
- Can divine design be observed between the supposed type and antitype?
- Does the New Testament designate or suggest type?

The following guidelines should be used when interpreting types:

- Observe whether the NT directly asserts a typological correspondence.
- Determine the historical sense of the OT type.
- Identify the specific point(s) of correspondence between the type and antitype.
- Identify the dissimilarities between the type and antitype.
- Identify how the antitype heightens or escalates the OT type.
- Do not hunt for more details than are legitimate.

Key Terms

Typology	Type	Antitype

Review Questions

1. What is meant by typology?
2. Why is typology a form of prophecy?
3. What are meant by type and antitype?
4. What is the significance of a type being called a shadow?
5. What are some examples of legitimate types and their antitypes?
6. How does a type differ from an illustration?
7. What are the characteristics of a true type?
8. What questions should be asked when working with types?
9. What guidelines should be followed when interpreting types?

Index of Terms

Analogy of faith 36, 157
Analogy of scripture 157
Anthropomorphism 138
Apocalyptic Literature 250
Apostrophe 139
Application 29, 161
Authority 9
Author's purpose 64
Background commentaries 42
Bible dictionary 41
Bible encyclopedia 41
Bible introductions 42
Bible surveys 42
Biblical hermeneutics 2
Canonization 157
Cohesion 74
Collocates 114
Comparative philology 115
Concordances 118
Connection 72
Connotation 111
Context of culture 50
Contextual meaning 111
Correlation 33
Cross-cultural 164
Cross-reference 158
Deductive reasoning 30
Definitions 117
Direct application 165
Discourse 72
Discourse analysis 73
Dispensation 163
Dynamic equivalency 12
Eisegesis 29
Embedded discourse 74
Epistle 186
Etymology 115
Euphemism 139
Exegesis 29
Exegetical commentaries 42
Exhaustive concordance 118
Exposition 30
Expository commentaries 42
Extensional definition 117
Figurative meaning 111, 136
Formal equivalency 12
Genre analysis 147
Genre competence 147
Genus and differentia 118
Gospel, gospel 172
Grammar 99

Grammatical analysis 99
Hendiadys 138
Hermeneutical guideline 2
Hermeneutical principle 2
HGRT method 34
Historical background 50
Historical occasion 58
Historical-critical method 157
Hook word 76
Hyperbole 139
Hypocatastasis 138
Inclusio 76
Indirect application 165
Inductive reasoning 30
Inerrancy 7
Infallibility 7
Inspiration 7
Intentional definition 118
Interlinear Bible 120
Interpretation 29
Interpretive grid 149
Irony 139
Lexical cohesion 74
Lexicons 43, 120
Linguistic structuralism 100
Linking pronouns 90
Literal translation 12
Literary context 72
Literary genre 35, 147
Logical connections 75
Mechanical layout 104, 105
Meiosis 139
Merism 138
Metaphor 138
Metonymy 139
Morphology 99
Narrative, Biblical 194
Observation 32
Occasional document 58
Onomatopoeia 112
Order 65, 89
Oxymoron 140
Parable 180
Paradox 140
Paragraph analysis 85
Paragraph arrangement 89
Paragraph development 88
Paragraph synopsis 93
Parallel passage 158
Paraphrase 13
Personification 138

Prejudices 18
Presuppositions 17
Pre-understanding 17
Prophetic Speech 240
Pronominal cohesion 74
Reasoning 30
Referent meaning 111
Revelation 6
Rhetorical analysis 73
Rhetorical connections 76
Rhetorical devices 76
Rhetorical outlines 79
Rhetorical situation 58
Rule of faith 156
Selectivity 65, 196
Semantic meaning 111
Semantic range 113
Shifts in cohesion 76
Simile 138
Situational context 58
Spatial cohesion 75
Spiritual illumination 20
Structure markers 75
Subject/actor cohesion 74
Subjectivity 16
Symbol 138
Synecdoche 139
Syntactic function 111
Syntax 99
Tapeinosis 139
Text 10
Thematic analysis 73
Theological interpretation 156
Theological wordbooks 43, 120
Theology 29
Thesis statement 64
Topic of paragraph 87
Topic sentence 87
Transitions 76
Translation 10
Typology 256
Unit boundary 76
Unity 36, 65
Usus loquendi 116
Verbal cohesion 74
Version 10
Vertical chart 80
Word Meanings 111
Word Study Fallacies 116
Zoomorphism 138

Made in the USA
Las Vegas, NV
14 May 2025

22184140R00149